The Horror Film

Inside Film Series

Also Available

Contemporary US Cinema	Dr Michael Allen
Film Noir	Dr Andrew Spicer
Spanish Cinema	Dr Rob Stone
The Western	David Lusted
Russian Cinema	Dr David Gillespie

Forthcoming Titles

Shakespeare on Film	Dr Judith Buchanan

The Horror Film

Peter Hutchings

Routledge
Taylor & Francis Group

LONDON AND NEW YORK

First published 2004 by Pearson Education Limited

Published 2013 by Routledge
2 Park Square, Milton Park, Abingdon, Oxon OX14 4RN
711 Third Avenue, New York, NY 10017, USA

Routledge is an imprint of the Taylor & Francis Group, an informa business

ISBN 13: 978-0-582-43794-4 (pbk)

British Library Cataloguing-in-Publication Data
A catalogue record for this book is available from the British Library

Library of Congress Cataloging-in-Publication Data
Hutchings, Peter.
   The horror film / Peter Hutchings.
     p. cm. — (Inside film)
   Includes filmography.
   Includes bibliographical references and index.
   ISBN 0-582-43794-6
   1. Horror films—History and criticism. I. Title. II. Series.

  PN1995.9.H6H837 2004
  791.43'6164—dc22

                               2004044281

Typeset in 10/13pt Giovanni Book by 35

CONTENTS

PREFACE

Horror has often been seen as both the most peculiar and the most predictable of all film genres. Its peculiar quality derives from the sorts of pleasures it seems to offer which, in the eyes of some at least, are perverse, weird and questionable. Its predictable quality lies in its apparent formulaic repetitiveness, with this most clearly manifesting itself in the preponderance of sequels within the genre. Of course, all film genres are repetitive to some degree, but in the case of horror it seems that this is a more pronounced and extreme feature than it is elsewhere.

This book takes issue with both these commonly held views of the horror genre. While the pleasurability of horror requires some explanation, this need not be founded on a sense of the psychopathology of either the horror film-maker or the horror audience. Horror might well be a distinctive part of our culture but for most of the time at least it operates firmly within the cultural mainstream rather than existing in some dank back-alley into which 'normal' people venture at their peril. As for horror's alleged repetitiveness, this just seems to be the opinion of those who are viewing the genre from a distance and missing, or discounting, the role that is played there by innovation and originality. In contrast, the view of horror offered by this book is one that is attuned to the commercial imperatives of the genre but at the same time is open to the idea that horror can be surprising and unpredictable and that its continued commercial success depends to a large extent on its mutability.

In fact, such is the variety apparent within the horror genre that it is hard to imagine any single book that could adequately sum it up. Accordingly, this book will not put forward either a single theory for explaining the genre (although, as will become clear, it will tend to favour those critical approaches that engage with horror in historical terms) or a chronological overview of the genre (although the reader will note that the first chapter focuses on the 1930s, horror's first decade, and the final two chapters engage with horror from the 1970s to the present day). Instead the book is structured around a series of issues that, in my view, are important and worthy of discussion. Some of these issues are longstanding ones in horror criticism – namely, genre definition, the role played by the monster, the uses (and abuses) of psycho-analytical theory in horror analysis, the extent to which horror is preoccupied with questions of otherness and difference. Here I set out the debates and suggest some ways in which those debates might be developed. Other chapters explore issues that have not featured much in previous horror criticism but a discussion of which can cast a new light on the genre – notably, horror's use of sound and the reliance of the genre on particular types of performance. The book's concluding two chapters form a case study of horror production from the 1970s to the present day. This will not be in the interests of producing any definitive conclusions about the horror genre. Instead, this overview of horror's most recent years will help to clarify its historical specificity, its changeability and its open-endedness.

LIST OF PHOTOGRAPHS

Slashers and post-slashers

Acknowledgements

We are grateful to the following for permission to reproduce copyright material:

Universal Studios Licensing LLLP for *Dracula* © 1931 Universal Pictures Corporation, *The Bride of Frankenstein* © 1935 Universal Pictures Corporation, *Son of Dracula* © 1943 Universal Pictures and *Frankenstein* © 1931 Universal Pictures Company, Inc.; MGM CLIP+STILL for *The Silence of the Lambs* © 1991 Orion Pictures Corporation, All Rights Reserved, *Carrie* © 1976 Metro-Goldwyn-Mayer Studios Inc., All Rights Reserved and *The Abominable Dr. Phibes* © 1971 Orion Pictures Corporation, All Rights Reserved; Warner Bros. Entertainment Inc. for *King Kong* © 1933 RKO Pictures, Inc.; All Rights Reserved; Miramax Film Corp. for *Scream*; Anchor Entertainment UK Ltd for *Halloween*; CANAL+ IMAGE UK LTD for *Circus of Horrors*; Charles O. Grigson (as Trustee for the Owners) for *The Texas Chainsaw Massacre*.

CHAPTER ONE

Defining horror

Read Marcus Aurelius. Of each particular thing, ask 'What is it in itself? What is its nature?'

(Dr Hannibal 'the Cannibal' Lecter, *The Silence of the Lambs*, 1991)

HOW DO YOU KNOW A HORROR FILM WHEN YOU SEE IT?

Defining what a horror film is should be easy. After all, 'horror film' is a widely used term. You will find it in film marketing: for example, a recent poster campaign for the American film *Jeepers Creepers* (2001) proclaimed it 'the best US horror movie in the last ten years' presumably on the confident basis that everyone looking at the poster would know what that meant. You will also find it in film reference books, listings magazines and as a section in most video rental outlets. As is the case for the other main film genres, including the western, the musical and the thriller, there is a familiarity about the designation 'horror film' and an accompanying assumption, both by the market and by critics, that audiences generally understand the term enough to organise their own viewing in relation to it, either – depending on their tastes – by actively seeking out horror films or by avoiding them like the plague.

Yet if one looks at the way that film critics and film historians have written about horror, a certain imprecision becomes apparent regarding how the genre is actually constituted. Not only do these critics and historians differ as to whether horror is a bad thing or a good thing, degrading or uplifting, mindless or thought provoking; they also sometimes differ as to which films should be thought of as horror films and which should not. This is particularly the case when attempts are made to separate out horror from the science fiction genre. For example, Stuart Kaminsky distinguishes horror from science fiction by arguing that 'horror films are overwhelmingly concerned with the fear of death and the loss of identity in modern society' while by contrast 'the science fiction film deals with fear of life and the future, not fear of death' (Kaminsky, 1974, pp.101, 111). That he then ends up discussing as horror films a number of titles thought of by many other critics as science fiction – notably *It Came from Outer Space* (1953), *The Creature from the Black Lagoon* (1954) and *Invasion of the Bodysnatchers* (1956) – simply demonstrates how indeterminate or ambiguous the generic identity of certain films can be.

Of course, it could be argued that these border disputes between genres are not in themselves especially numerous or significant, and that while there might be moments in film history where genres intersect – horror and science fiction in the 1950s, for example, or 1980s generic hybrids such as *Aliens* (1986) and *Predator* (1987) – the broader generic categories remain intact, i.e. most horror films are unequivocally horror rather than anything else. However, the more one thinks about the horror genre, the more one comes to realise how many films there are which appear to exist on generic borders and which can be classified in one direction or another. Consider, for example, the procession of films about serial killers that have appeared in American cinema since Hitchcock's *Psycho* in 1960. Slasher films like *Halloween* (1978) and *Friday the 13th* (1980), 1990s slasher-revival films such as *Scream* (1996) and *I Know What You Did Last Summer* (1997) as well as the likes of *The Silence of the Lambs* (1991), *Seven* (1995), *Copycat* (1995) and *Kiss the Girls* (1997), to name but a few, all boast thriller or whodunnit narrative structures with no obvious supernatural elements (although such elements do creep into some of the numerous sequels to *Halloween* and *Friday the 13th*). In the past some of these, notably the slasher films, have more commonly been thought of as horror, while others, including *Seven* and *Copycat*, have tended to be seen as violent thrillers. But it is easy to envisage scenarios in which either the slasher films are drawn into a discussion of crime cinema or the more expensive, up-market psychological thrillers are seen as horror films (and indeed the fact that this chapter is headed by a quote from *The Silence of the Lambs* implies a claim for the film as a horror text).

A sense of the serial-killer film being only loosely anchored in a particular genre is underlined by the fact that in one major study of horror cinema, *The Philosophy of Horror* by Noel Carroll, films of this type are explicitly excluded from the discussion of the aesthetics of horror, while another major study of the genre, *Men, Women and Chainsaws: Gender in the Modern Horror Film* by Carol Clover, principally focuses on serial-killer/slasher films (Carroll, 1990; Clover, 1992). One could worry over the question of who is right out of these two scholars, but it is probably more profitable to consider how the definitions of horror they and other critics propose function as interventions into the horror genre rather than as disinterested meditations on the nature of horror. In other words, critics do not simply assume or rely upon a pre-existing, well-established group of films when they write about horror but instead will often work to shape a group of films, including some and excluding others, in order to produce their own particular idea of what horror is.

This process of placement, whereby critics and historians position various films within or outside horror, is not only apparent for more recent types of film but also applies for earlier forms of horror cinema. For example, while most accounts of horror history published in the past thirty years refer to the German productions *The Cabinet of Dr Caligari* (1919) and *Nosferatu* (1922) as horror films, it is clear that these films were neither produced nor originally marketed as horror films but instead as 'art movies' (Elsaesser, 1989). Their designation as horror films is therefore retrospective, with Carlos Clarens' classic 1967 study of the genre, *An Illustrated History of the Horror Film*, perhaps the first sustained attempt to view them in such a way (Clarens, 1967). Much the same can be said of *King Kong* (1933). Now widely thought of as a 'horror classic', historians of 1930s US cinema have convincingly demonstrated that at the time of *King Kong*'s production and original release it was not thought of principally as a horror film but instead more as a jungle adventure movie. Along with other jungle adventure movies (such as the 1932 production *The Most Dangerous Game*), it only subsequently comes to be classified as a horror film (Berenstein, 1996; Erb, 1998). Even the 1931 version of *Dracula*, starring Bela Lugosi as the Count and seen by many as inaugurating the 1930s US horror boom, was originally marketed as a morbid romance, a thriller and a shocker but not as a horror film. In fact, the evidence suggests that the term 'horror film' itself did not become widespread until later on in the 1930s.

Matters are made yet more complicated by the fact that the film industry itself is not especially consistent in the way it defines and promotes horror cinema. Sometimes it will market particular films as horror in one context and then re-market them as belonging to another genre in a different context (and vice versa). One thinks here of the way in which Universal Studios sought to repackage some of its classic horrors from the 1930s and 1940s – including *Dracula*, *Frankenstein* (1931) and *The Wolf Man* (1941) – as science fiction during the SF boom of the 1950s (Altman, 1999, pp.78–9). Ironically, later on in the 1950s those very same films would be packaged again as horror when they featured in the very popular horror film seasons screened on American television, while one of the 'classic' SF films from the 1950s, *The Creature from the Black Lagoon*, would be repackaged as horror in the late 1990s as part of the Universal Horror Video Collection.

What audiences make of this apparent generic fluidity is not always clear, but recent accounts of horror fandom suggest that, at the very least, the fan section of the horror audience does not passively accept industrial designations of the genre. For example, Mark Jancovich has noted the way in which some horror fans saw *Scream* and its various sequels, all of which were sold as horror films, as 'inauthentic' horror rather than 'the real thing'. Jancovich cites one horror internet fan site in this regard:

> *This new rash of movies masquerading as Horror flicks are driving classics off the shelves and good movies out of the theatres. Above all else, they are giving the genre a bad name. Do you want your kids to grow up thinking a Horror movie is only possible if Neve Campbell, Jennifer Love Hewitt or Sarah Michelle Geller stars in it? I don't think so.*

> (Jancovich, 2000, p.30)

(For the benefit of readers unfamiliar with this sort of material, Neve Campbell and Jennifer Love Hewitt are the young stars of, respectively, the *Scream* trilogy and the *I Know What You Did Last Summer* films, while Sarah Michelle Geller – star of the television series *Buffy the Vampire Slayer* – appeared in *I Know What You Did Last Summer* and *Scream 2* and was killed off in both.)

Bearing all this in mind, the task of defining what a horror film is becomes rather more difficult than might originally have been supposed. In part, this has to do with the fact that the numerous definitions of horror cinema do not fit together into a cohesive whole. But it also has to do with the way in which a significant number of films are constantly being reclassified so far as their generic affiliations are concerned, with the industry, critics and sectors of the audience all working to construct their own versions of horror.

This difficulty in pinning horror down once and for all is actually part of a broader problem with defining genres. Given that film genres are marketing categories that audiences and film-makers need to know about and in some way understand in order for those genres to prosper, it is perhaps surprising that critical attempts to identify and delineate those properties that character-ise particular genres are often so problematic. It is significant in this respect that when genre first became a major focus of interest in the study of film during the 1970s, it formed part of a more general turning away from what were perceived as the excesses of auteurism. Auteurism, looking at cinema in terms of directors, had been a controversial, cutting-edge development in film criticism during the 1950s and 1960s, especially in its insistence that artists of value and distinction were to be found working within the Hollywood studio system. But by the 1970s auteurism itself was increasingly perceived as old-fashioned and somewhat elitist in its outlook, with its focus on the uniquely talented individual film director often operating at the expense of an understanding of other aspects of cinema, notably cinema's existence as a medium of popular entertainment. Auteurism, which as Alan Lovell has noted 'used the common critical tool of traditional artistic criticism (the author expressing the personal vision)', tended to put a distance between the way that auteurist critics saw film and the way that audiences saw them, with this being particularly the case for those mainstream entertainment films upon which so much auteurist activity had been concentrated (Lovell, 1975, p.5). Even when directors' names were used as part of a film's marketing – with examples including Alfred Hitchcock, Cecil B. DeMille or, more recently, Steven Spielberg or Ridley Scott – these seemed to operate more as 'brand names' than as promises of artistic or auteurist integrity.

Why do audiences go to see mainstream entertainment films? Not because of auteur-directors apparently but rather because of stars and genres, with these deployed within a particular narrative-based format. The study of genres was thereby legitimised as a way of thinking about cinema in terms of its popular appeal to audiences. Yet immediately genre criticism stumbled over the question of definition. 'Genre is what we collectively believe it to be' stated Andrew Tudor confidently in a classic early piece of genre criticism, with that use of a 'we' that incorporated critics, audiences and film-makers an important assertion of how a genre-based approach to cinema would be different from an auteur-based one (Tudor, 1973, p.139). However, it quickly became apparent that it was not clear what we collectively believed, nor, for that matter, whether we collectively believed anything at all so far as genres were concerned. Defining the object – i.e. establishing what thing you will discuss before going on to discuss it – therefore became in the case of genre study not just a preliminary to genre analysis but itself a significant problematic that required considerable effort and sophistication to work through.

To a certain extent, matters were helped by the fact that much of this 1970s definitional work was organised around the western genre which, fortuitously, turned out to be one of the easiest mainstream genres to define (although even here there were problems). In searching for that 'Factor X' that bound together all the films belonging to a particular genre, one could point to the western's specific geographical and historical setting, to a fairly consistent set of visual conventions and devices, and, perhaps more contentiously, to a number of themes that, according to some critics, all westerns addressed, notably the conflict between civilisation and the wilderness. In effect, critics sought to identify that which was distinctive visually about a genre – its iconography – and that which was distinctive in thematic or structural terms. Problems arose when deciding which films to include and exclude. This was even the case with an 'obvious' genre like the western where numerous B movies that in various ways might have challenged the dominant critical definition of the western and its significance were not considered either because they were simply not available to critics or, in the case of the popular singing-cowboy films, because they were probably just too embarrassing for those critics who wanted to stress the 'seriousness' of the western format.

A 'chicken and egg' type of problem is apparent here that is common to all genre definitions, namely deciding what comes first – the genre or the definition of the genre? How can one decide which films belong to a particular genre without a definition of that genre, and yet how can one form such a definition without knowing in the first place which films belong to that genre (Tudor, 1973, pp.135–8)? During the 1970s, when much of this genre theory was being formed, there did not seem to be an easy solution to this problem, and most critics ended up asserting their own definitions, with this leading to some partial accounts of genres (many of which have since been challenged by other critics). In retrospect, the most interesting feature of this problem is that it was only a problem for critics, not for the film-makers and audiences who seemed able to negotiate their way through various genres with ease, with this in turn suggesting that the basis of their knowledge of genre was in certain respects very different from that of genre critics and theorists.

If defining the western was not as straightforward as might have been supposed, it was as child's play compared to defining the horror film. Unlike the western, horror films have no distinctive iconography to bind them all together. They are not limited to any particular historical or geographical setting: a horror film can take place anywhere (any town, country, planet) in any historical period (past, present, future). So far as the genre's stylistic identity is concerned, while one can detect stylistic approaches that are popular and even dominant at certain moments in the genre's history – a visually expressionistic approach in the 1930s, for example, or a relatively realist approach in the 1970s – such approaches are not common across the genre as a whole.

In the face of such eclecticism, critics have often become preoccupied instead with what might be termed horror's inner workings, its themes and underlying structures as well as its social function, and have used this as a basis for genre definition. Here notions of repression and the monstrous have become very important. As Robin Wood, one of horror's most lucid critics, has put it, 'the true subject of the horror genre is the struggle for recognition of all that our civilization represses or oppresses, its re-emergence dramatized, as in our nightmares, as an object of horror, a matter for terror, and the happy ending (when it exists) typically signifying the restoration of repression' (Wood, 1986, p.75).

Other critics have taken issue both with Wood's politico-ideological readings of horror and with his reliance on some psychoanalytical terminology. However, there is a general agreement that horror films present us with fearful and unpleasant events and experiences but usually do this in a way that renders those events and experiences pleasurable and/or 'safe'. Of course, this begs all sorts of questions. How is something as subjective as fearfulness defined in this context? By what process does fearfulness become entertainment? Is this feature of the genre its sole property, or can it be found in some non-horror films as well (and if so, what use is it to a basic definition of the horror genre)? Certainly if one wishes to see scary monsters *per se* as a defining feature of horror, one has to deal with the fact that other types of film – science fiction, fantasy, crime (if one thinks of the serial killer as a monster) – also have scary monsters in them, as well as the fact that not all films thought of as horror contain monsters. Or if, following Wood's lead, horror films are about repression, one also has to take into account that repression can be seen as an important element in various westerns, melodramas, thrillers and musicals.

Most critical accounts of horror engage with some or all of these issues, and out of this emerges, as noted above, numerous definitions and delineations of the horror genre as different critics adopt their own particular stances. It seems from this that the prospect of coming up with a model of horror cinema that would enable us to identify definitively which films are horror and which films are not remains as distant as ever.

Recent developments in genre theory have suggested ways around this problem. In particular, 1970s genre theory's concern with defining genres has itself come to be seen as problematic inasmuch as it presupposes that there is a cohesive body of films pre-existing the critical work of definition which only needs to be discovered and described by the observant critic. It has already been noted in this chapter that in fact industrial and fan-based definitions of horror are far from cohesive or consistent, and that, for the market at least, horror – and, for that matter, other genres as well – exists as a provisional grouping of films subject to significant alteration as the requirements of the market change. One might also argue that, so far as it can be ascertained and measured, the audience's understanding of horror is similarly fragmented, pragmatic and short-term. In other words, neither the industry nor audiences think about the horror genre as either a historical or a theoretical totality; instead they operate on a much smaller scale, interested only in what is relevant to them in the context within which their engagement with horror is situated.

It seems from this that those critical attempts to define horror in totalising terms, to come up with a definition that exceeds localised uses of the term, often operate on an abstract level, constructing what in effect is an ideal of horror that is seen to lurk behind a whole range of horror films. This approach results in accounts that stand at some distance from industrial and audiences' perceptions in a manner comparable with those auteurist approaches against which genre theory itself can be seen as a kind of reaction. Different accounts of the horror genre therefore offer competing accounts of what the horror-ideal might be. Genre theorist Rick Altman describes this situation well in his book *Film/Genre*.

> *Genres are not inert categories shared by all (although at some moments they certainly seem to be), but discursive claims made by real speakers for particular purposes in specific situations. Even when the details of the discourse situation remain hidden, and thus the purpose veiled, we nevertheless do well to assume that generic references play a part in an overall discursive strategy.*

> (Altman, 1999, p.101)

It does not follow that all these definitions of horror carry the same weight, however. Some have clearly gained widespread support. For example, it would be hard today to find anyone – an audience member, a critic or a film-maker – who would not accept that *Dracula* films are horror films (although, as we have seen, the 1931 *Dracula* was initially marketed as a weird thriller rather than as a horror film). In fact, one has to wonder whether Universal's attempt in the early 1950s to sell *Dracula* as science fiction was likely to win the assent of audiences who had grown accustomed to thinking of the film as horror. But this consensual position on *Dracula* has only been achieved through the suppression or marginalisation of ways of thinking about *Dracula* – both the original 1931 production and its literary and theatrical sources – in relation to other generic groupings. Nor is it unimaginable that future readings of *Dracula* films may relocate them, or some of them, in relation to other genres, genres that might not yet be in existence. Saying that *Dracula* films are horror films is not the same, therefore, as saying that they are essentially and irrevocably horror films. Rather it is an indication that these films are widely perceived as horror within particular contexts.

This section began by asking the question 'How do you know a horror film when you see it?' By now the answer should be a little clearer. The ways in which you recognise any film as horror is dependent upon the context within which you see the film. Someone in the 1930s is likely to have a very different notion of how horror is constituted from someone in the 1970s (and not everyone in either the 1930s or the 1970s is likely to agree on what films are horror). Moments of consensus do appear – moments when there is a convergence of industrial and critical designations of horror – but these moments are themselves subject to historical change.

What this means is that a definition of horror cinema cannot simply be achieved by reeling off a list of films. The horror genre is much more amorphous and unpredictable than this, and in order to understand this amorphousness and unpredictability, one needs to explore how shifting understandings of horror – industrial, critical and, where the evidence is available, audience-based understandings – are themselves an integral part of generic definition and generic history.

At the same time, one has to be aware that any new account of horror – such as that provided by this book – necessarily represents an intervention into this process of definition. At certain points I will no doubt refer to particular films as horror that some readers might not accept as part of the genre (*The Silence of the Lambs*, for example). Given that there can be no fixed, once-and-for-all list of horror films, this is unavoidable. Such an approach might well prove an affront to those who consider that studying an object involves keeping a distance from that object and thereby protecting one's own objectivity. In the face of this, I would argue that such 'objectivity' is an illusion, a denial that one is always operating from a particular, limited perspective. In the case of horror, writing about the genre involves to a certain extent becoming part of the genre, contributing towards the process of generic development in its broadest sense, and in some small, modest way having an effect not only on what horror is but also on what horror might be. Perhaps the most striking and exciting feature of horror cinema in this respect is that, like one of its own shape-shifting monsters, it is always changing, always in process. At the very least, I hope that this book can give a sense both of the imaginative energies involved in this process and of all those moments in film history when something called horror has left its mark.

WHERE DID THE HORROR FILM COME FROM?

One way of thinking about the identity of horror cinema is to consider its origins. Where did the horror film begin? In historical terms, the answer to the question is clear. Horror cinema began in the early 1930s in the American film industry. In other words, the early 1930s marked the point where the term 'horror' became understood – by the industry, by critics, by audiences – as designating a particular type (or, as we shall see, types) of film, with the recognition of this term apparent not just in America but in other countries where American films were distributed. For example, in 1933 the British film censors actually came up with a new classification, the H certificate, specifically for this new category of film.

It follows from this that when critics designate films made before the early 1930s as horror films, they are doing so retrospectively. As already noted, while German films *The Cabinet of Dr Caligari* and *Nosferatu*, along with *The Student of Prague* (1913) and *The Golem* (1913), might well anticipate and be an influence upon later horror production, they were not deemed to be horror films when they first appeared. Much the same can be said for a small number of films produced within the American film industry before 1930, films which to our eyes look like horror films and which are often classified as such in discussions of horror cinema but which were categorised differently at the time of their original release. These include two early versions of *Frankenstein*, the first produced in 1910, the second – under the title *Life Without a Soul* – in 1916, as well as *The Werewolf* in 1913 and two versions of *Dr Jekyll and Mr Hyde* in 1920 (one of which starred John Barrymore as the troubled doctor). To this list can be added several Lon Chaney films from the 1920s, notably *The Hunchback of Notre Dame* in 1923 and *The Phantom of the Opera* in 1925. The presence of such films in the pre-1930s period showed that when horror cinema did emerge, it did not come from thin air, so to speak, but instead often drew upon and reworked elements already present within cinema.

Many critics have also seen gothic literature as providing another important source for the horror film. However, establishing the precise nature of the connection between gothic and horror is complicated by the fact that the term 'gothic' itself can be just as vague and imprecise as the term 'horror'. Used as a historical term, gothic refers not just to a period of literary history but also to a period of architectural history (and, more recently, has been applied to a youth subculture as well as to a brand of romantic fiction). So far as literature is concerned, the original gothic period ran from about 1760 through to about 1820. The English and Irish novels deemed by literary historians to be part of what was a kind of literary cycle or movement included Horace Walpole's *The Castle of Otranto* (1764), Ann Radcliffe's *The Mysteries of Udolpho* (1794) and *The Italian* (1797), Matthew Lewis' *The Monk* (1796), Mary Shelley's *Frankenstein* (1818) and Charles Maturin's *Melmoth the Wanderer* (1820). Although this work is very diverse, literary historian David Punter has identified some of the elements underpinning it: 'an emphasis on archaic settings, a prominent use of the supernatural, the presence of highly stereotyped characters and the attempt to deploy and perfect techniques of literary suspense' (Punter, 1996, p.1).

But 'gothic' has also been used in a broader sense to designate an approach apparent in both European and American literature throughout the nineteenth and twentieth centuries. Of particular interest here so far as the later development of both horror and science fiction cinema is concerned is a cluster of novels published in Britain in the late-Victorian period which are sometimes referred to as 'decadent gothic'. These included Robert Louis Stevenson's *The Strange Case of Dr Jekyll and Mr Hyde* (1886), Oscar Wilde's *The Picture of Dorian Gray* (1891), H.G. Wells' *The Island of Dr Moreau* (1896) and Bram Stoker's *Dracula* (1897), all of which have been repeatedly adapted for cinema.

The relationship between gothic and horror is not always clear. In some instances, the terms are used as if they are interchangeable, while in other circumstances 'gothic horror film' denotes a type of horror cinema reliant on period settings (Hammer horror, for example). The more common approach is to see gothic literature as a precursor to and influence upon horror cinema. However, it is worth noting that very few gothic novels have actually been adapted for the cinema, with this particularly applying to the initial outpouring of gothic literature in the 1760–1820 years. Of these, only *Frankenstein* and *The Monk* have been filmed (and the 1972 production of *The Monk* – scripted by Luis Bunuel and directed by Ado Kyrou – played down the original novel's horror-like elements). Inasmuch as they display an interest in gothic literary texts at all, horror film-makers have tended to focus, with the notable exception of *Frankenstein*, on the late-Victorian gothic novels, works which in many respects are very different from the original gothics. The other significant fact about the cinematic adaptations of gothic novels that do exist is that none of them is even remotely faithful to the literary originals, with this applying to all film versions of *Frankenstein*, *Dracula* and *Dr Jekyll and Mr Hyde* from the 1930s onwards.

Given that horror production in the genre's initial formative phase during the 1930s was based almost entirely in the United States, it is striking that the work of American gothic writers such as Charles Brockden Brown and Nathaniel Hawthorne did not feature at all in 1930s American horror films. Only the writings of Edgar Allan Poe were used, albeit in a 1932 film version of *Murders in the Rue Morgue* that arguably owed more to *The Cabinet of Dr Caligari* than it did to Poe's original story. (*The Black Cat*, from 1934, and *The Raven*, from 1935, took their titles from Poe but very little else.) So why did those American film-makers who turned to gothic literature for their sources turn to British gothic rather than the American version?

Answering this involves thinking about what happened to certain gothic novels in the period in-between their publication and their entrance into horror cinema, namely that they – and notably *Dracula*, *Frankenstein* and *Dr Jekyll and Mr Hyde* – were adapted for the stage. In fact, an explanation for many of the differences between the 1930s film versions of *Frankenstein*, *Dracula* and *Dr Jekyll and Mr Hyde* and the literary originals is that the films drew upon theatrical adaptations which had already taken considerable liberties with what were often sprawling literary narratives in order to make them work on stage. The popularity of stage versions of certain gothic novels highlights a quality of gothic that was important to the development of horror cinema but which is sometimes overlooked in critical accounts of gothic – its commercial value. This was especially the case with *Dracula*. Published in 1897 by Bram Stoker, himself someone who worked in the commercial theatre, it was adapted for the British stage by Hamilton Deane in 1924 and subsequently revised for the American stage by John L. Balderston in 1927, with this transatlantic version providing the basis for the famous Universal

1930s horror icon: Bela Lugosi as Count Dracula in *Dracula* (1931). Courtesy of Universal Studios Licensing LLLP.

film that starred Bela Lugosi as the Count (for details, see Skal, 1990). The attractiveness of the *Dracula* story to Universal clearly had more to do with its status as a recent commercial success within the American market than with its status as a British gothic text. In other words, if there had happened to have been, say, a successful stage version of American novelist Charles Brockden Brown's gothic masterpiece *Wieland* playing on Broadway in the late 1920s (which there wasn't), we might well have had a film adaptation of that in addition to, or instead of, the version of *Dracula* that appeared in 1931, and the subsequent development of the horror film could have been quite different.

Two more theatrical events that arguably were of significance in the development of the American horror film were the productions on Broadway of *The Bat*, by Avery Hopwood and Mary Roberts Rinehart, in 1920 (based on Rinehart's classic American crime novel of 1908, *The Circular Staircase*) and *The Cat and the Canary*, by John Willard, in 1922. Both were crime thrillers – the Bat in the Rinehart play was not a vampire but instead a master crook – that took place largely in dark, possibly haunted houses, with all sorts of bizarre events going on in the shadows. As one might expect from crime thrillers, everything is explained in the end and the criminals revealed and caught, but for a while these narratives toy with the idea of the supernatural.

The substantial and long-lasting box-office success of *The Bat* and *The Cat and the Canary* led to further plays of a similar ilk, and Hollywood adapted a number of these while also coming up with its own original versions of what has come to be known as the haunted house spoof. *The Bat* was filmed in 1926 and, as *The Bat Whispers*, in 1930 (with another version coming along in 1959). The first film adaptation of *The Cat and the Canary*, stylishly directed by German émigré Paul Leni, appeared in 1927, and two more versions were released in 1930, *The Cat Creeps* and *La voluntad del muerto*, the latter of which was a Spanish-language version shot on the same sets as *The Cat Creeps* but with a different cast and crew. (Universal, the studio that produced *The Cat Creeps*, produced a Spanish-language version of the 1931 Lugosi *Dracula* in similar circumstances. Some critics, notably David Skal, have suggested that this version of *Dracula* is better than the English-language one; see Skal, 1990, pp.153–78.) A fourth version, this time reverting to the title *The Cat and the Canary* and starring Bob Hope in his first major film role, was produced in 1939; and in 1978, a fifth rendition of the tale made a somewhat belated appearance. Other films of this type from the 1920s included D.W. Griffith's *One Exciting Night* (1922), *The Last Moment* (1923), *The Monster* (1925), *Unknown Treasures* (1926), *The Gorilla* (1927), *The Terror* (1928) and Paul Leni's haunted theatre drama *The Last Warning* (1929).

It is interesting to compare theatrical adaptations of gothic novels with these haunted house spoofs in terms both of setting and of tone. If we take as an example of the former the John Balderston stage version of *Dracula*, we find, perhaps surprisingly given that we now tend to associate *Dracula* films with period costumes, that it is set in the 1920s and that, unlike Bram Stoker's novel, the play takes place entirely in England. (The novel's Transylvanian scenes had been cut for reasons of economy but would be reinstated in the 1931 Universal film production.) The tone throughout, as it would be for all versions of *Dracula* until Hammer's 1958 rendition of the story, is relentlessly humourless, and the non-American foreignness both of Dracula and his world is stressed as much as possible. By contrast, the haunted house spoof tends to be set firmly within contemporary America, with not only American heroes and heroines but also American villains. It also usually boasts comedic elements, with the extreme and potentially supernatural and horrific events of the narrative not meant to be taken too seriously.

Historians of the horror film have often argued that monsters in 1930s US horror cinema are, in the main, non-American, with their activities usually taking place on foreign shores safely distant from America. From this perspective, horror itself becomes a kind of foreign intrusion into American cinema, with some of its non-American sources including British gothic literature and German Expressionist cinema. Underlining this is the fact that the two main stars of 1930s US horror, Bela Lugosi and Boris Karloff, were, respectively, Hungarian and English, and a number of important horror film-makers from this period were also not American – for example, the English film director James Whale who was responsible for *Frankenstein* in 1931 and *Bride of Frankenstein* (1935), among others, and the German cinematographer and director Karl Freund who photographed the Lugosi *Dracula* and directed *The Mummy* (1932) and *Mad Love* (1935).

However, such an understanding of 1930s horror tends to be based on one specific type of horror from the period, the horror films produced by Universal Studios (including *Dracula*, *Frankenstein* and *The Mummy*). If one looks at horror films produced by other studios, one can quite easily find narratives set in contemporary America. The significance of the 1920s haunted house spoof in this respect is that it demonstrates that in the years leading up to the formation of the horror film there were numerous examples within American popular culture of fictions involving fear, madness and horror located in recognisable contemporary American landscapes. It follows that while in certain circumstances, the gothic circumstances of Dracula and Frankenstein, the monster might well be foreign, elsewhere monsters sometimes turned out to be much closer to the American home.

In other respects, and despite its modernity, the haunted house spoof can reasonably be seen as belonging, if distantly, to the gothic. As Punter notes, ' "Gothic" fiction is the fiction of the haunted castle, of heroines preyed on by unspeakable terrors, of the blackly lowering villain, of ghosts, vampires, monsters and werewolves' (Punter, 1996, p.1). While there might not be any castles in the haunted house spoof, there are cavernous, castle-like houses along with terrorised heroines, unspeakable terrors, sinister villains, and the threat – if not the actuality – of ghosts and supernatural monsters. In fact this type of fiction can be related to the 'supernatural-explained' mode of gothic fiction associated with novelist Ann Radcliffe, whose work often contained apparently supernatural happenings that ultimately turned out to be part of a criminal conspiracy.

As noted above, there are very few film adaptations of gothic novels in the 1930s (or thereafter, for that matter). Similarly, there are not that many haunted house spoofs in the same period. Yet the influence of gothic literature can arguably be traced in certain films in terms of their settings and some of their themes, while the influence of the haunted house spoof is also readily apparent, usually (but not exclusively) in films that have contemporary settings, including *Doctor X* (1932), *The Old Dark House* (1932) and *Mark of the Vampire* (1935, a remake of the Lon Chaney film of 1927, *London After Midnight*), to name but a few. Importantly, however, the popular entertainment market mediates this kind of influence. There is no evidence that the makers of either the 1931 *Dracula* or the 1931 *Frankenstein* had much respect for or interest in the gothic literary originals, nor that the creators of the haunted house spoof had read, or even knew about, Ann Radcliffe's work. Instead they were all drawing upon and reworking material that had a proven contemporary commercial life either in theatre or in cinema itself.

Any account of horror that sees it as emerging from gothic literature, or as itself an expression of a gothic mode that underpins a range of cultural texts from the eighteenth century to the present, inevitably ends up marginalising the economic forces at work in the creation of horror cinema. One can understand why certain critics shy away from the commercial realities of the horror film. Given that horror has frequently been criticised for being exploitative, those critics concerned to defend it often seek to raise its status through associating it with areas of 'serious' culture (albeit areas of culture such as gothic literature that when they first appeared were themselves sometimes accused of being exploitative). The term 'horror' itself can become somewhat embarrassing and vulgar in this respect, doubly vulgar in fact because not only is it a marketing term but it also describes a crude bodily sensation that stands at some distance from the 'higher' feelings that culture is meant to instill in us. Yet the reality of horror cinema, both in its initial formation and in its subsequent development, is above all else a vulgar commercial reality, and any account of horror cinema needs to engage with the brute forces of the market.

SEQUELS AND CYCLES IN 1930S US HORROR

Understanding commercial film production necessarily involves having to come to terms with the film sequel and the film cycle. While, as we have seen, definitions of genre often operate on a level of generality that can obscure localised deployments of generic terms, sequels and cycles of films usually have a historical specificity to them. They exist in relation to particular times and particular places, and they offer an intermediate stage between the uniqueness of individual films and the formulaic nature of generic production. Genre theorist Rick Altman has argued that cycles of films function as proprietary brand names which are owned, developed and exploited by particular companies – for example, the series of movies at MGM during the 1930s and 1940s featuring Andy Hardy, or the detective films featuring 'The Falcon' at RKO in the 1940s. In this, they are quite different from film genres which are not owned by anyone. It follows that it makes more sense in economic terms for a production company to develop its own profitable film cycles than it does for it to make more general all-purpose genre films (although, as Altman notes, smaller companies with no valuable properties of their own often have little choice but to 'borrow' elements from other successful films for their own – usually low-budget – productions in a manner that hopefully does not leave them open to prosecution for breach of copyright: Altman, 1999, pp.113–21).

Like all film genres, horror can be seen as proceeding via successive waves of sequels and cycles as initial commercial hits are exploited by the company fortunate to own the films in question, while other companies seek to find their own way to cash in on that success. One might go further and argue that, so far as an understanding of genre history is concerned, the follow-up films are more important than the films that spawned them inasmuch as they reveal patterns of generic development not immediately apparent from just looking at the initial work. Bearing this in mind, it is worth considering the role of cycles and sequels in the 1930s, the inaugural decade of film horror.

As noted by most historians of horror cinema, the main producer of horror films in this period was Universal Studios. One of the smaller of the eight companies that dominated the American film industry, Universal had experienced some commercial success during the 1920s with macabre work such as *The Hunchback of Notre Dame*, *The Phantom of the Opera*, *The Cat and the Canary* and *The Man Who Laughs* (1928), although its transition into a 'horror factory' was not a smooth one, with Carl Laemmle, the head of the company, disliking the new horror films produced by his son, Carl Laemmle Junior. Nevertheless, it was Universal that inaugurated the 1930s horror boom with the release in 1931 of *Dracula* and *Frankenstein*, and the same studio was also responsible for the introduction into sound cinema of the mummy in *The Mummy* and the werewolf in *The Werewolf of London* (1935). All four of these represented potential 'brand-name' products or, to use a more modern term, 'franchises', properties that could generate profits across a range of films, and certainly in later years Universal was prepared to defend its 'ownership' of these properties in the courts, notably throughout the 1960s and 1970s when it engaged in a legal battle with the family of Bela Lugosi over who owned rights to images of Lugosi as Dracula. (Universal eventually won the case; for an interesting discussion of some of the legal ramifications, see Gaines, 1992, pp.175–207.)

By contemporary standards, however, Universal was slow off the mark in producing sequels to these four films. Nowadays if a film, and especially a horror film, is commercially successful, one can expect to see a sequel in 1–2 years – perhaps a little longer if it was a big-budget film. By contrast, the first Frankenstein sequel, *Bride of Frankenstein*, appeared in 1935, four years after the original, and the second, *Son of Frankenstein*, in 1939, while *Dracula's Daughter* (in which Dracula only appears as a briefly glimpsed corpse) came out in 1936, five years after *Dracula*, and Dracula himself would not be seen in a Universal film until the 1940s. Horror fans would have to wait even longer for another mummy or werewolf film, with *The Mummy's Hand* appearing in 1940 and *The Wolf Man* in 1941, and in any event both of these proved to be re-workings of the mummy and werewolf stories rather than sequels to the 1930s films (although they themselves subsequently generated several sequels).

This tardiness can in large part be assigned to the absence in the 1930s of what might be termed an established 'sequel culture'. Serials – weekly twenty-minute episodes usually with a cliffhanger ending setting up the next episode – were a popular part of the cinema-going experience, and there were also series of feature films structured around particular characters – the aforementioned Andy Hardy films, for example, or numerous Charlie Chan and Mr Moto detective films. But the idea of making a film that in some way followed on chronologically from a previous film, as opposed to a film that simply featured a returning character, was a novel one. Matters were complicated further for Universal when it quickly became apparent from the critical and public response to *Dracula* and *Frankenstein* that the figures of fascination, the potential brand names, were not Frankenstein or Van Helsing, Dracula's nemesis, but rather the monsters themselves. Unfortunately Universal had killed off both these monsters at the end of the films in which they appeared (and had also killed off the mummy and the werewolf for good measure).

A well-established convention in the various sources, gothic and otherwise, from which the new horror cinema drew, was that the monster had to be destroyed in the course of the narrative. The problem confronting Universal, therefore, was how to bring back a profitable monster, and the solutions it devised to this problem have informed horror film production ever since. One approach, the *Dracula's Daughter* approach, is not to bring the monster back at all but instead to replace him with another monster, in the case of *Dracula's Daughter* a female vampire. The *Scream* films from the 1990s adopted a similar method by keeping the killer's distinctive mask from one film to the next but having different killers behind it for each film. The other, more influential approach is to bring back the 'destroyed' monster, either by retrospectively finding a loophole in the plot of the original film that enables the film-makers to claim that the monster did not die really, or by actually resurrecting the dead monster. *Bride of Frankenstein* exemplifies this approach. In this film, it turns out that the monster was not destroyed by the fire that apparently consumed him at the end of the original 1931 *Frankenstein* but is merely waiting in the ruins of the old mill for the next film to begin. The 'resurrection' option would not figure much in 1930s cinema, but it would be important in Universal's 1940s horror films where Dracula, Frankenstein's monster, the mummy and the wolf man would all repeatedly be brought back from the dead.

It follows that one of the things Universal was attempting to work out during the 1930s was what a horror sequel was. This involved finding a way of resolving the apparent contradiction between the narrative imperative that dictated the monster must die (not until the 1960s would it become acceptable for a horror monster to be left alive at the end of a film) and the commercial imperative dictating that the monster must survive. The fact that there were no obvious precedents for this kind of operation goes some way to explaining the awkwardness of the opening sequence of *Bride of Frankenstein*, with Mary Shelley, Percy Shelley and Lord Byron wheeled on to explain how the narrative of *Bride of Frankenstein* connects with the 1931 *Frankenstein* film. By contrast, *Son of Frankenstein* handles itself as a sequel far more confidently, and by having the new Baron assert that the monster is indestructible, this third Universal Frankenstein film usefully justifies the monster's future appearances in all the sequels to come.

Historians of the horror film have sometimes made a great deal of the fact that a number of post-1960s horror films have 'open' endings in which the monster is not defeated, with this narrative 'openness' itself seen as expressing an ambivalence about, or even a critique of, dominant social values. Whether or not this is the case (and it will be discussed later in this book), it is certainly true that a number of Universal horror films from the 1930s and 1940s also depended upon a kind of narrative openness, albeit one with a commercial function. While, say, Frankenstein's monster is destroyed in *Son of Frankenstein* and the mummy is destroyed at the end of *The Mummy's Hand*, audiences and film-makers by this stage confidently expected these creatures to return, and hence the endings themselves became in effect pro-forma events not to be taken as too final.

The 'sequelisation' of horror initiated by Universal during the 1930s accelerated in the 1940s, with Dracula, Frankenstein's monster, the wolf man and the mummy appearing regularly alongside each other in multi-monster narratives such as *Frankenstein Meets the Wolf Man* (1943), *House of Frankenstein* (1944), *House of Dracula* (1945) and, ultimately, *Abbott and*

The horror sequel: Elsa Lanchester as the female monster in *Bride of Frankenstein* (1935). Courtesy of Universal Studios Licensing LLLP.

Costello Meet Frankenstein (1948). Critics have often seen this 1940s work as entailing a falling away in terms of quality from the 1930s films. Budgets and production values were generally lower in the 1940s than they had been in the 1930s, and an increasing reliance on sequels – with virtually every 1940s Universal horror film a sequel of some kind or other – apparently denoted a more openly exploitative approach to the horror genre than before. Because of this, it has become common in histories of horror for 1930s Universal horror to be considered as a separate entity from 1940s Universal horror, with the former deemed more original, innovative and imaginative.

This negative perception of sequel-heavy 1940s Universal horror is often intertwined with a prejudice against the sequel itself as a particular cinematic format, with the sequelisation process seeming to mark the moment where innovation ends and exploitation begins. Given the importance of sequels and cycles of films in the subsequent development of the horror genre, it is worth pointing out here that the original 1930s Universal horrors – along with later 'original' horror films that spawned sequels – were just as much creatures of the market as the sequels that followed and were just as much exploiting previously existing material (in the form of stage adaptations, etc.). Equally, sequels themselves afforded all sorts of opportunities for film-makers to innovate and engage imaginatively with the material, with this happening more often in 1940s Universal horror than has sometimes been acknowledged.

If one defines a horror cycle as a series of films featuring a particular character (usually a monster), then there is really only one such cycle in 1930s horror, the Frankenstein cycle, with the 1931 *Frankenstein* followed by *Bride of Frankenstein* in 1935 and *Son of Frankenstein* in 1939. (As already noted, *Dracula* only generates one sequel in which the Count himself does not appear.) However, the term 'film cycle' has also been used by historians of cinema to designate a group of films emanating from a particular studio, films which are seen as sharing certain stylistic or thematic features – for example, the horror films produced by Val Lewton at RKO during the 1940s, or the horror films produced in Britain by the Hammer company from the late 1950s through to the early 1970s. From this perspective, all of Universal's horror films from the 1930s might be seen together as comprising a Universal horror cycle, although this presupposes, of course, that they share a common identity.

A survey of the films themselves reveals that virtually all of them – with the exception of *The Raven* – are set away from America but that the majority also have contemporary settings. (1940s Universal horror would be more open to the idea of bringing the monster to America, in *Son of Dracula*, the *Mummy* series and, not least, in *Abbott and Costello Meet Frankenstein*.) Many historians of the horror film have claimed that the monster in 1930s US horror is invariably foreign. Robin Wood has pointed out some of the implications of this: 'the foreignness of horror in the 1930s can be interpreted in two ways: simply, as a means of disavowal (horror exists, but is un-American), and, more interestingly and unconsciously, as a means of locating horror as a "country of the mind", as a psychological state' (Wood, 1986, p.85). Similarly, Andrew Tudor has argued that 1930s horror is set in an 'elsewhen', a space apart from an everyday American reality (Tudor, 1989, p.123). This quality is often linked to the fact that these horror films were being produced during the Great Depression, with the implication being that the films offered an escape into an unreal world away from the depredations of a grim economic reality.

Regardless of the relation of horror to the Depression (an issue to which we will return shortly), it is clear that this understanding of horror is based primarily on the Universal horror film. It is also clear that it entails an 'averaging-out' process by which differences between films are elided in order that a cohesive identity might be assigned to a particular group of films, in this case the Universal horrors. However, if one looks at the films themselves, some very striking differences can quite easily be found. For example, director James Whale's British-set films The Old Dark House and The Invisible Man (1933), with their predominantly British casts and their eccentric sense of humour, have a distinctive character of their own; and one wonders whether in fact they would have been classified as horror films at all if they had not been directed by the man who made Frankenstein. Similarly, the playful use of expressionistic devices apparent in Whale's horror work generally should not be lumped together with the more ponderous expressionistic style of Murders in the Rue Morgue or Son of Frankenstein. If one considers setting alone, one finds that the feudal European settings of the Frankenstein and Dracula films have little in common with the starkly modernist European landscape conjured up by Edgar Ulmer's The Black Cat, and while The Mummy might 'borrow' some of its narrative from Dracula, its Egyptian setting and its attitude to things foreign is quite distinct from its vampiric predecessor.

It seems from this that while the majority of 1930s Universal horror films deployed notions of the 'foreign', no uniform treatment of foreignness was apparent. Nor was there uniformity in terms of style or tone. So far as the latter was concerned, some of the films, notably those directed by James Whale as well as The Black Cat, had their tongues placed firmly in their respective cheeks while others exhibited none of this or any other kind of humour.

1930s Universal horror emerges from this as a heterogeneous grouping of films that are connected only in a loose, fairly general way. This does not mean that Universal horror was not perceived as a distinctive entity at the time, for clearly it was. But the nature of that entity had more to do with its status as a particular brand name than it did with the inherent qualities of the films themselves. Universal became associated with horror, as would

Hammer films in the 1950s and 1960s, because it made more successful horror films over a longer period of time than did any of its competitors. In doing this, it helped to develop some of the key horror stars – Boris Karloff, Bela Lugosi – and other horror specialists (directors, cinematographers, screenwriters) who would subsequently go on to do notable work not just for Universal but for other studios as well. Someone going to see a Universal horror film in the 1930s is likely to have expected a non-American setting, particular stars (Karloff, Lugosi, etc.) and a narrative involving particular types of monster (including vampires, werewolves, mad scientists, etc.), just as decades later audiences for Hammer horror would have anticipated period settings, stars such as Peter Cushing and Christopher Lee, and particular monsters. But these very general expectations, and the brand name with which they are associated, should not be confused with or used to define the films themselves, which are often more distinct from each other than the brand name suggests.

This sense that 1930s horror in general was rather more varied than sometimes supposed is yet more apparent if one looks at the films produced by companies other than Universal, in particular a cluster of films that appeared in the early 1930s. Notable among these were Paramount's *Dr Jekyll and Mr Hyde* (1931) and *Island of Lost Souls* (1932), Warner Brothers' *Doctor X* and *Mystery of the Wax Museum* (1933) and MGM's *Freaks* (1932). Of these, *Dr Jekyll and Mr Hyde* was clearly a 'quality' production, boasting a prestigious director in Rouben Mamoulian and high production values as well as an already-established star in Fredric March (whose performance in the film won him an Oscar). By contrast, *Island of Lost Souls*, with its story of a mad scientist's horrifying experiments, seems a much more opportunistic attempt to cash in on Universal's success. Based on H.G. Wells' novel *The Island of Dr Moreau*, the film explored the sexual tensions involved in a scenario where men take control of the reproductive process in a far more perverse manner than did the 1931 *Frankenstein* (although Universal's *Bride of Frankenstein*, now often seen as a camp or gay film, would go even further in this respect). It also managed to convey the sadistic cruelty of its scientist's surgical activities so effectively that the British censors banned it until 1958 (and it did not receive a public screening in Britain until 1967).

It is clear that the figure of the mad scientist was an important one in many US horror films of the 1930s and 1940s. However, just as one does not find absolute consistency in Universal horror's treatment of foreignness, one should not expect the mad scientist always to be presented in the same way by US horror films in general. Having said this, Frankenstein and Doctor Moreau in *Island of Lost Souls* have more than a little in common: both are foreign (played by English actors Colin Clive and Charles Laughton respectively) and both aspire to control life itself. Accordingly, each of these characters compares himself with God (although Frankenstein's dialogue to this effect was cut from the 1931 film *Frankenstein* in the mid-1930s, for reasons of 'decency'). By contrast, the portrayal of science and the scientist in Warner Brothers' *Doctor X* takes us in another direction.

Doctor X is a whodunnit set in contemporary America. Its narrative deals with the attempt to track down the Moon Killer, a serial murderer who strangles and mutilates his victims. The main suspects are scientists working at Doctor Xavier's Research Institute, all of whom, with their eccentricities and arrogance, potentially fit the description of 'mad scientist'. Ultimately, in true whodunnit fashion, the murderer turns out to be the least likely suspect, an American scientist apparently incapable of strangling anyone because he only has one arm. It is revealed that the scientist in question has developed 'synthetic flesh' with which he can replace his missing limb, strangle his victims and then remove the body parts he needs to continue his experiments. Unlike Frankenstein and Doctor Moreau – whose aims are massively anti-social and who accordingly live apart from society – the scientist's motive in *Doctor X* is in itself a reasonable one. He wants to help the physically handicapped: 'I'll make a crippled world whole again,' he explains as he prepares to kill his next victim. Here the insanity lies instead in the scientist's methods.

The Frankenstein films from the 1930s, *Island of Lost Souls* and the 1931 production of *Dr Jekyll and Mr Hyde* all located their scientists within a moral, or moralistic, framework, with the scientist's actions deemed as transgressive of God's law, and with the scientist himself frequently accused of playing at being God. The extent to which this morality was meant to be taken seriously, and the extent to which it just provided some cover for the film's fascination with the scientist's illicit activities, can only really be decided by detailed reference to specific films (although generally it could be argued that these films are not as moralistic as they are sometimes made out to be). One thing is clear, however, and that is that *Doctor X* lacks this moral dimension. Instead it locates its scientist within an investigatory framework where ethical issues do not matter very much and the focus instead is on capturing the criminal.

Arguably the main reason why both *Doctor X* and *Mystery of the Wax Museum* are different from other horrors of this period has to do with the studio where they were produced. Warner Brothers was associated at this time with a realist style of film-making, as exemplified by its gangster films (including *Little Caesar* in 1930 and *The Public Enemy* in 1931) and its musicals (commencing with *Gold Diggers of Broadway* in 1929), and this realism is more than evident in its horror productions from the early 1930s, both of which were directed by Michael Curtiz who would go on to direct, among many others, *The Adventures of Robin Hood* (1938) and *Casablanca* (1942). Not only are they set in contemporary urban America (although

Mystery of the Wax Museum has a short European-set prologue) but they also offer versions of the street-wise, wisecracking character who would feature in gangster films and musicals as well. In *Doctor X* it is a newspaper reporter played by Lee Tracy hot on the trail of the Moon Killer while in *Mystery of the Wax Museum* it is again a reporter, albeit a female one this time, played by a fast-talking Glenda Farrell as if she has just wandered in from a *Gold Diggers* musical (and indeed Farrell herself would go on to appear in *Gold Diggers of 1935* and *Gold Diggers of 1937*).

Another distinctive feature of these Warner Brothers horrors – and one which stands in a certain tension with their realist qualities – is the way in which they, in a very self-conscious manner, invite an audience to think about its own relation to scenes of fear and horror. In *Doctor X*, for example, Dr Xavier devises an experiment to trap the Moon Killer. All the suspects will be chained to chairs and forced to watch a re-enactment of one of the Moon Killer's murders, and the killer's emotional reaction will be such that his identity will be revealed. Unfortunately, the one scientist left unchained turns out to be the Moon Killer, and the remaining scientists, including Doctor Xavier himself, watch helplessly as the killer menaces Doctor Xavier's daughter. This sequence is one of the earliest examples from horror cinema of an attempt to dramatise what it means to be a horror audience and to witness scenes of terror. The sequence stresses both the voyeuristic appeal of the experience – with the male scientists concealed in darkness spying on the scantily dressed female victim – and the powerlessness it involves, with neither the scientists nor the audience able to intervene when the potential victim is threatened. In a different but related way, *Mystery of the Wax Museum* uses the location of the wax museum itself to explore the public appetite for horrifying experiences. The sense one gains here of films drawing an audience's attention to cinema in various ways was alien to the Universal approach to horror during the 1930s, but it can also be traced in RKO's *King Kong*, the first part of which is about the making of a film, and MGM's *Mad Love*, parts of which are set in a Grand Guignol theatre, and it would subsequently become an important part of the horror genre.

A key feature of genre theory since the 1970s has been to establish what links together films belonging to a particular genre. Within such a context, any differences between genre films can become something of a problem inasmuch as they threaten a sense of generic unity, i.e. if these films are too different from each other, then perhaps they do not belong to the same genre after all. Difference is often seen in this respect as something that is contained by repetitive generic formula, with genre films different from each other only in limited, carefully circumscribed ways. Or difference becomes an expression of the historical development of a genre as sets of generic conventions gradually change over time.

Clearly an approach to horror that seeks to establish that 1930s US horror films are all more or less the same is going to have problems engaging with the sheer heterogeneity of the genre at this time. Connections between these films can be made, but these links need to be seen as operating across a whole range of differences to do not just with stylistic and thematic factors but also with the creative personnel and studios involved in the production process. It is all very well to assert, as some historians of horror have asserted, that horror of this period is organised around a series of stock figures, including the mad scientist, Frankenstein's monster, the vampire, etc., but such an approach fails to recognise that there are significant differences between the various cinematic treatments of these figures. Take the mad scientist, for example. As already noted in this chapter, Universal's Frankenstein is different – in terms of location and motivation – from the mad scientist in *Doctor X* (or, for that matter, *Dr Jekyll and Mr Hyde*). However, one might go further and argue that director James Whale's decidedly camp Frankenstein in the first two Frankenstein films is distinct from the rather more sombre view of the scientist offered us by director Rowland Lee in the third Frankenstein film, *Son of Frankenstein*. Holding up the mad scientist as a figure of cohesion within the horror genre in this period necessarily involves transforming him into an average or essential figure, with this in turn obscuring the specific narrative and stylistic contexts within which this figure is presented and developed.

Similarly, thinking about 1930s horror in terms of its relation to particular notions of modernity can be illuminating so long as one maintains an awareness that different films address modernity in different ways. Clearly, a sense of the modern is important to a lot of 1930s US horror films. One finds a fascination in many films with modern technology, not just the technologies of science but also the technologies of communication and transport. Even those Universal horror films set in an apparently feudal Europe are replete with images of trains, planes and automobiles; and the drama of many of these films, Universal and otherwise, can be seen to revolve around a confrontation between that which is perceived as modern and that which is perceived as ancient or atavistic. Yet the way in which this confrontation is managed varies considerably from one film to the next, ranging from the relatively straightforward depiction of American progressiveness versus European backwardness in *Son of Frankenstein* to the subtler distinction apparent in *Doctor X* between different forms of modernity, the alienating modernity of science and the modernity of urban life (with the latter exemplified by the wisecracking journalist), with both of these contrasted with the primal cannibalistic urges of the Moon Killer.

One other common way of connecting 1930s US horror films together is to see them as responses to, and even expressions of, fears and anxieties associated with the Great Depression. This connection between text and context is most often made in relation to the Frankenstein films, with Frankenstein's monster identified as a powerless proletarian figure with which an economically disempowered audience might identify. (See, for example, O'Flinn, 1986.) Such readings of individual films are often interesting, and something could certainly be made in this regard of the pathos with which some 1930s movie monsters (notably King Kong) are invested. (For a pertinent discussion of Kong, see Carroll, 1984.) However, readings of this type run the risk of oversimplifying both historical context and film text. So far as the former is concerned, it should be clear that not everyone in America during the 1930s experienced the Depression in the same way, that different social groups (divided by class, race, gender, ethnicity) experienced it in ways specific to their own positions within society. Constructing a reading of any film, horror or otherwise, on the basis of there being a shared audience experience of the Depression can therefore be misleading inasmuch as it neglects divisions within American society and tends to view the Depression itself as a monolithic historical fact of which the films themselves are just a reflection. It is interesting in this respect to compare a reading of the 1930s Frankenstein monster in terms of the proletariat with other readings which see that monster either as embodying a coded representation of blackness or as part of a broader play with gender identity within the films in question (Berenstein, 1996; Young, 1996). At the very least, such readings demonstrate that there is something ambiguous or multifaceted about these films, and any readings that assume 1930s audiences all experienced the films in the same way fly in the face of our current understanding of the complex ways in which cinema audiences actually respond to and make sense of what they see.

Matters are made yet more complicated by the sheer variety of films on offer during the 1930s. There is no single type of horror film in this period, no single stylistic approach or thematic identity. Instead there are different types of horror competing for the public's attention, with Universal's horror films proving the most consistently successful in the market place. Connections can be made between films, but these are not totalising connections, i.e. they do not pull all horror films together into a cohesive unit. Certainly there was a growing awareness on the part of both film-makers and critics during the 1930s that a new cinematic category had emerged, but what actually went into that category was subject to constant renegotiation throughout the decade as different groups attempted to exploit the success of other films. To give just a few examples of this, the main reason why MGM's *The Mask of Fu Manchu* (1932), Columbia's *The Black Room* (1935) and Universal's *Tower of London* (1939) were, and continue to be, thought of as horror films is arguably that they starred Boris Karloff, an established horror icon. So far as the narrative content of the films themselves are concerned, it makes more sense to see *The Mask of Fu Manchu* as an exotic adventure story (as three

26

previous Fu Manchu films produced at Paramount and starring Warner Oland as the evil Doctor were seen as exotic adventures) and *The Black Room* and *Tower of London* as historical melodramas. Here the designation 'horror' operates, as it so often does in the history of the horror film, in a short-term, opportunistic manner. Similarly, a cinematic oddity like MGM's *Freaks* ends up in horror partly because Tod Browning, the man who made the 1931 *Dracula*, directed it but mainly, one feels, because no one could think of any other generic category where it might belong. *Freaks* controversially featured real-life freaks, and its disturbing representations of 'abnormal' human bodies can be seen as undermining the special effects-generated body horror on display in the likes of *Doctor X* and *Mystery of the Wax Museum*. In this respect, *Freaks* functions as a kind of anti-horror film, and its presence within horror underlines how broad and capacious that category can be.

Looking at 1930s US horror in this way shows how important it is to be sensitive as much to the differences between horror films as to their similarities. As we will see, later periods of horror production are more visibly organised around particular cycles and sequels, but even there heterogeneity is constantly apparent, with the various relationships of particular groups (including film-makers and audiences) to horror formed within the different contexts (industrial, social, national, creative, etc.) within which those groups are operating. It can be argued here that it is this quality of horror, that which makes it so difficult to define on a once-and-for-all basis, which actually makes it so interesting and lively an area of culture, and that the history of horror's commercial development after the 1930s has more of an innovative and imaginative dimension to it than has sometimes been supposed.

HOW DOES HORROR DEVELOP?

One of the more pervasive and influential models of the history of horror cinema sees it in terms of distinct consecutive periods of development, each of which is characterised by a particular type of horror film. A snapshot of horror's development from the 1930s through to the 1970s might well look something like this.

1930s: Universal horror – *Dracula, Frankenstein, The Mummy*, etc.
1940s: Val Lewton's productions at RKO – *Cat People* (1942), *I Walked With a Zombie* (1943), *The Seventh Victim* (1943), etc.
Second wave of Universal horror production – *The Wolf Man, House of Frankenstein* and various Abbott and Costello films.
Early 1950s: US science fiction/horror – *Creature from the Black Lagoon, It Came From Outer Space, The Thing from Another World*.

Late 1950s: British horror, especially films produced by Hammer – *The Curse of Frankenstein* (1957), *Dracula* (1958), *The Mummy* (1959), *Curse of the Werewolf* (1961).

Post-1968:   The modern/contemporary US horror film – *Rosemary's Baby* (1968), *Night of the Living Dead* (1968), *The Exorcist* (1973), *The Texas Chainsaw Massacre* (1974), etc.

Post-1978:   The slasher film – *Halloween* and *Friday the 13th*.

This particular version of horror's history usefully identifies some important centres of activity within the genre. However, as should already be clear from this chapter's discussion of 1930s horror, it also provides an overly stream-lined picture of generic development, one which does not always take enough account of the range of different horror films available in any given period. In locating the development of horror along an American–British axis, it also marginalises other significant areas of horror production, for instance Italian horror, Spanish horror and Mexican horror. A tendency to see horror in terms primarily of American and British production, with European production only acknowledged so far as its 'art' or 'avant-garde' sectors were concerned, was especially evident in writings about horror from the 1960s and 1970s. For example, in two widely read and fairly representative examples of this type of horror history, Carlos Clarens' *An Illustrated History of the Horror Film* (first published in 1967, subsequently published in a new edition under the more user-friendly title *Horror Movies: An Illustrated Survey* (1968)) and Denis Gifford's *A Pictorial History of Horror Movies* (first published in 1973), Italian, Spanish and Mexican horror are either discussed briefly in passing or not mentioned at all. By contrast, recent critical work on Italian horror cinema in particular has assumed a prominence in writings about horror that reflects not only the sheer volume of horror production in Italy but also the quality and distinctiveness of many of these films.

Even the most cursory glance at the Italian horror film reveals that it does not fit neatly into the historical schema outlined above. Certainly the numerous Italian period horror films that appear from the early 1960s onwards can be related to the Hammer horror films inasmuch as they were seeking to appeal to those audiences who had already made Hammer such a success. (Much the same could be said for the series of Edgar Allan Poe adaptations directed by Roger Corman in America during the early 1960s.) In fact, in a number of these films the Italian film-makers even adopted English-sounding pseudonyms in order to make the films themselves appear more English, i.e. more like Hammer. At the same time, however, Italian cinema was also starting to produce what have come to be known as *giallo* films, lurid psychological thrillers in contemporary settings that often featured acts of sexual or sexualised violence. (*Giallo* – the Italian word for yellow

– referred to the yellow covers of the Italian pulp fiction from which these films drew their inspiration.) Some horror critics have argued that this type of film does not belong to the horror genre in any meaningful way, while others have seen it as comprising an important development within horror, one which in its focusing on extreme psychological states and scenes of sexual violence anticipates later American horror films. But its precise place within a cyclical model of horror history is not clear. Simply viewing it as an early version of the American slasher films of the late 1970s and early 1980s arguably misrepresents it, for in many important respects the Italian *giallo* is different from that type of film. Nor can it simply be seen as an attempt to cash in on the box-office success of Hitchcock's *Psycho* (1960). While there might be a shared emphasis on representing madness within contemporary settings, the *giallo* favours a far more baroque and artificial approach than that adopted by Hitchcock. In any event, *Psycho* itself sits rather uneasily within a horror history that suggests that period horror is not supplanted by contemporary horror until the late 1960s.

It seems from this that at the very least account needs to be taken not only of differences within particular types of horror – for example, Italian period horror is quite distinct thematically and stylistically from British or American period horror – but also of the way in which types of horror overlap chronologically. If one looks, say, at horror in the late 1960s, clearly period horror was not swept away by contemporary horror but continued in various forms, especially in Britain, through to the mid-1970s (and resurfaces at various points later on), with some interesting work done in this area, while contemporary-setting horror films, especially in America, were only inter-mittently present until the huge success of *The Exorcist* in 1973 marked this type of horror as ripe for development and exploitation.

It is also clear that the relative importance of period and contemporary horror varies from one country to the next. For example, in the 1960s contemporary horror seems more firmly established within Italian cinema – primarily via the *giallo* format – than it is elsewhere. In Britain, Hammer did produce a series of contemporary-set psychological thrillers in the 1960s that were clearly designed to exploit the success of *Psycho* (although the plots of these films borrowed more from the French thriller *Les Diaboliques* than they did from Hitchcock's film), but these tended to be 'poor relations' to the better-known period films. This did not mean that British contemporary horror films were absent during the 1960s and 1970s, just that they were being produced by companies other than Hammer, for example Anglo-Amalgamated and Amicus. It follows that any account of British horror in this period that fixates solely or mainly on Hammer gives a distorted view of the relation between period and contemporary horror within British cinema. In America the situation was different again, with a mini-cycle of contemporary-set teen-horror films appearing in the late 1950s (including notable titles *I Was a Teenage Werewolf* and *I Was a Teenage Frankenstein*), *Psycho* in 1960, a mini-cycle of period adaptations of the stories of Edgar Allan Poe in the early 1960s, some early 'splatter-gore' films (including *Blood Feast* in 1963 and *Two Thousand Maniacs* in 1964) from cult director Herschell Gordon Lewis, and then little sustained horror production until the early 1970s when American horror did turn very decisively to the contemporary for its settings and its subjects.

If we look at the development of horror cinema from the 1970s onwards, the idea that any one type of horror can define a period of horror production becomes even harder to sustain. This is unsurprising, perhaps, given that this section of horror history is more familiar to us than those earlier periods of horror where a number of the films concerned have long since sunk into obscurity. Of course, there are obvious groupings to be found in modern horror – the American 'slasher' film or, to use *Variety's* piquant term, 'teenie-kill-pic' from the late 1970s and early 1980s, the 1980s horror franchises (including the *Nightmare on Elm Street* and *Friday the 13th* films), and the revival of the slasher format in the 1990s. However, one also needs to take into account, to name but a few, a significant number of films about zombies and cannibals from both Europe (especially Italy and Spain) and America, continuing production of the Italian *giallo* throughout the 1970s and 1980s, US serial killer films from the 1980s onwards, ghost stories of various kinds, Asian horror cinema, and so on.

Three films released in 2001 testify to the broadness of the horror category. *The Others* is a ghost story that harks back both to *The Innocents* (1961) and *The Haunting* (1963) but is also a film made in the shadow of the huge box-office success of another film about ghosts, *The Sixth Sense* (1999). By contrast, *Brotherhood of the Wolf* is a French production that mixes period drama with martial arts action scenes and a horror scenario involving a ferocious beast stalking through the French countryside. As this description might suggest, the film offers an eclectic mix of pop-cult references provocat-ively intermingled with the more stately values associated with the French heritage drama. Meanwhile *Jeepers Creepers* presents itself as a no-frills horror movie harking back to the brutal simplicity of low-budget 1970s horror and generally (but not entirely) avoiding the self-parodic approach endemic in US horror since the success of *Scream*. Each of these films is positioned differently – by the film-makers, by the films' marketing, to a certain extent by the critical responses to the films – in relation to horror, with each connected to different groups of films within horror history.

Instead of seeing horror proceeding in monolithic, lumbering fashion, relying on just one type of horror at a time, one needs to maintain both a sense of the constant variety of horror production and a sense of how this horror production often involves the creation of retrospective pathways back through horror history. This is most visibly the case with the horror sequel, which very obviously refers back to an earlier film, but it also has a more general importance in horror, with a range of horror film-makers (including those responsible for *The Others*, *Brotherhood of the Wolf* and *Jeepers Creepers*), linking their work in different ways, for commercial and creative reasons, to what has gone before in the genre. As noted above, film scholars, and audiences too, can and do create their own pathways through horror as well, providing their own definitions of what horror is for their own purposes. Horror emerges from this as comprising not just various groups of films produced within different historical and national contexts but also the responses to and understandings of those films generated by film-makers, audiences and critics.

So far as this book is concerned, the critical method implied by this way of seeing the genre involves focusing on specific sites of production – production of films and of meaning – rather than trying to come up with some global theory of what horror is and what horror does. Having said this, it is worth noting here some broader features of horror's history that do have a noticeable material effect on the genre's variegated and international develop-ment. In particular, one needs to be aware of the significant shift that occurs in horror production at some point in the mid-1950s and which can be seen effectively to divide horror into two distinct areas or regimes. The first of these regimes runs from the early 1930s through to the early 1950s, and it is characterised by the dominance of the American horror film. Of course, one can find a few non-American horror films in this period, and the input of non-American creative personnel into American horror was a significant one, but, nevertheless, film horror is almost entirely American-produced up until the 1950s. The second horror regime commences in the late 1950s and it is characterised by production of horror films on an international basis. America no longer had a monopoly on the genre, and one can find significant centres of production throughout the 1950s and 1960s in Britain, Italy and Spain, with non-European countries entering the genre thereafter.

A number of factors were instrumental in causing this shift from one horror regime to another. The traditional Hollywood studio system, the home of most American horror production throughout the 1930s and 1940s, was broken up in the first half of the 1950s as a result of US government anti-trust legislation, with this in turn opening up opportunities for independent producers, both in America and abroad. (In particular, the British company Hammer, subsequently a market leader in the horror genre and the success of which encouraged other European companies to produce their own horror films, benefited from this new American openness to their low-budget products.) The position of cinema within western society was also changing in the 1950s. Cinema attendances fell at this time largely as the result of leisure activities being relocated within the domestic household, with the most visible expression of this increased emphasis on the home being the growing importance of television as a mass medium. The average age of the cinema audience declined, and cinema became more of a young person's medium than it had ever been before. At the same time, both America and much of western Europe saw a gradual relaxation of film censorship, with this facilitating the production of new forms of film horror.

One can also point to broader shifts and changes occurring within western society during the 1950s and developing thereafter, with these the products both of increasing affluence and of Cold War/nuclear-age politics. Clearly one should not generalise too much about these shifts, which relate to the ways that gender, class and race function within society, and their precise impact upon horror is best established through detailed discussions of specific groups of films. However, it does seem that these changes, and the changes to cinema itself as a particular medium, helped to shape both a new institutional space for the production of horror films and, arguably, to create new cultural milieux within which horror could operate and flourish.

A number of horror historians, notable among them Andrew Tudor, have seen horror's development in terms of a move from closed narratives (where the monster is definitively destroyed) and a relative security about social authority towards open narratives (where the monster is not always definitively destroyed) and a relative insecurity about social authority (Tudor, 1989). To a certain extent, this sort of development could be mapped on to the structure I have just outlined, with the closed forms of horror associated with the first American regime and the socially conformist practices of the traditional Hollywood studio system and the open forms of horror with the second international regime and a greater willingness generally to question social norms. Ultimately, however, this is just too neat a picture of the genre. I have already suggested that notions of narrative openness are significant within US horror of the 1930s and 1940s; and other critics have argued that a number of these films do engage in critical fashion with a whole range of normative social attitudes and values. So far as post-1950s horror is concerned, one could reasonably point out that an 'open' ending does not necessarily equate with an 'open' social attitude – as some critics (although not Tudor) assume – and that in all fundamental aspects so-called 'open' horror narratives tend to be just like any other traditional narratives, i.e. they have a beginning, a middle and a conclusion. The content of the conclusion might be different, but it is still a conclusion. In other words, the narrative is not open in the way that, say, an avant-garde film might be open, provocatively refusing the pleasures of closure in order to draw an audience's attention to the nature of the cinematic institution itself.

In an article on the films of Howard Hawks, Robin Wood warns against overly general approaches to Hawks' work that obscure 'the local significances that arise from the fusion of context and concrete realization'. Instead, Wood argues, 'the life of a film is in its detail' (Wood, 1976, pp.205–6). In large part, this chapter has followed Wood's advice in arguing that the life of the horror genre is in its detail. Of course, there are connections to be made between horror films, and one can also identify elements that underpin significant sectors of the genre (as I have already suggested in discussing regimes of horror), and this book will seek to explore some of those connections and shared elements. At the same time, an approach to horror needs to be open to what might be termed here its liveliness, the way in which it exists in process, in incessant change. Looking back at 1970s genre theory, one sometimes detects a quiet desperation on the theorists' part as their attempts to define once and for all a particular genre, in effect to pin it down and stop it moving, are constantly confounded by the unexpected emergence of some generic variant that does not fit into their schema. Horror, surely one of the more protean of the mainstream genres, is particularly hostile to being pinned down. As I hope this book will demonstrate, the main reason for this is that, to borrow a phrase from Frankenstein, it's alive, alive.

CHAPTER TWO

A world of monsters

What's the boogeyman?

(Halloween, 1978)

THE HOUSE IS THE MONSTER

In the late 1950s, film director Roger Corman was trying to persuade exploitation specialists American International Pictures to fund his horror adaptation of Edgar Allan Poe's classic short story *The Fall of the House of Usher*. 'But where's the monster?' asked the AIP executives, obviously finding it difficult to imagine a horror picture which did not feature a monster. 'The house is the monster,' replied Corman, who subsequently got the funding and made the film. Whether or not one believes this often-told anecdote (Samuel Arkoff, co-head of AIP, offers a different version in Naha, 1982, p.29), it does underline the importance of monsters to the horror genre. Monsters abound in horror, and to a certain extent the history of horror cinema is also a history of monsters. This does not mean that all films thought of as horror have monsters in them or that horror cinema has a monopoly on the representation of monsters. But it does mean that in order to grasp what is distinctive about the horror genre, it is helpful to have some sense of what the function of the monstrous is within it.

Critics and historians of the horror genre have offered numerous explanations and theories of the monstrous, with these relating both to 'monsterdom' in general and to particular horror monsters. Some of this work focuses on the nature of the monstrous itself. What makes a monster a monster? Obviously one necessary element is that the monster has to be dangerous and that it does harm to the people it encounters. But simply being dangerous is not in itself enough to bestow monster status. Villains in general

– whether in thrillers, westerns, melodramas, and even some musicals – are all dangerous but they are rarely seen as monsters. Bearing this in mind, one possible way of separating out horror monsters from villains in other genres is by stipulating that these monsters should not only be dangerous but 'impure' or 'unnatural' as well.

This way of thinking about the monster often draws upon the anthropological work of Mary Douglas, and especially her book *Purity and Danger*. In this, Douglas argues that societies develop a meaningful social order through imposing classificatory systems upon 'an inherently untidy experience' (Douglas, 1984, p.4). In other words, order is created and managed through the division of objects and/or properties into distinct groups which are perceived as separate and discrete – categories such as living (as opposed to dead), human (as opposed to animal/non-human), male/female, young/old, etc.

From this perspective, the horror monster is a kind of pollutant; it embodies a crossing of borders and a transgressive mixing of categories. So far as our common-sense way of understanding the world is concerned, the horror monster is a thing that simply should not be. As Noel Carroll puts it in his book *The Philosophy of Horror*,

> they [monsters] are un-natural relative to a culture's conceptual scheme of nature. They do not fit the scheme; they violate it. Thus, monsters are not only physically threatening; they are cognitively threatening. They are threats to common knowledge . . . monsters are in a certain sense challenges to the foundations of a culture's way of thinking.

> (Carroll, 1990, p.34)

Carroll goes on to identify the different ways in which this can happen. Monsters can be categorically interstitial or contradictory, i.e. they blur or undermine distinctions between categories such as, for example, the living and the dead (the vampire, the zombie, the mummy, Frankenstein's monster, more recent creations such as Freddy Krueger and Candyman), human and animal (the werewolf), or human and vegetable (the 'intellectual carrot' monster in the 1951 version of *The Thing*). They can also be incomplete, with various body parts missing; for example, the headless horseman in *Sleepy Hollow* (1999), the reanimated severed hands that wander through *The Beast with Five Fingers* (1946) and *Dr Terror's House of Horrors* (1964), or the disembodied brains that feature in *Fiend Without a Face* (1958). Or they can be formless, such as the shapeless monsters in the 1958 and 1988 versions of *The Blob* and the 1982 version of *The Thing*.

A related way of thinking about the monster involves the concept of abjection. The theoretical inspiration here is provided by Julia Kristeva's

The Powers of Horror, a book that, like Douglas' *Purity and Danger*, shows no interest at all in horror cinema but from which nevertheless horror critics have borrowed extensively. Kristeva identifies the abject as that which does not 'respect borders, positions, rules' and which 'disturbs identity, system, order' (Kristeva, 1982, p.4). Abjection is described as a process integral to the formation of the self, one that involves the exclusion of those elements that might threaten or undermine the individual's sense of him- or herself as a distinct entity. Hence various bodily fluids and substances passing from inside the body to outside become abject inasmuch as they breach the body's borders. Similarly, the sight of our own internal organs is abject because it reminds us of our connection with a biological world against which – according to Kristeva at least – our identities have been constructed. In this respect, the ultimate abjected object becomes the human corpse, an object from which identity itself has been expelled.

In abjection we have a concept that has the potential to help us understand the biological nature of many horror monsters, not only in the way in which they confound distinctions between human and animal but also in their association with gross biological processes. One thinks here of the organic sliminess of numerous monsters as well as the way in which monsters often make visible or foreground aspects of human biology in a manner that renders that biology disgusting. A good example is provided by David Cronenberg's 1986 version of *The Fly*, in which the mutating scientist develops a form of external digestion, i.e. he vomits digestive fluids on to his food before actually ingesting that food. Significantly, much of this biological horror relates specifically to female biology, with menstruation, pregnancy and childbirth all providing potent sources of horror and the monstrous. (See Creed, 1993 for a discussion of this.) This does not just apply to female monsters – with examples including the menstrual telekinetic female in *Carrie* (1976), the woman who reproduces parthenogenetically via an external womb in *The Brood* (1979), the alien mother in *Aliens* (1986) – but also has a broader purchase within horror, with the biological itself sometimes implicitly gendered as 'feminine' as opposed to the more 'masculine' virtues of rationality and self-control.

The sexual politics of horror cinema, and in particular the potentially gynophobic and misogynist elements that can be seen to run through many horror films, will be discussed later in this book. What is important to note here is that the abject does not simply designate that which is disgusting and which threatens identity. The abject also offers a source of fascination and desire, seductively drawing our attention to the limits of our selfhood even as we seek to distance ourselves from that experience. As Kristeva puts it, 'abjection itself is a composite of judgement and affect, of condemnation and yearning' (Kristeva, 1982, pp.9–10). Applying this to some of the horror films mentioned above, one can argue that the bloody sights of the parthenogenetic Nola in *The Brood* and the menstrual Carrie are not simply disgusting – although they are certainly that in some respects – but also invite and play to the fascinated gaze of the spectator. (Whether or not this is implicitly a male spectator is another issue to which this book will return at a later stage.) Similarly, Douglas, in her book *Purity and Danger*, identifies transgressive crossings of categorical borders as moments not just of danger but also of potential empowerment (Douglas, 1984, pp.94–113).

Whether influenced by Douglas or Kristeva, this sense of the monster as an entity that breaches and potentially undermines a particular way of making sense of the world bestows upon the monster itself an ambiguous status. On the one hand, horror films can be seen to reaffirm social categories by driving out the 'unnatural' monster, but on the other hand the very existence of the monster reveals that these categories can be breached, that they – for all their apparent 'naturalness' – are fragile, contingent, vulnerable. In this respect, monsters not only represent threats to the social order but can also offer new possibilities within and transformations of that order.

Other critical approaches to the horror monster are less concerned with the nature of the monster itself and more interested in what the monster might represent. In other words, the question being addressed is not so much 'What is a monster?' as it is 'What do monsters mean?' Of particular importance in this respect are various psychoanalytical and socio-historical readings of horror that usually view the monster as either a symptom of or a metaphor for something bigger and more significant than the ostensible reality of the monster itself. The key difference between this way of thinking about the monster and the anthropology-based way outlined above is that here the monster's true significance is hidden beneath the surface and requires analysis of some kind to bring that significance out into the open. By contrast, the monster's categorical interstitiality or contradictoriness, or its abjected status, is usually on the surface, manifestly obvious for all to see.

The next chapter of this book will deal with the benefits and disadvantages of the psychoanalytical method as applied to an understanding of horror cinema. Suffice it here to note that psychoanalytical readings of horror tend to view the monster as an expression of fundamental psychological processes that underpin the films or the culture from which the monster emerges. For example, James Twitchell and Walter Evans both consider the horror monster as a figure that embodies in a coded manner fears and anxieties about adolescent sexuality. Twitchell argues that 'modern horror myths prepare the teenager for the anxieties of reproduction' while for Evans the power of monsters is related to 'that dark fountainhead which psychically moves those masses in the American film and TV audiences who desperately struggle with the most universal, and in many ways the most horrible of personal trials: the sexual traumas of adolescence' (Twitchell, 1985, p.7; Evans, 1984, p.54). The physical and psychological changes associated with adolescence – the sprouting of body hair, the rush of hormones, a lack of physical co-ordination, intense and confused sexual drives, etc. – are seen as the key to understanding the appeal of such horror monsters as the vampire (the trauma of sexuality), Frankenstein's monster and the werewolf (the trauma of lack of control over one's body), with the horror films themselves acting as a kind of juvenile therapy. The assumption here, of course, is that horror films are primarily for adolescents, not something that is always borne out by the evidence, although Walter Evans, as if in acknowledgement of this, suggests somewhat cryptically that 'Adolescents . . . may be of any age' (Evans, 1984, p.61).

By contrast, Robin Wood offers a more politicised engagement with the horror monster, one that seeks to combine psychoanalytical concepts with Marxist ideas about social oppression. For Wood, the monsters in horror are expressions of social and psychological repression (with the two inextricably linked) that can reveal truths about the political and social structures within which we all live (Wood, 1986). Others have seen the monster in terms of the representation of sexual difference, with the monster figured sometimes as a 'non-phallic' threat to male identity and power and sometimes as a 'phallic' threat to independent women (for example, Clover, 1992; Neale, 1980; Williams, 1984). Monsters can represent the id (i.e. the unconscious) or the superego (i.e. the conscience) and, where critics disagree over a particular monster's significance, they can sometimes be seen as representing both. (For example, see the contrasting discussions of Freddy Krueger, the monster from *The Nightmare on Elm Street* films, in Hutchings, 1996 and Rathgeb, 1991.)

As if this were not enough, horror monsters have also been interpreted as expressions of or as metaphors for socially specific fears and anxieties. From this perspective, monsters help audiences (and perhaps film-makers as well) to engage with and come to terms with those fears. For example, as already noted in the previous chapter, the 1930s Frankenstein monster, as well as various other monsters from that decade, might be viewed as articulating concerns about mass unemployment and an accompanying sense of powerlessness (O'Flinn, 1986). Similarly, horror monsters from the 1950s could be metaphors for the nuclear bomb or for some of the tensions associated with social change during that decade (or both), while 1980s and 1990s monsters might be metaphors for, among other things, AIDS. (On the 1950s see Biskind, 1983 and Jancovich, 1996; on the 1980s see Guerrero, 1990.) Interestingly, this 'monster as social metaphor' approach often assumes that audiences – and sometimes film-makers as well – are unaware, or at least not fully aware, of the true social significance of the horror monster. That is to say, the figure of the monster might help an audience to deal in imaginative terms with some troubling aspect of their social existence, but it does so in a manner that is dependent upon no one, perhaps not even the film-makers, noticing what is actually going on. As with the psychoanalytical method, meaning here lurks beneath the surface, is figurative rather than literal, and requires some critical effort to get at it.

It is difficult, if not impossible, to fit these various approaches to the monster together into a cohesive whole. Adding to the complexity of the situation is the fact that it is not uncommon for critics to mix approaches, with socio-historical, psychoanalytical and anthropological terms interming-ling with each other in discussions of particular monsters. For example, Barbara Creed's book *The Monstrous Feminine* deploys the concept of abjection in both a psychoanalytical and an anthropological manner, while Robin Wood's work on horror uses psychoanalytical concepts within a broadly socio-historical approach.

It is also clear that there is a tension in a lot of this work between providing an account of monsterdom in general terms and trying to explain specific horror monsters. Does defining the monster simply involve the identification of a general function – the monster function – into which all horror monsters can be inserted? Perhaps so, but only to a limited extent. As noted above, monsters are threatening and generally they will chase and kill, or attempt to kill, their victims, and this will be so whether it is Frankenstein's monster, the werewolf, the vampire, the serial killer, Pinhead in the *Hellraiser* films, Candyman, Hannibal Lecter, the demon in *Jeepers Creepers* (2001), and so on *ad infinitum*. Similarly, one can usually identify the way in which monsters breach categories or (although this is a more contentious point) enact psychoanalytical scenarios. However, this consistency in monster function can arguably only be achieved through reducing monsters to the most basic level of their existence. Some accounts of horror make a point of doing this in their attempts to discover structures and concepts that underpin all horror films. As should be clear from the previous chapter, this book is concerned instead as much with the differences between horror films and horror monsters as with what they might all have in common. It is clear that horror monsters from the 1930s are very different in important respects from contemporary horror monsters. Moreover, at any given point in the history of horror, there will be significant differences between monsters, with these differences deriving from the various contexts (authorial, industrial, national, etc.) within which the monsters in question are being deployed. Any approach to monsterdom that seeks to marginalise or efface these differences in the interests of producing a neat cohesive model of the monster's meaning can lead us therefore to an overly simplistic view of the horror genre in general. Horror's gallery of monsters comprises a richly varied if somewhat motley crew. While there might well be some shared familial resemblances, each monster has its own distinct identity and history, and in order fully to understand horror monsterdom in general, one needs to come to terms with particular monsters. To demonstrate this, we can now turn to two horror monsters, the first a true horror star, Count Dracula, the second a more recent arrival, the serial killer.

PRINCE OF DARKNESS

'You think I don't watch your movies? You always come back,' Buffy Summers informs Dracula as she stakes him for a second and final time in the opening episode of Season Five of the television series *Buffy the Vampire Slayer*. Buffy is right, of course, for the history of Dracula in popular culture is a history of his constant regeneration, as the Count keeps appearing at different times, in different places and in different forms, from his introduction in Bram Stoker's 1897 novel up until present day. Not only does he feature in stage, film and television adaptations of the novel; he also exists as an independent, free-floating character who stars or guests in narratives that have little or nothing to do with Stoker's novel.

One possible explanation for the ceaseless popularity of Dracula in our culture is that he represents a fundamental truth about humanity. In other words, our fascination with the figure of the vampire is bound up with a need to explore some essential feature of our own nature. Critics, and especially those with psychoanalytical leanings, have wasted no time in identifying the appeal of Dracula as being in this respect primarily a sexual one. The encounter with the vampire, it seems, is erotic, with the penetrative biting and the sucking of blood it involves part of a transgressive non-genital sexual exchange between vampire and victim. Through this encounter – if one believes the critics, that is – all sorts of sexual anxieties (to do with infantile complexes, relation with parent figures, etc.) are articulated in such a way that, according to one critic, the Dracula narrative 'turns out to be a quite blatant demonstration of the Oedipus complex . . . a kind of incestuous, necrophilous, oral-anal-sadistic all-in-wrestling match' (Richardson, 1991, pp.418–19).

Whether or not one accepts this as an explanation of Dracula's meaning so far as any particular telling of the Dracula story is concerned, problems arise when these ideas are applied to the whole range of representations of Dracula, not just those in cinema but also those in culture generally. Take, for example, a scene that is crucial to many psychoanalytical readings of the novel, the scene where Dracula forces Mina to drink blood from a cut on his chest. 'With his left hand he [Dracula] held both Mrs Harker's hands, keeping them away with her arms at full tension; his right hand gripped her by the back of the neck, forcing her face down on his bosom. . . . The attitude of the two had a

40

terrible resemblance to a child forcing a kitten's nose into a saucer of milk to compel it to drink' (Stoker, 1993, p.363). On a literal level, the scene depicts an unpleasant act of violence directed at Mina (Mrs Harker). From a psychoanalytical perspective, however, the scene can also be viewed as having a sexual dimension, with Mina's drinking the Count's blood carrying distinct connotations of enforced fellatio and rape. The latter reading involves thinking about the scene in figurative terms and suggesting that its 'true' meaning was probably not consciously put there by the author nor was it consciously available to the novel's original readership. In other words, the meaning of the scene, which crystallises the perverse, non-genital sexuality embodied by the vampire, is locked away in the unconscious and requires analysis to get at it.

Anyone looking for a cinematic rendition of this scene in the various Dracula films produced by Universal Studios during the 1930s and 1940s would be disappointed for it does not appear anywhere – not in the Bela Lugosi 1931 *Dracula*, nor in the 1936 sequel *Dracula's Daughter* (in which, in any event, Dracula is only briefly glimpsed), *Son of Dracula* (1943, with Lon Chaney Junior as the Count), *House of Frankenstein* (1944, John Carradine as the Count), *House of Dracula* (1945, Carradine again) or *Abbott and Costello Meets Frankenstein* (1948, which featured Lugosi's second and final appearance as Dracula). In fact, there is no on-screen biting in any of these films, and at no point does Dracula sport fangs. This does not mean that the film-makers were not aware of the vampire's erotic appeal. After all, the 1931 *Dracula* was released on Valentine's Day under the slogan 'The story of the strangest passion the world has ever known'. But this eroticism is, for reasons of censorship if nothing else, more low-key than in the novel, ethereal rather than physical, with much more being made by the film-makers of Dracula's mesmeric dominance of women than his sexual seduction of them.

By the time the British company Hammer released its first version of *Dracula* in 1958 (with Christopher Lee in the title role), censorship had relaxed somewhat, and Hammer was able to offer a more robustly physical and sexual rendition of the vampire's story, with various buxom, negligee-clad women succumbing to the Count's seductive power in full view of the camera. Despite this new openness, however, there was still no sign of a scene in which Mina drinks Dracula's blood. In fact, one would have to wait until 1965, and Hammer's *Dracula – Prince of Darkness*, for horror cinema's first very tentative attempt at such a scene. Here Dracula confronts his intended female victim, bares his chest and cuts himself so that the blood flows – and that is as far as he gets for he is almost immediately interrupted by the arrival of the forces of good. For its later Dracula films, Hammer would often return to Stoker's novel for ideas – for example, versions of Renfield, a character absent from the 1958 *Dracula*, show up in both *Dracula – Prince of Darkness*

Another Dracula: Lon Chaney Junior in a publicity still for *Son of Dracula* (1943). Courtesy of Universal Studios Licensing LLLP.

(where he is called Ludwig) and *Scars of Dracula* (1970), and the scene in the novel where Dracula scales a wall in lizard-like fashion finally appears in *Scars of Dracula*. The scene in *Dracula – Prince of Darkness* in which the Count cuts open his chest should be seen in this light, although its severe truncation renders it a decidedly enigmatic moment, one which members of the audience unfamiliar with Stoker's novel must have found baffling. Why did

Hammer not allow the scene to progress further? Perhaps because it was just too perverse for the rather strait-laced Hammer film-makers who, for all the iconoclasm of their work, tended to adhere to a fairly conventional moral outlook. (Of course, one should also consider why Hammer bothered to include a version of the scene that was stripped down to the point of incomprehensibility. Answering this would probably involve thinking about the speed with which Hammer was churning out horror films throughout the first half of the 1960s, a speed which meant that sometimes elements were included in films without being thought through or fully integrated into the overall narrative.)

Finally, in the 1979 version of *Dracula* (in which Frank Langella plays the Count), a woman gets to drink Dracula's blood. However, the tone of the scene is quite different from Stoker's version. Stoker stresses both the violence involved in Dracula's encounter with Mina and her subsequent traumatisation. The 1979 film presents the scene in a much more ambiguous way. Although it begins with Dracula announcing that he will be master of this woman (here, in a film which switches round virtually all of Stoker's characters' names, renamed Lucy Seward), the scene that follows is presented as a love scene, and the drinking of blood a consensual act involving no physical violence from Dracula. Throughout the film Lucy has proved far more assertive than previous Dracula heroines, and it is never clear to what extent she is coerced into a relationship with the Count and to what extent she wills it herself. The film concludes with her apparently still on Dracula's side, smiling enigmatically as a shape that might or might not be the Count flies off into the distance. The assertiveness of the heroine is taken yet further in Francis Coppola's film *Bram Stoker's Dracula* (1992) when Dracula (played by Gary Oldman), having opened up a wound on his chest, decides that it would be for the best if Mina did not drink of him. Mina has other ideas, however, pushes him back on the bed and starts sucking away. (By the time we get to Buffy's encounter with Dracula in 2000, matters are even more forthright. After drinking the vampire's blood – decorously from his arm rather than from his chest – Buffy proceeds to beat up Dracula and then stakes him.)

We seem to have travelled some distance from the violated heroine presented by Bram Stoker in 1897 to the altogether more proactive Mina presented in Coppola's film, with this journey involving multiple re-imaginings of Dracula as he and associated characters are constantly modified to make them relevant and engaging for successive audiences. Arguably it is here, in the creative work of regeneration, that one finds a key to understanding Dracula's cultural significance. It should be clear that Dracula is in no way a fixed, stable figure but exists perpetually in a state of flux, with this having implications for the way in which he is viewed and interpreted by film-makers, audiences and critics. Instead of seeing the Count as an entity emerging spontaneously from some inner recess of our collective psyche (as some psychoanalytical accounts would have it), it is perhaps more apt to think of him as a focus for cultural and economic activity as film-makers periodically seek to resurrect the vampire in a form that will be both interesting and profitable. This does not mean that psychoanalytical approaches cannot illuminate the Count's significance at any point in the creative development of that figure, but it does suggest that any interpretation of Dracula that views him independently of the history of his various manifestations in culture (with these involving appearances not just in cinema but on the stage, in literature and on television as well) fails to engage with the creative energies that have helped keep Dracula alive over the decades.

A survey of the various Draculas shows certain trends and tendencies emerging over time. For one thing, as should be apparent from the discussion above of the scene where Mina drinks Dracula's blood, the female non-vampire characters in Dracula films become increasingly powerful and independently minded. In Stoker's novel, they are essentially helpless creatures requiring the protection of men, and their passivity continues unabated – through all the Universal and Hammer Dracula films – until the 1970s. As already noted, the female lead in the 1979 *Dracula* is different, more assertive and, so far as one can make out, not particularly wanting to be rescued from Dracula. To a certain extent, her appearance can be seen as reflecting changing social mores in the 1970s, and especially the inroads made by feminism during this period into traditional patriarchal assumptions about what women were and how they should behave. It is significant in this respect that strong, assertive female characters begin to show up elsewhere in the horror genre in the late 1970s, notably in slasher films such as *Halloween* (1978) and *Friday the 13th* (1980) and the various sequels and 'rip-offs' that followed. It quickly became a convention of this type of film that the monster would be defeated not by a male hero, as would have been the case in earlier types of horror, but instead by a teenage female, dubbed 'the final girl' by Carol Clover (Clover, 1992). Whether this final girl can be seen as a positive, progressive representation of women is another matter, however. Certainly the slasher films were heavily criticised, by feminists and others, in the late 1970s and early 1980s for what was perceived as their misogynist terrorisation of women. More recently, Carol Clover has argued that these films are more complex and ambiguous than previously supposed, although she too holds back from seeing the slasher as 'progressive' in any straightforward way. (The slasher film will be discussed in more detail in Chapter 9.)

Comparable ambiguities are apparent in the treatment of Lucy in the 1979 *Dracula*. On the one hand, her intelligence and assertiveness are presented as attractive features, and in this she can be seen potentially as a positive representation of the female. But on the other hand, the film is very much concerned to 'contain' Lucy via a romantic liaison with a male, and in the world the film conjures up of inadequate males – this is the Dracula film where, uniquely, Dracula stakes a doddering Van Helsing – the only male up to the task appears to be Count Dracula himself. As noted above, this contradiction – between seeing Lucy as an independent character and presenting her as an object to be fought over by men – remains unresolved at the film's enigmatic conclusion.

The 1979 Dracula also offers a further development of something already apparent in earlier versions of Dracula, namely the transformation of the Count himself into a romantic figure. It is hard to think of Stoker's Dracula in this way. While occasionally urbane, he is never described as physically attractive; on the contrary, he is, more often than not, utterly repulsive. This sense of the vampire is carried over into the first major cinematic adaptation of the novel, F.W. Murnau's Nosferatu (1922), in which the actor Max Schreck provided a memorably animalistic version of the Count. However, the casting of Bela Lugosi in the 1931 Dracula (he had also played the part on Broadway) marked a first step in the cinematic domestication of the Count, transforming him from the wild thing envisaged by Stoker into something more dapper and civilised. Not especially handsome by contemporary standards, Lugosi nevertheless received considerable fan mail from a female audience. Later Draculas – notably those played by Christopher Lee, Frank Langella and Gerard Butler in Dracula 2000 (2000) – would similarly benefit from matinée-idol good looks and, in comparison with Stoker's Dracula, would exhibit a youthfulness and vitality often lacking in the male characters surrounding them. Dracula films also increasingly present the vampire as a mournful, lonely figure seeking out the one woman who will make his life meaningful, with this reaching its culmination in Coppola's Dracula and Dracula 2000. Associated with this is a tendency to view Dracula in more sympathetic terms as a rebel or outsider whose defiance of social authority has potentially a noble dimension – implicitly in the 1979 Dracula, explicitly in the 1992 version. (It is interesting in this respect that in recent years the vampire has been presented – in the novels of Anne Rice, in the television series Angel – as a hero whose sensitivity marks him as superior to run-of-the-mill humans. It seems that the transformation of the vampire from villain to something altogether more positive is now complete.)

Stoker's original 1897 novel can be seen as a kind of invasion narrative in which the vampire, a mysterious figure from the East, threatens to invade both British society – via the proliferating infectiousness of vampirism – and the British body, with this clearly answering to various social anxieties in Britain in the late-Victorian period. In contrast, cinema has never shown much interest in the idea of invasion but instead has presented the story of Dracula as a perverse romantic one. One possible reason for this shift of emphasis is that it focuses the narrative and makes it more linear and manageable for film-makers, as opposed to the sprawling and disjointed narrative structure provided by Stoker. In addition, anxieties about alien incursions from the East would not have especially concerned American and British audiences and film-makers from the 1930s onwards, when Dracula was making his mark in cinema, whereas the idea of Dracula as 'the terrifying lover who died yet lived' (to borrow a phrase from the poster for the 1958 *Dracula* produced by Hammer) seems to lend itself much better to development as a story concept.

The persistence of Dracula over decades also means that representations of this figure, especially the post-Lugosi ones, are produced in the full knowledge of, and often as a response to, what has gone before. This particularly relates to what might be termed the 'I am Dracula' moment, the moment where each film has to introduce its own version of the vampire. For instance, the introduction of the Count in Hammer's 1958 film mimics Bela Lugosi's famous appearance on the castle staircase in the 1931 film (a scene which many remember as Dracula's first appearance, although by then he has in fact already appeared twice in the film). Again Dracula stands at the top of a staircase and proceeds down it towards his English visitor, not Renfield, as in the 1931 version, but instead, as in the novel, Jonathan Harker. (Although Terence Fisher, the director of the Hammer *Dracula*, claimed in interviews not to have seen the Lugosi film, elsewhere, in other interviews, he displayed a knowledge of the staircase scene. The 1931 Lugosi *Dracula* was still being shown in British cinemas in the mid-1950s and was also beginning to show up on American television, so it is possible that the audience for the Hammer *Dracula* would have also been able to make a comparison between the Universal and the Hammer versions.) The parallels between the two scenes serve mainly to underline their differences from each other. While the Lugosi version presents us with a large, gloomy set through which a squat, thickly-accented vampire moves slowly and ponderously, Hammer gives us a smaller, cosier castle, with Dracula himself moving with speed and grace and speaking with an impeccable English accent. The fact that the Hammer version was in lurid Eastmancolor rather than black-and-white also served to distinguish it from its predecessor and was a selling point on the poster for the Hammer film. It is clear that at least part of the effect of Hammer's sequence depends on its both invoking the Lugosi version and at the same time differentiating itself from that version. Later Dracula films too, including Hammer's own sequels to the 1958 *Dracula*, would also constantly be looking backwards, referring to and borrowing from earlier Dracula films if only to show how different, special and up-to-date the latest version actually was (with Coppola's 1992 film especially assiduous in this respect).

The self-consciousness this involves is apparent in other areas as well. The 1931 film gives considerable time and space to the need to convince those of its characters who do not believe in vampires that such things actually exist. Later *Dracula* films are much less patient with such people. Jonathan Harker in the 1958 Hammer *Dracula*, for example, is not the unsuspecting innocent found in Stoker's novel but instead a vampire hunter who already knows all about the undead. Given the persistent popularity of Dracula in our culture, the question addressed by each film gradually becomes not so much 'Why should sane, rational people believe in vampires?' as 'How is it possible for anyone not to have heard of Dracula?' By the time we get to *Dracula 2000* and *Buffy the Vampire Slayer*, the air is thick with awkward jokes about and references to Dracula as a popular fictional character.

This short overview of patterns and tendencies in the development of Dracula has, of course, only scratched the surface. There is more to the Universal Dracula than Lugosi, for instance, with both Lon Chaney Junior and John Carradine providing interesting variations on the Count. And what about the comedy Draculas played by George Hamilton in *Love at First Bite* (1979) and Leslie Nielsen in *Dracula – Dead and Loving It* (1995)? Or the European Draculas, not just Max Schreck in *Nosferatu* but also Klaus Kinski in *Nosferatu the Vampire* (1979), Christopher Lee in the Spanish *El Conde Dracula* (1970) and Udo Kier in *Blood for Dracula* (1973). There are also some notable television Draculas: in America John Carradine in 1956 and Jack Palance in 1973, in Britain Denholm Elliot in 1969 and Louis Jourdan in 1977.

The more one considers the commercial reality of Dracula, the harder it becomes to find any single interpretation that can bind together all versions of the Count into a cohesive whole. His appearance changes over time, moving from the dapper vampire offered by Lugosi and Lee to the more Bohemian, long-haired look preferred by Gary Oldman and Gerard Butler. His relationship with the characters who surround him also shifts from one film to the next. The fact of his foreignness, something vital to the novel, is played up in some films (the 1922 *Nosferatu*, the Lugosi version) and played down in others (the 1958 and 1979 versions, for example). Even those elements that might be seen to define Dracula in a very fundamental way – the sexual dimension of vampirism, Dracula as a figure transgressively crossing the barrier between life and death – turn out to be not in themselves meaningful but rather are only made meaningful by film-makers who inflect and revise them for their own purposes.

Of course, this begs the question of why it is that Dracula has been so successful and has such a sustained presence in horror in comparison with some other horror monsters. Compare Dracula in this respect with the mummy, a monster that has been around in horror cinema for decades but which has generated neither the number nor the range of interpretations associated with Dracula, largely, it could be argued, because of the limitations inherent in the concept of the mummy itself. Notwithstanding the inventiveness of film-makers such as Karl Freund (director of *The Mummy* in 1932) or Seth Holt (director of *Blood from the Mummy's Tomb* in 1971, an adaptation of Bram Stoker's novel *Jewel of the Seven Stars* (1903)) and the reworking of the mummy in recent action adventures *The Mummy* (1999) and *The Mummy Returns* (2001), the history of mummy films in general suggests that there is only so much you can do with a cloth-wrapped ancient Egyptian. By contrast, the Dracula narrative as initially envisaged by Bram Stoker in 1897 offered a greater potential for meaningful development, with its heady mix of passion, death, aristocracy and the supernatural. Importantly, however, Dracula has only become an important, long-lived cultural icon because of the subsequent elaborations of his identity, many of them bold and imaginative, produced by film-makers, writers and artists. In other words, Dracula has remained alive because cinema, and to a lesser extent other media, has kept him moving, changing, transforming. And, if Buffy the vampire slayer is right, there is more still to come, for if the history of horror tells us anything, it is that Dracula always comes back.

KILLING MACHINES

While Dracula is a venerable horror monster that is long established in the genre, the serial killer represents a more recent development in the world of monsterdom. It could be argued that, unlike Dracula, the serial killer is not a proper horror monster at all. For one thing, unlike all major preceding horror monsters the serial killer exists in real life as well as in fiction. In his book *The Philosophy of Horror*, Noel Carroll defines horror monsters as 'any being not now believed to exist according to reigning scientific notions' (Carroll, 1990, p.35). Such a definition clearly applies to vampires, werewolves and ghosts, and, if stretched a little, it can also apply to pseudo-scientific entities such as Frankenstein's monster which, in the 1930s versions at least, tended to be the product of a fictional science that existed at some distance from real science (although Hammer's 1960s Frankenstein films, made in an era of significant surgical-medical advances, would close that distance somewhat). But such a definition would seem to exclude serial killers from horror monsterdom for while most of us do not believe that vampires or werewolves actually exist, it is hard for anyone to deny the existence of real-life serial killers.

However, Carroll does qualify his definition by pointing out that while some monsters might exist in reality, 'their presentation in the fictions they inhabit turn them effectively into fantastical beings' (Carroll, 1990, p.37). Carroll illustrates this point by reference to *Jaws* (1975), a film in which the shark behaves in a manner hitherto unknown in the history of sharks, demonstrating superior intelligence and a preternatural ability to survive attempts to kill it. Similarly, the serial killer in film fictions can be seen as quite different from real-life serial killers. So far as can be made out, the reality of serial killers is a sad, dreary one, with the killers themselves pathetic, dysfunctional and rather tedious individuals who murder in a desperate attempt to install significance in their empty, meaningless lives. By contrast, serial killers in films are considerably more exciting. Sometimes they are powerful and virtually indestructible (in this respect, not unlike the shark in *Jaws*, a monster which has some affinities with the serial killer). On other occasions, they can be charming, articulate, cultured and altogether more intelligent and sophisticated than the people trying to catch them. Serial killer Hannibal Lecter, to date 'star' of four films, is undoubtedly the epitome of the latter type. Joan Smith has noted of him that 'a real serial killer once observed that Hannibal Lecter . . . was entirely unconvincing: anyone as charismatic as Lecter, he pointed out, would not need to commit murder' (*The Guardian G2*, January 8, 2002, p.12).

As is the case with Dracula, the concept of the serial killer, in both fact and fiction, has its own distinct history. The term itself was not coined until the mid-1970s but since then has often been used retrospectively to describe crimes from earlier periods, most notably the Jack the Ripper killings that took place in London in 1888. (As social historian Judith Walkowitz has noted, the Ripper killings offered a curious mixture of fact and fiction, with much of the 'Jack the Ripper' phenomenon, including the name itself, an invention of the media: Walkowitz, 1992.) The concept of the serial killer does not really gain much purchase in cinema until *Manhunter* (1986), *Henry – Portrait of a Serial Killer* (1986) and *The Silence of the Lambs* (1991), although thereafter it rapidly becomes a widely used term. Again, however, the term has been used retrospectively to refer to cinematic representations of killers that were not labelled as 'serial killers' at the time of their production.

Of particular significance in this respect are four films directed by Alfred Hitchcock: *The Lodger* (1926), which draws some of its inspiration from the Ripper killings, *Shadow of a Doubt* (1943), in which the murderer of a series of women returns to his small-town home, the classic horror-thriller *Psycho* (1960) and *Frenzy* (1972), in which an obsessive repeat-murderer stalks through Covent Garden. Of these, it is *Psycho* that sets one influential pattern for representing the serial killer, namely the serial killer as psychological case study. Here the obsessive actions of the killer – in this case Norman Bates (although this also applies to a certain extent to Uncle Charles, the killer in *Shadow of a Doubt*) – are seen to derive from some trauma in the killer's past and/or from some underlying mental condition. For Norman Bates, the trauma relates to his murder of his mother and her lover, and his subsequent killings emanate from his attempts to deny that his mother is dead.

Robert Bloch, who wrote the novel upon which the film of *Psycho* was based, took as his inspiration the real-life serial killer Ed Gein, a mother-fixated recluse who not only killed people but also dug up corpses from the local cemetery and took to wearing human skin. Other films about Gein, notably *Deranged* (1974) and *Ed Gein* (2000), have followed the 'case-study' approach in their exploration of the killer's bizarre relationship with his mother as the source of his aberrant behaviour. (Ed Gein was also one of the sources for *The Texas Chainsaw Massacre* in 1974 and *The Silence of the Lambs*. After Jack the Ripper, he has the somewhat dubious distinction of being the serial killer who has most influenced the development of horror cinema.) Similarly, the murderous behaviour of the Tooth Fairy, the serial killer in *Manhunter* and in *Red Dragon* (2002, an adaptation of the same novel that had inspired *Manhunter*) and of Buffalo Bill in *The Silence of the Lambs*, is shown as having a basis in the warped psychologies of the killers, psychologies that need to be understood in order that the killers can be caught. Hence the importance in both films of the profiler, the person who can see into the mind of this particular type of monster.

A contrasting use of the serial killer can be found in a 1964 Italian film *Sei donne per l'assassino* (literally 'Six Bodies for the Killer', although the English release title was *Blood and Black Lace*), a *giallo* directed by Italian horror maestro Mario Bava. In this, a masked, black-gloved figure stalks female models working for a fashion house and murders them in a variety of extremely violent ways, including strangulation, stabbing, burning, suffocation and drowning, with the film itself sparing no details of these killings. At the end of the film, it is revealed – in a plot twist that anticipates the *Scream* films – that there are two killers using the mask disguise, one male and one female, with the male motivated by greed and the woman by her love for the man and her need to protect herself from blackmail. Here the serial killers are not presented as 'ill' but instead just as criminals. More importantly, the film's emphasis is not so much on either the identity or the motivation of its killers, both of which are revealed in a very desultory way, as it is on showing these killers as killing machines, as faceless, impersonal, emotionless murderers who efficiently despatch a series of female victims and show none of the mental trauma displayed by, say, Norman Bates in *Psycho*. As has been noted by critics, in both approving and disapproving terms, the killings themselves are presented as aesthetically pleasing spectacles, featuring inventive uses of colour, light, camera movement and editing, with the killer acting as the masterful organising agent behind the spectacle.

Connections can be drawn between a *giallo* like *Sei donne per l'assassino* and the American slasher film of the late 1970s and early 1980s. As with the *giallo*, in the slasher the monsters tend to be presented as killing machines rather than as psychological case studies as they kill off a series of teenage victims with mechanical efficiency. While *giallo* and slasher alike offer explanations for their killers' behaviour, these are sketchy at best and rarely involve a sustained exploration of the killer's psychology. In the slashers, for example, the killer is often motivated by a desire for revenge for some unpleasant act directed against it or against a loved one in the past – note in this respect *Terror Train* (1980), *Prom Night* (1980) and *The Burning* (1980) as well as more recent films such as *Cherry Falls* (2000) and *Valentine* (2001). Of course, there are also differences between the *giallo* and the slasher. The killers in *Sei donne per l'assassino* are mature and sophisticated individuals, and their choice of disguise, weapons and scenarios of death reflects a sense of style. By contrast, the slasher-killer is usually presented as immature and with his violence often betraying an inarticulate child-like rage. But in all these films – *giallo* and slasher alike – the serial killer tends to be masked and/or constantly lurking in darkness, not there as a psychologically individuated character but rather as a principle of threat and violence.

Hannibal Lecter – in *Manhunter*, *The Silence of the Lambs*, *Hannibal* (2001) and *Red Dragon* – can be seen to combine some of the elements associated with different types of serial killer. He displays the sophistication and culture of the *giallo* killers and, especially in *Hannibal*, is very much the stylish serial killer about town. However, while he is not masked (other than when he briefly dons human skin and a restraining mask in *The Silence of the Lambs*) and has a compelling, charismatic personality, he is never offered up for the psychological case-study approach. (The novel *Hannibal* does tentatively explore his psychology, but these elements are not present in Ridley Scott's adaptation of the novel.) In this, he is presented as a different type of serial killer from the Tooth Fairy in *Manhunter* and (especially) *Red Dragon* and Buffalo Bill in *The Silence of the Lambs*, for while both of these 'lesser' serial killers are ultimately knowable in psychological terms, Lecter himself remains supremely enigmatic.

But there is more to Lecter than this. The combination he offers of charm and brutality is reminiscent of that displayed by classic villains in Gothic literature – with examples including Montoni in Ann Radcliffe's *The Mysteries of Udolpho* (1794), Count Fosco in Wilkie Collins' *The Woman in White* (1860) and Silas in J. Sheridan LeFanu's *Uncle Silas* (1864) (Hutchings, 1996). His intellect links him with other criminal masterminds, from Dr Mabuse, the criminal mastermind who featured in several Fritz Lang films, to any number of megalomaniac villains in James Bond films (all of whom in any event can be seen as lineal descendants of the original Gothic villains). He is also the latest in a long line of mad psychiatrists that stretches back to the 1930s. A composite monster, then, Lecter represents a curious mixture of the old and the new, and it is arguably this quality, which facilitates a constant shifting back and forth between different persona (psychiatrist, raconteur, cannibal, etc.) that renders him both so fascinating and so appalling. (John Doe in *Seven* and Daryll Lee Cullum in *Copycat* are close relatives of Lecter in this respect, similarly enigmatic and masterful although lacking Lecter's chilling charm.)

Critics and theorists have offered a variety of explanations for the popularity of the fictional serial killer. One response, which is especially associated with the slasher film, is to see this fascination with the killer as an expression of misogyny, a misogyny that is apparent in the killers, in the films and in the broader culture that supports the films (for example, Clover, 1992; Williams, 1984). Another is to view the serial killer, not just the fictional ones but the real ones as well, as a product of and response to a society that is becoming increasingly depersonalised and fragmented (Jancovich, 1992, pp.104–9). The effectiveness of such interpretations is to a large extent determined by the specificity of their definitions of the serial killer itself, for, as we have seen, there are distinctive types of serial killer existing in culture, with different aesthetic and narrative strategies associated with each, and arguably different meanings as well. As is the case with Dracula, the more general the interpretation, the more likely it is to miss important differences between fictional (and real) manifestations of the serial killer.

Of course, this does not mean that general issues regarding the cultural significance of the serial killer are unworthy of attention. Something clearly needs to be said about the fact that most serial killers – not just in fiction but in reality as well (although what the relationship is between fiction and fact so far as serial killers are concerned is not always clear) – are male. This in itself does not automatically support any charge of misogyny; not all films about serial killers feature women as their main victims, although many do. But it can be connected with the fact that the majority of horror monsters are also male. Why should this be? Such is the variety of horror monsterdom, there is probably no single answer to this question. However, constantly posing the question in different contexts and in relation to different groups of films can help to illuminate the complex sexual politics of the horror genre.

Another general issue, which has already been raised in the previous chapter, relates to whether the serial killer actually belongs to the horror genre. Some would consider many of the films cited above as thrillers rather than as horror films. One possible response here is to identify Gothic or horror-specific elements within a range of serial killer films in order to justify their inclusion within the horror genre. Such elements might include a reliance on notions of repression, especially so far as the relation between past and present is concerned, or the sheer amount of violence and gore on offer in many serial killer films. It is also possible to view the serial killer, for all his realist credentials, as an impure or interstitial creature, as someone who breaches social categories of meaning in a manner akin to that of Dracula and other 'classic' monsters. Noel Carroll's suggestion that Norman Bates in *Psycho* can be seen as blurring distinctions between living and dead and between male and female can be applied to other serial killers as well, for this is an area of horror cinema rich in images of not only deathly pale-faced murderers but also ambiguously gendered ones (Carroll, 1990, p.39; for a discussion of gender ambiguities in the American slasher film, see Clover, 1992). In addition to this, the serial killer can be taken as an important vehicle for a fairly broad change occurring in horror from the 1960s onwards, one that involved an increasing stress in the genre on contemporary settings and psychopathological dramas. As noted in the previous chapter, this change does not happen uniformly across the different horror-producing countries, and the serial killer takes different forms at different times in, say, Italy, America and Britain, but it does seem that this particular monster, while not restricted just to horror, does occupy an important place in the historical development of the horror film.

Seen in this way, the many faces of the serial killer direct us to some questions – about the gender politics of horror, about the way that the horror film changes over time – that can perhaps more profitably be explored through analysis of particular serial killers in the contexts within which they were produced by film-makers and received by audiences. Stressing the relative modernity of the serial killer should not obscure one further general point, however, which is that most horror monsters are in a sense serial killers. They kill a series of victims within particular narratives, and the more successful of them continue killing from one film to the next. Dracula and Frankenstein's monster, the werewolf, and the Moon Killer from *Doctor X* (1932) are all serial killers. So are Freddy Krueger from the *Nightmare on Elm Street* films, Candyman and Jason from the *Friday the 13th* films. From this perspective, serial killing becomes a basic function of all monsters, another way of thinking about the threat they pose.

So, for example, when in *Halloween* the serial killer Michael Myers survives being stabbed in the neck, in the eye and in the chest and, shortly thereafter, being shot six times at point blank range and falling out of an upstairs bedroom window, something very fundamental is being said not just about this particular serial killer but also about monsterdom in general, and that is that monsters, and not just Dracula, always come back. But as a brief survey of representations of Dracula and the serial killer demonstrates, they do not always come back the same. They change, they mutate, they transform in their ongoing attempts to surprise and confound us. Because of this, critical accounts both of monsterdom in general and specific monsters are constantly struggling to keep up with the inventiveness that forever pushes onwards the horror genre and its monsters. After all, what single 'explanation' of vampirism could possibly encompass not just all versions of Dracula but also the poetic subtleties of Carl Dreyer's *Vampyr* (1932), Harry Kumel's *Le Rouge aux lèvres* (1971) or Guillermo del Toro's *Cronos* (1993) as well as, say, the martial-arts vampirism of *Blade* (1998)? Similarly, what theorisation of the serial killer could encompass all the variations played by cinema, and culture in general, on that monster, with faceless and impersonal killers intermingling with killers possessing distinctive personalities as well as more local variants such as the one noted by Steven Schneider: 'the creative merging of realistic serial killers with demonic, otherworldly forces, in films such as *Exorcist III* (1990), *The Frighteners* (1996), and *Fallen* (1998)' (Schneider, 2000a, p.176)?

While horror offers a world of monsters, each horror monster within that world has its own specific place and its own time. It might be a Transylvanian castle in the nineteenth century. It might be a cabin in the woods in contemporary America. Or a motel. Or a cellar. Or a sewer. Or even a spaceship at some point in the future. And each monster has its own distinct characteristics and moves through the history of horror in its own particular way. Although it might seem strange to invoke a need for sensitivity in the context of a discussion of monsters, it is clear that any attempt to explore monsterdom does need to be sensitive to all these specificities, to all the little peculiarities and differences that make each monster the distinctive thing that it is. Only in this way can we come to understand the world of monsters in general.

CHAPTER THREE

All in the mind?
The psychology of horror

This is no dream. This is really happening!

(*Rosemary's Baby*, 1968)

THE HOUSE OF SECRETS

Imagine this scenario. A man is trying to find out who is responsible for a series of murders. His investigation eventually leads him to an abandoned and reputedly haunted house. There the man discovers a child's painting on a wall, a painting that seems to depict a child stabbing his father. Later on, the man finds the father's decaying body hidden away in a sealed room. He makes the obvious deduction. After murdering his father, the child has grown up to become the serial killer responsible for the more recent murders. The deduction proves to be wrong, however, for it is the mother who is revealed as the killer while the child is simply a traumatised witness to her crime. The murders under investigation were all motivated by the mother's desire to keep the killing of her husband a secret.

This is not a scenario made up for the purposes of this book. It belongs to a real film, *Profondo Rosso* (1975) directed by renowned horror auteur Dario Argento. *Profondo Rosso* is a *giallo* of sorts, albeit one that takes the *giallo* format into new areas, exploring aspects of psychology that previous *gialli* had generally left untouched. It is certainly the case that aficionados of the psychoanalytical method could make, and indeed have made, much of *Profondo Rosso*. Given that so much psychoanalytical writing about cinema concerns itself with discovering meanings in films that are not immediately apparent to the casual observer, meanings that are hidden from view, it is worth identifying some elements in *Profondo Rosso* that could lend themselves to analysis of this kind.

The murder of the father

The murder depicted in the painting on the wall, a murder that is also shown us via a flashback sequence, might be seen as a coded and rather warped representation of what Freud termed 'the primal scene'. According to Freud, this is the moment when the child witnesses, or fantasises about witnessing, its parents having sex, with this act perceived by the child as a violent, potentially murderous one. The scene's organisation around a child's viewpoint with a child's song playing on the soundtrack, its focusing on familial tensions, and the way in which it is shown to impact upon the child's subsequent sexual development, all attest to its functioning as an expression of something essentially psychological. The fact that the child grows up to be gay can be seen in this respect, in the film's terms at least, as deriving from that child's 'misidentification' in relation to this scene as he, perhaps understandably, identifies with the powerful mother rather than with the dead father. (*Hands of the Ripper*, a British horror film from the 1970s, offers a neat reversal of this by having a female child witness her father stabbing her mother to death in what could be interpreted as yet another primal scene. While the male child in *Profondo Rosso* subsequently adopts the 'feminine' position, the girl in *Hands of the Ripper*, identifying with her father, grows up to exhibit some decidedly 'masculine' qualities.) From this perspective, *Profondo Rosso* offers a distinctly Freudian view of sexual tensions within a family unit, tensions that can both facilitate and sometimes block a journey towards heterosexual maturity. (On Argento, see Hunt, 1992; Knee, 1996; McDonagh, 1991; Mendik, 2000: on *Hands of the Ripper*, see Hutchings, 1993a, pp.180–3.)

The house

The house itself can also be characterised in psychoanalytical terms. The hidden room features in this respect as an expression of something that has been repressed psychologically by the characters associated with the house. Within the Freudian approach, things repressed do not simply disappear but remain present, albeit hidden, within the mind, just as the hidden room, an irrefutable sign of a past crime, waits patiently behind a wall for the inevitable moment of its discovery, a moment which marks the return of the repressed.

The investigator

One could also consider the psychology of the investigator who is not here a professional detective but instead Marc Daly, a musician (played by David Hemmings) who is himself a troubled figure personally implicated in the murder investigation. Significantly, so far as *Profondo Rosso*'s 'primal scene' is concerned, it is hinted that he too has a difficult relationship with his father, and the film also goes to some lengths to show him as inadequate in his dealings with women. (He is probably the only cinema hero to lose an arm-wrestling contest to the film's heroine.) Carlo, Marc's best friend, turns out to be the child glimpsed in the film's primal scene, and the fact that the film sets up a doubling relationship between Marc and Carlo – two pianists who dress similarly and who often balance each other in the film's compositions – suggests that in investigating these killings, Marc is also to a certain extent investigating himself and his own psyche. The secret of the haunted house is therefore his secret as well and, as if to confirm that throughout the film Marc is confronting anxieties about his own sexual identity, *Profondo Rosso* concludes with him contemplating his own reflection in a pool of blood.

One could go further and point out that *Profondo Rosso* depicts a world full of strong women, weak men and dysfunctional or broken families, a world where women are often associated with 'phallic' objects such as knives, and men, especially Marc and Carlo, are feminised in various ways. The corpse in the hidden room could be seen in this respect as not merely the body of a father but also as symbolising the principle of patriarchal authority in this world, an authority that has been supplanted by the actions of a rebellious, powerful woman. Seen in this way, *Profondo Rosso* itself could be interpreted as a response to, or a reaction against, feminist ideas and discourses that, during the period in which the film was produced, were interrogating in a very visible and public manner notions of patriarchal authority.

Admittedly this is an overly compressed account of *Profondo Rosso*, lacking in supportive detail and reliant on insufficiently explained psychoanalytical concepts. It is more of a gist of a reading than the reading itself, but it does give a sense of what a psychoanalytical interpretation of *Profondo Rosso* might look like. What needs to be considered now is the validity of this way of thinking about not just *Profondo Rosso* but horror cinema in general. Engaging with psychoanalysis is arguably an essential part of any account of the horror film, if only because so many interpretations of horror rely on psychoanalytical concepts. But at the same time, the psychoanalytical method is quite a contentious one, and the readings of horror it has generated are far from universally accepted.

Take the account of *Profondo Rosso* outlined above, for instance. While in a more developed form it might be able to offer an explanation of what is going on in the film, that explanation can be contested in all sorts of ways. In particular, its dependence on finding meanings that are tucked away behind or concealed by apparently innocuous narrative events can lead to accusations of reading too much into the film, of producing interpretations that have more to do with the psychoanalytical critic's imagination than they have to do with the film itself. Why do you need the concept of the primal scene to explain a crime, the ostensible function of which in the film is perfectly clear? On what basis can a knife be seen as a phallic object? Why should the hidden room or the father's corpse symbolise anything? Isn't this reading just a product of wishful thinking, a desperate attempt to manufacture a hidden significance when in fact everything about this and other films is perfectly clear? And as for the concepts themselves, do we really believe that, say, the primal scene has any credibility as a description of a stage in human development, and, for that matter, do we believe in psychoanalysis at all as a way of explaining human behaviour?

Assessing the usefulness of psychoanalysis to an understanding of horror cinema is a complicated enterprise for a number of reasons. For one thing, psychoanalysis itself is far from being a singular, cohesive approach but has many distinctive variants, including the Freudian, the Jungian, the Lacanian and the Kleinian, to name but some. For another, when psychoanalytical concepts are deployed in film criticism, they are often intertwined with concepts associated with other ways of thinking about culture, be these historicist, poststructural, postmodern, Marxist or anthropological. These concepts are also used within different contexts to address different aspects of cinema, from the nature of the cinematic experience itself to detailed analysis of specific films. As this all tends to generate a variety of approaches, it becomes hard either to accept or reject psychoanalytical film criticism in its totality. Both positive and negative perceptions of it do not necessarily apply to every approach that offers itself as psychoanalytical.

It also needs to be noted that psychoanalysis is not just a theory (or theories) about human behaviour or a tool for understanding culture. It is also a way of thinking about what it means to be human that has become widely disseminated in western culture to the extent that many people – including film-makers – will be familiar with concepts and practices associated with it, including, say, the unconscious and the interpretation of dreams. It is fairly easy to demonstrate that psychoanalysis, in various forms, plays a part in cinema. In particular, it has informed modes of characterisation. The idea that characters are not always fully aware of the reasons for their behaviour and that their real psychological motivations are revealed symptomatically through dreams or slips of the tongue is apparent in a wide range of films. What it is useful to think about here is the extent and the nature of the role of psychoanalysis within horror. Understanding how psychoanalytical ideas function in the horror film can, perhaps, make it easier to assess how convincing are the psychoanalytical interpretations of horror produced by various critics and theorists.

THE MIND OF HORROR

The most visible sign of horror cinema's awareness of psychological matters is the presence within numerous horror films of psychoanalysts, psychiatrists and other mental health specialists. (However important the distinction might be in real life between psychoanalysis, psychology, psychiatry and psychotherapy, it is fair to say that horror cinema tends to lump them all together.) Horror is by no means the sole cinematic location for such figures. From the 1930s onwards, they began to appear in a range of film genres, including melodramas, thrillers, comedies and even musicals. Nevertheless, certain patterns of usage are apparent in horror's representation of mental health specialists, and these point, to a limited extent, to a distinctive generic position on the psychological itself.

The first thing to say about horror's version of the mental health expert is that he or she (and it is usually a he) is rarely the hero of the film in which he or she appears. Heroic psychoanalysts and psychiatrists, those who in some way make things better for their patients, exist elsewhere in cinema, for example in melodramas such as *Now Voyager* (1942) and *The Three Faces of Eve* (1957). Generally kept in supporting roles then, horror's version of this figure can usually be placed in one of three categories – the murderous, the compromised and the ineffectual. A relatively small cluster of murderous, psychotic psychiatrists comprises what is probably the most memorable category, representing as it does such an extreme inversion of the psychiatrist-as-hero type. The most famous example is, of course, Dr Hannibal Lecter who is joined by, among a few others, Dr Elliott (played by Michael Caine) in *Dressed to Kill* (1980) and Dr Decker (played by David Cronenberg) in *Nightbreed* (1990). (Murderous psychiatrists also occasionally show up in the thriller genre, notably in *Spellbound* in 1945 and in *Shock* in 1946.) The compromised psychiatrist is also relatively rare; he or she is a figure who generally starts out with good intentions but whose professional authority is undermined by personal problems or personal feelings for their patients. One thinks here of Dr Judd in *Cat People* (1942) and Dr Pritchard in *Hands of the Ripper* (1971). Both are meant to care for their troubled, potentially murderous female patients but exacerbate these women's problems by falling in love with them; the women concerned end up killing them both. In a different way, Dr Raglan in David Cronenberg's *The Brood* (1979) is compromised by his intense focus on yet another dangerous female, Nola, with this ultimately leading to several violent deaths, including Raglan's own. While Raglan is not strictly a psychiatrist or psychoanalyst and instead specialises in a weird form of therapy called psychoplasmics, the idea of the professional compromised by personal feelings still stands.

The psychiatrist is in: Hannibal Lecter (Anthony Hopkins) and Clarice Starling (Jodie Foster) in *The Silence of the Lambs* (1991). Courtesy of MGM CLIP+STILL.

Alongside these spectacular examples of psychiatrists gone bad, one can place a larger, more unobtrusive group of mental health specialists whose main function in the horror genre, not to put too fine a point on it, is to be proved wrong. Take as an example of this the psychiatrist from *The Exorcist* (1973) who calmly hypnotises Regan, a twelve-year-old girl apparently possessed by a demon, only to be reduced to a screaming wreck when she grabs him very powerfully by the genitals. Or the psychiatrist in *Candyman* (1992) who patiently, and perhaps a little smugly, watches as Helen, a woman accused of a brutal murder, seeks to summon the supernatural being called Candyman who, Helen claims, is responsible for the murder. The incantation is spoken, Candyman dutifully appears, and the psychiatrist is gutted with a very big hook. Not all psychiatrists suffer in this extreme way, of course, but instead just suffer the indignity of seeing their pronouncements and beliefs about human nature undermined or disproved by the narratives in which they appear. One thinks here of the various specialists in the *Nightmare on Elm Street* films who claim that Freddy Krueger, a demented child murderer with blades attached to his fingers, is simply the fantasy of some troubled juveniles while in the meantime Krueger just gets on with killing his victims.

Or, in other films and other cycles, those who claim that there are no such things as vampires, werewolves, ghosts, etc. (To a certain extent, the psychiatrist who appears at the end of *Psycho* can be assigned to this category. He offers a reasonable explanation of Norman Bates' behaviour, but the film's final scene, in which a smiling Norman stares enigmatically into the camera, undermines any sense that the case of Norman Bates has been explained away.)

What links all these figures together – the murderous, the compromised and the ineffectual – is their association with social authority and rationality. So far as their authority is concerned, the generally negative presentation of this figure in horror films speaks of a distrust of the expert. Some historians of horror have seen such distrust as a distinctive feature of the more modern, post-1960s forms of horror. However, this attitude can readily be found in earlier types of horror film as well, although there it is usually directed against the scientist rather than against the mental health expert. The turn to contemporary settings in horror from the 1970s onwards arguably provides the main reason why the psychiatrist, who is generally thought of as a contemporary figure, appears more frequently in post-1960s horror films than before.

This overturning of the rationality embodied by the mental health specialist also becomes part of a play with notions of belief and disbelief that in particular can be found in the supernatural horror film. It is a way of dealing with the fact that what we as an audience encounter in such films are entities and events in whose existence in reality we generally do not believe but, for the purposes of watching the film at least, we are in some way prepared to believe. (For an interesting discussion of notions of belief in horror, see Carroll, 1990, pp.59–96.) Horror films help us in making the transition from a disbelieving 'There's no such thing as vampires' to a credulous 'Look out, it's Dracula!' by dramatising the overcoming of those beliefs to which in reality we might generally subscribe. For example, take Dr van Straaten, the psychiatrist who features in the Ealing film *Dead of Night* (1945). Although surrounded by people who claim to believe in the supernatural, he calmly and reasonably insists that there is a rational explanation for what might appear to be manifestations of the supernatural. Unfortunately for Dr van Straaten, however, he is appearing in a ghost story, one of the best known in horror history. Because of this, an audience knows that he must be wrong, and that audience is thereby distanced from what are likely to be its own beliefs. Or think of the psychiatrist in *The Exorcist* who, along with all the other medical experts who appear in that film, is the sort of person we might well want to consult about our own problems. But this is a horror film, and we know that the girl is actually possessed by a demon, so the medical experts become narrow-minded fools whose final suggestion to Regan's mother, that she arrange an exorcism for 'therapeutic' reasons, underlines the humiliation of their defeat and leaves the way open for the chief exorcist Father Merrin, an indefatigable believer in the supernatural.

The mental health expert is not the only figure deployed within horror who serves this function, but he (or, less commonly, she) is perhaps better suited to it than most inasmuch as many horror films that raise the prospect of the supernatural vacillate, if only for a while, between psychological and supernatural explanations of events in the narrative. Henry James's short novel *The Turn of the Screw* (1898) provides an important precedent here and, famously, never resolves the question of whether the governess who narrates the story is mad or haunted. By contrast, horror films dealing with the supernatural do tend to resolve this tension in favour of the supernatural explanation, with this often involving the discrediting of the psychiatrist or some other voice of rational social authority. (It is interesting that the horror spoof discussed in Chapter 1 also sets up a tension between the rational and the supernatural, although here the tension is resolved in favour of the rational as the events of the narrative are revealed as the work of criminals rather than of ghosts or monsters.)

Caught up in this vacillation between belief and disbelief, with his or her authority constantly undermined, the mental health expert does not emerge from horror as a particularly positive figure. This is even the case for those more 'realistic' horrors featuring serial killers, where the psychiatrist is sometimes called upon to provide an explanation for the serial killer's activities, but where that explanation never leads to an amelioration of the killer's problems. So far as horror is concerned, you cannot cure a psychopathic monster, and those who think they can – notably the psychiatrists who release Norman Bates into the community in *Psycho 2* (1983) on the grounds that he has recovered his sanity – are sadly misguided. Perhaps horror's ideal mental health expert in this respect is Dr Sam Loomis, the psychiatrist in *Halloween* (1978, named after a character from *Psycho*), who will have no truck with psychological explanations of the killer Michael Myers but throughout the film insists instead that Myers is pure evil. In reality, Loomis would be a very bad psychiatrist, but the film invites us to endorse his antipsychological views. It is as if he, alone among all the psychiatrists and psychoanalysts who show up in horror, realises that he is in a horror film and modifies his beliefs accordingly.

It follows from this that one should not assume, as some psychoanalytical interpretations of cinema assume, that horror films are 'innocent' of psychoanalysis or that the people responsible for making such films have no knowledge of it. The presence of psychiatrists and psychoanalysts within horror is in this respect merely the tip of a large iceberg, pointing as it does to a much broader knowledge of and familiarity with psychoanalytical concepts that manifests itself in a variety of ways, in the formation of character and motivation, in patterns of symbolism. This might not be clinical or theorised knowledge, but it is knowledge or an awareness that is arguably widespread in – and to a certain extent popularised by – generic cultural forms. This has implications for the ways in which we might interpret horror films. The sort of psychoanalytical interpretation of *Profondo Rosso* offered earlier could in fact be focusing on elements that are not 'hidden' at all but rather are manifestly present, consciously put there by the film-makers concerned. Or, if one is not willing to assign that amount of intentionality to horror film-makers, it might be argued that notions of, say, the unconscious are so well established as part of a cultural or cinematic repertoire that they function as conventions that can be used to organise their films without the film-makers needing to know about what those concepts mean either in clinical practice or in psychoanalytical theory. The extent to which this way of thinking about the role of psychoanalysis in the horror genre impacts upon, or undermines, some of the more important and influential psychoanalytical interpretations of horror is an issue that will be addressed towards the end of this chapter. Prior to that it is necessary to consider what forms these psychoanalytical approaches have taken.

SEXUAL DIFFERENCE

Psychoanalytical concepts and approaches have been used in the interpretation of a wide range of cultural forms. But it is the medium of cinema that has often been seen as the most appropriate location for the psychoanalytical method. The fact that the experience of cinema is played out in darkness and involves an audience's contemplation of images that are simultaneously intensely real and illusory suggests a relationship with, or resemblance to, a state of dreaming. As Parker Tyler, one of the first film critics to deploy psychoanalysis in the study of cinema, put it back in 1947: 'From the capacity of the screen for trick illusion, plus the dark-enshrouded passivity of the spectator, issues a state of daydream' (Tyler, 1971, p.30). This association between cinema and the dream has been promoted by a body of psychoanalytically informed theories about the nature of the cinematic experience that do not especially concern themselves with individual films or types of film. (See in particular the work of Jean-Louis Baudry, 1986a and 1986b.)

However, other critics have engaged with the idea of cinematic dreaming in relation to specific types of film. For example, Robin Wood has suggested that entertainment films are especially amenable to forms of psychoanalytical analysis inasmuch as, like dreams, their meaning is not immediately apparent either to those who make them or to those who receive them.

Popular films, then, respond to interpretation as at once the personal dreams of their makers and the collective dreams of their audiences, the fusion made possible by the shared structures of a common ideology. It becomes easy, if this is granted, to offer a simple definition of horror films: they are our collective nightmares.

(Wood, 1986, p.78)

The reference here to ideology is part of Wood's strategy for connecting horror films with political beliefs and values. It represents one way of using psychoanalytical concepts, and we will return to it later in this book when 1970s horror cinema, the main focus of Wood's work on horror, is discussed.

What will be explored here are those psychoanalytical approaches to horror that are more explicitly concerned with the ways in which horror cinema might reproduce, re-enact, simulate or in some other way relate to psychological processes and complexes. One version is the account of the genre (already mentioned in the previous chapter) that sees it as helping its audience to come to terms with essentially adolescent anxieties (for example, see Evans, 1984; Twitchell, 1985). However, other approaches reject this idea of horror's serving an adaptive or therapeutic function and offer instead a view of horror as a genre preoccupied with matters relating to sexual difference. Much of this work derives from, or is influenced by, important developments in film theory associated with the British periodical *Screen* during the 1970s, in particular an article by Laura Mulvey entitled 'Visual Pleasure and Narrative Cinema' (Mulvey, 1975). In this, Mulvey argued that mainstream cinema is organised around a male gaze at and mastery over the female body. The woman in cinema functions as a site of visual pleasure but at the same time she is also a source of anxiety for the male spectator. This is because the woman lacks a penis and therefore represents for the male the possibility of castration. According to Mulvey, cinema seeks to deal with this 'lack' either through a sadistic voyeurism, a punishing of that female body (an approach associated by Mulvey with the films of Alfred Hitchcock) or through a fetishistic overvaluation of that body, stressing its 'perfection' through endowing it with attributes that stand in for what was missing, i.e. the female lack (an approach associated by Mulvey with the films that Josef von Sternberg made with Marlene Dietrich).

This way of thinking about the cinema has been refined, elaborated, criticised and reworked ever since, not least by Mulvey herself, but its central tenets about sexual difference still carry some weight, especially in critical writings about horror. For example, in his 1980 book *Genre*, Steve Neale argues that the horror genre is primarily concerned with anxieties about castration. He relates this in particular to the centrality within the genre of the monster, a figure that in various ways embodies a form of difference which horror narratives strive to manage and contain: 'Hence the monster may represent the lack, but precisely by doing so it in fact functions to fill the lack with its own presence, thus coming to function as a fetish, simultaneously representing and disavowing the problems of sexual difference at stake' (Neale, 1980, p.44). Similarly Karen Hollinger has argued that the fact of most movie monsters being male is 'an expression of the connection between the image of the monster and the filmic representation of castration anxieties' (Hollinger, 1996, p.297).

One obvious problem with focusing on castration as horror's key problematic, the issue with which it is supposed constantly to engage, is that, in terms of its narratives, horror is a remarkably castration-free zone. While infamous video nasties *I Spit On Your Grave* (1978) and *Cannibal Holocaust* (1979) feature castrations, it could be argued that these films, like many of the 'nasties', exist on the margins of the horror genre and make more sense when seen in relation to other cinematic categories. So far as mainstream horror is concerned, a hatchet blow to a male groin in *Friday the 13th Part 3* (1982), a briefly glimpsed castration in *Candyman* and, most spectacularly, a castration by speargun in *Carrie 2: The Rage* (1999) are the only examples that immediately spring to mind. (Perhaps not coincidentally, *Carrie 2* is one of a small number of horror films to be directed by a woman.) While the assiduous researcher could probably track down a few more castration-related incidents, it is clear that castration *per se* is not a major feature of the horror genre. So if one wishes to establish castration as central to horror's operations, one has to explain why it is so important when, in literal terms, it is barely there at all. Clearly a figurative or symbolic reading is required, such as that offered earlier for *Profondo Rosso*, with, say, the knives of the slasher-killer or Dr Judd's swordstick in *Cat People*, broken in the course of that film's narrative, being seen as possessing a covert phallic significance. Perhaps inevitably, this leads us back to the oft-repeated criticism of psychoanalytical interpretations, namely that they read too much into the films in question, manufacturing significance rather than discovering it.

One might also question the prioritising of sexual difference over other forms of difference – to do with class, race, nationality, etc. – in the psychoanalytical model for the formation of identity. Surely this identity, in reality or as expressed in culture, involves something more complex and subtle than the simple division of the human race into females and males? (See Chapter 5 for a further discussion of this.) The centrality of castration to the 'sexual difference' approach to horror, and the associated sense that horror is primarily a genre about masculinity for a male audience, also makes it difficult to engage with the fact that women too form part of the horror audience, and in certain periods of horror's history an important part.

In her 1984 article 'When the Woman Looks', written in response to the burgeoning popularity of the slasher film, Linda Williams addresses some (although not all) of these issues. Like Steve Neale, she associates the monster with castration. However, for Williams castration operates in horror not as a source of fear and anxiety but rather as part of a reassuring fantasy that covers over something yet more disturbing about sexual difference, namely that the woman whose body represents the threat of castration is not herself castrated. While this might seem fairly obvious to those who do not support the psychoanalytical approach, it did represent a striking intervention into psychoanalytical film theory in the early 1980s. The idea here is that the possibility of the female's 'non-phallic' power is contained or curtailed through marking that female as 'castrated' and thereby rendering her as something less than a man rather than as someone different from a man. From this perspective, the cutting and slashing of the female victims in slasher films becomes part of a masculine fantasy that these women are castrated, are inherently weak and wounded, when in fact they are not.

As Williams notes, this opens up a space within the 'sexual difference' model of horror for women, both female characters in films and female spectators for those films. While critical of the slasher film, Williams does provocatively argue against the idea that horror in general is simply about monsters terrorising female victims. She identifies in this respect what she sees as a covert acknowledgement of female power in many horror films, an acknowledgement that is dependent upon similarities between the status of the monster and the status of the female victim:

> Clearly the monster's power is one of sexual difference from the normal male. In this difference he is remarkably like the woman in the eyes of the traumatised male: a biological freak with impossible and threatening appetites that suggest a frightening potency precisely where the normal male would perceive a lack.

(Williams, 1984, p.87)

Theorising about the source of that feminine non-phallic potency can lead, in psychoanalytical film criticism at least, to the maternal, and in particular to infantile memories of the mother as an all-powerful figure, memories that can be reactivated in horror films in order to produce fear and anxiety. The archaic mother or the pre-Oedipal mother figures in this respect as an engulfing force that stands at some distance from the objectified, 'castrated' woman found elsewhere in psychoanalytical film theory. Associated with abjection (a concept discussed in Chapter 2), this figure can arguably be found lurking behind not just some of horror's female monsters – for example, the witch Asa in Mario Bava's *La maschera del demonio* (1960) or the eponymous heroine of

Carrie (1976) – but the ostensibly male or gender-neutral ones as well. For example, Roger Dadoun has argued that while Dracula is a phallic figure, he is so much associated with locations of a 'uterine, enveloping quality' that he also needs to be seen as an expression of the archaic maternal: 'The Dracula form, the phallus-fetish, stands out against the background of the archaic mother and is part of that background' (Dadoun, 1989, p.55). Or, to give another example, the shape-shifting monster in John Carpenter's 1982 version of *The Thing* can also be seen as embodying qualities linked with the archaic maternal, notably its grossly biological nature, its formlessness and its engulfing powers (see Hutchings, 1993b for a discussion of the film in these terms). In her study of the monstrous-feminine in horror, Barbara Creed has gone so far as to argue that the association of the archaic maternal with fears of engulfment, of being swallowed up, means that this figure is more generally present in all horror films 'as the blackness of extinction – death' (Creed, 1993, p.28).

Where this leaves sexual difference is not always clear. Fears of the archaic mother should, presumably, operate equally for males and females. However, most accounts of horror that see it in these terms assume that this archaic level of significance is hidden behind or periodically erupts through the castration-centred model of identity outlined above. It seems from this that those horror films that are most amenable to this kind of reading are those that in some way dramatise the emergence of the maternal into a previously secure male order. A good example of this is the aforementioned *La maschera del demonio*. In this, cult horror star Barbara Steele plays two roles. The first is Katia, the daughter in a noble household who respects her father, does what she is told by men, and generally personifies all the 'proper' patriarchal virtues. But Steele also plays Asa, an altogether more dangerous figure. Asa, a distant relation of Katia, is a witch who was burned to death by her family after having a mask – the mask of Satan – nailed into (as opposed to on to) her face. In the course of the film she is resurrected and proceeds to attack Katia's family and tries to swap places with Katia herself.

Asa lives in an abject, archaic world. She spends most of the film in a dank dungeon surrounded by cobwebs, insects and bats, and her gaze alone is enough to master men, swallowing them up mentally if not physically. Male attempts to master her – not just the burning but the wounding of her face via the mask – figure in this respect as attempts to mark her as 'castrated', as subject to male definitions of her identity. Her resistance to this reveals a non-phallic potency that, according to this reading at least, is ultimately the power of the archaic mother. Given that good girl Katia and bad woman Asa are both played by the same actress, the film also disturbingly seems to imply that lurking behind all women is this otherness, this archaic power. (For more on *La maschera del demonio*, see Jenks, 1992.)

If this focus on the archaic maternal takes psychoanalytical readings of horror in one direction, the influential work of Carol Clover on the American slasher film suggests another way forward. Clover's reading of the slasher, in her book *Men, Women and Chainsaws: Gender in the Modern Horror Film*, takes issue with earlier feminist criticisms that treated it simply as an expression of misogyny. For Clover, the slasher is full of images of ambiguous gender identity, of male killers with feminine attributes and of female heroes (the final girl) with masculine attributes. While, using the terms associated with Laura Mulvey, this can be seen as part of the slasher's attempt to resolve a castration complex either 'through eliminating the woman (earlier victims) or reconstituting her as masculine (Final Girl)', Clover suggests that there might be more going on in these films (Clover, 1992, p.50).

In doing this, Clover focuses on something that had not overly concerned earlier psychoanalytical accounts of sexual difference in horror, namely the male response to these films. Previously this had been considered straightforward and unproblematic; horror films, and to a certain extent entertainment cinema generally, sought to assuage male anxieties about castration, and that was that. The problematic issue, the issue that required critical attention, was the place of the woman within this. For Clover, however, the phenomenon of the predominantly male adolescent audience for the slasher film rooting for a female hero, the final girl, is not wholly explicable by reference to any notion of castration anxiety. The final girl might well be 'phallicised' and fetishised in various ways, but nevertheless she is still a female functioning as an identificatory figure for men. Could it not be that the slasher's treatment of gender is in this respect more playful than previously supposed, and that, as Clover puts it, part of the thrill for its audiences 'lies precisely in the resulting "intellectual uncertainty" of sexual identity' (Clover, 1992, p.56)? While Clover is reluctant to see the slasher as a progressive form, her sense of the complexity of the likely responses to the films by audiences suggests ways of understanding horror that lead us away from the male-centred castration-fixated models of horror proposed by earlier psychoanalytical critics and, arguably, points towards what has since come to be called queer theory, an approach that explicitly focuses on notions of unstable gender identities. (More on this in the next chapter and on the slasher in Chapter 9.)

As the 'sexual difference' approach to horror has developed, an increasing sense of the complexities of specific types of horror has been brought into play. The sorts of statements that one might have found in the earlier work – statements such as 'Horror invariably engages with castration anxiety' – are now much more likely to be qualified or subject to critical debate. Accompanying this is a growing awareness of the aesthetic and generic levels of mediation that intervene between the ways in which films operate and the ways in which humans function psychologically. In fact, the 'truth' value of psychoanalysis, the idea that concepts such as 'castration anxiety' might mean something in reality as well as in culture, has become less important as films themselves have become a focus for critical interest. In other words, psycho-analytical film criticism seems to take on a life of its own as it grows apart from other uses, especially clinical uses, of psychoanalysis itself.

THE UNCANNY

Freud's concept of the uncanny offers an approach to the horror film that differs in important respects from the 'sexual difference' approach outlined above. For one thing, Freud acknowledges that the uncanny is not just a phenomenon observable in clinical terms but that it also has an aesthetic or cultural dimension. This can be contrasted with the way in which the approaches to cinema associated with notions of sexual difference have often relied on psychoanalytical concepts that were not originally designed for cultural analysis and which sometimes seem inappropriate so far as under-standing the specificities of the cinematic medium are concerned.

Freud identifies the uncanny, or *unheimlich*, as a sensation or feeling that relates to beliefs, ideas or experiences that have been repressed or surmounted but which still linger inside us. The German word '*unheimlich*' possesses a resonance in this respect that the English 'uncanny' lacks, for the *unheimlich* can mean both something that is strange and something that is homely. According to Freud, certain events in real life or, in a different way, occurr-ences in fiction, can reactivate repressed or surmounted mental elements in a manner that for the individual involved combines a feeling of strangeness with a weird sense of the familiar: 'this uncanny is in reality nothing new or alien, but something which is familiar and old-established in the mind and which has become alienated from it only through the process of repression' (Freud, 1990, pp.363–4).

In his article 'The Uncanny', Freud lists a number of potential sources for the uncanny. Among them, perhaps unsurprisingly, is the castration complex; and indeed Freud himself provides a lengthy account of Hoffman's story 'The Sandman' in these terms, with the eye injuries that feature there related to anxieties about castration that have been repressed but which are now returning in a strange but ultimately familiar form. As we have already seen, a similar approach has been applied to horror by adherents of the 'sexual difference' model, and references to the uncanny often feature in their accounts of horror as a way of thinking about the nature of an audience's relationship to the events taking place on screen.

Another potential source for the uncanny, according to Freud, is the con-tinuing influence upon us all of what he sees as an animistic conception of the universe, one characterised 'by the subject's narcissistic overvaluation of his own mental processes; by the belief in the omnipotence of thoughts' (Freud, 1990, p.363). Freud associates this view of the world, in which one believes in the magical powers of one's own thoughts, with both primitive societies and infantile fantasies, suggesting that perhaps 'each one of us has been through a phase of individual development corresponding to this animistic stage in primitive men' and that although we move beyond or surmount these beliefs, they remain with us as a kind of residue liable to be reactivated as uncanny feelings (Freud, 1990, p.363). Freud gives as an example the scenario of wishing someone dead and then learning that this person has died. The rational response to this would be to label it a mere coincidence, but there is the possibility here of an uncanny feeling that perhaps it was the thought that magically caused the death.

Given that monsters such as the vampire, the werewolf and the mummy (to name but a few) seem to belong to an older, more primitive view of the world and command our interest despite our modern rationality, the uncanny offers one potential explanation for the fascination they exert. Indeed, in a recent article on horror, Steven Schneider argues that 'the stars of classic reanimation tales – mummies, zombies, the Frankenstein monster – can be viewed as more or less distinct embodiments of our surmounted belief in the ability of the dead to return to life' (Schneider, 2000a, p.174). Schneider also antici-pates one possible criticism that could be made of this approach, namely that many horror films operate in a manner comparable to fairy tales, i.e. they conjure up worlds that are postulated as completely separate from the everyday world of the horror audience. Freud explicitly excludes fairy tales from the uncanny because they take place wholly within animistic worlds and therefore do not involve what Freud has termed 'a conflict of judgement as to whether things which have been "surmounted" and are regarded as incredible may not, after all, be possible' (Freud, 1990, p.373). In other words, classic horror stories about the dead returning to life are so obviously fantasies set in unreal locations that they do not have any significant implications for our own belief systems; there is no conflict of judgement, therefore notions of the uncanny do not apply. In response to this, Schneider argues that while these classic horrors might now seem like 'R-rated fairy tales', this is only because 'our overfamiliarity with the fictional worlds these monsters inhabit has rendered ineffective their efforts to horrify, since they no longer engender in us the requisite conflict of judgment' (Schneider, 2000a, p.176).

This is an appealing view of the horror genre, one that seeks to incorporate into its theoretical framework a sense of horror's historical mutability (although Schneider would need to provide more evidence to support his claim that earlier audiences for classic horror films responded to them in the manner that he claims they did). However, there are problems here, some associated with Freud's own ideas about the uncanny, others with the application of these ideas to the analysis of horror. This chapter has already discussed some of these issues in relation to the castration complex, so it would be more useful to move on to the question of surmounted belief, something seen by Freud as an important source of the uncanny. One does not require much expertise in anthropology to realise that Freud's ideas about primitive societies and their beliefs are crude in the extreme. These ideas also rely upon a teleological model of human development that is built around a belief in the innate superiority of modernity, with human progress largely defined as our delivery as a race from an irrational, childish past to a modern rational maturity. Freud clinches this teleology through drawing an analogy between primitives and infants, both caught up in a world of animistic beliefs subsequently to be dispelled in the course of their respective developments, with the reactivation of those beliefs via the uncanny functioning in this respect as a kind of atavistic regression.

Having said this, the assumption that a belief in the dead coming back to life is a surmounted belief actually raises some important questions. Is this really a primitive and/or infantile belief? How do we define 'primitive' in this context (and are we entirely sure we know what infants think about the issue)? An array of anthropological studies reveals that the belief systems of early societies were complicated things, and every belief operating within these societies needs to be properly contextualised in order for its significance to be fully understood rather than simply being abstracted from its context and filed under the category 'primitive'. Similarly, the assumption that the inhabitants of modern society, from whom the audiences for horror cinema will be drawn, absolutely do not believe that the dead can come back is also, in various ways, questionable. It might not be a widespread literal belief, but religious notions of resurrection still have the power to command belief in our society. Rationalists such as Freud might not approve of this and indeed might prefer to see religious feelings as surmounted, primitive beliefs, but the rationalists are not necessarily the dominant social force they would like to be. This is significant inasmuch as resurrection is an important feature in the horror genre, and one that often carries religious connotations. Instead of marking bodily resurrection in horror as something that derives from a surmounted belief, one might more profitably relate its various treatments to the national and historical contexts from which they emerge. For example, some interesting comparisons could be made between the Catholic iconography associated with resurrection in certain Italian horrors (notably *La maschera del demonio*) and the more Protestant treatment of the theme in some British horror films, relating this in particular to the religious discourses in circulation within the respective countries at the time of the films' production. It does not follow that these films are in themselves religious, but it does suggest that horror perhaps deploys religious ideas more commonly than is sometimes supposed and not necessarily in the context of surmounted belief. This does not mean that the uncanny cannot aid an understanding of horror films, but the more specific and contextualised the usage, the more convincing the resulting interpretations are likely to be.

One possible example of a productive deployment of the concept of the uncanny in relation to horror cinema involves using it to illuminate the way in which certain films relate notions of history, be this a psychological history or a social history, to particular constructions of cinematic space. Clearly this involves moving away from a consideration of purely psychological matters to aesthetic ones, but since we are dealing with cinema here rather than directly with the human mind, such a movement is arguably all to the good. In effect, what is being discussed here via the concept of the uncanny is the presence within films of themes or ideas that are rarely spelled out explicitly but which are used by the film-makers to organise their characters' exploration of dangerous and illicit spaces.

Perhaps the best-known example of this in the horror genre is Robert Wise's *The Haunting* (1963), adapted from Shirley Jackson's classic ghost story *The Haunting of Hill House*. Several critics have noted an ambiguity in the status of the house that provides the main location for both novel and film. (See, for example, Newman, 1990.) On a literal level, this house is simply a haunted house, one that is being investigated by a team led by a parapsychologist to determine whether ghosts actually exist. At the same time, however, there seems to exist a relationship between the various spectral manifestations associated with the house and events in the past life of Eleanor, a member of the investigative team. The odour in parts of the house inexplicably remind Eleanor of her recently deceased mother; a ghostly banging on a wall during the night is initially mistaken by a sleepy Eleanor for the sound that her ailing mother used to make when summoning Eleanor. One of the stories told about the house's past also parallels Eleanor's own story – a companion looking after an increasingly demanding old lady who one night ignores the old lady's knocking only to discover that she has died. This sense of the haunting focusing on Eleanor is made most explicit in the message that mysteriously appears on a wall shortly after Eleanor's arrival: Help Eleanor Come Home. While most of these elements are present in both novel and film, Wise's film accentuates them. It repeatedly places Eleanor as a reflection in various mirrors and shiny surfaces within the house as if to literalise the idea that the house is in some fashion reflecting Eleanor. It also underlines the way in which Eleanor gradually becomes part of this haunted house by giving her a ghostly voice-over that at the end of the film, after Eleanor's death, becomes literally the voice of a ghost.

The relevance of the uncanny to this scenario should be clear. For Eleanor herself, the house is an uncanny location. She has never been there before, it is a strange place to her; and yet it has a familiarity about it that makes no rational sense but nevertheless elicits her belief that Hill House is, in some weird way, her home. How the audience for *The Haunting* perceives this is another matter, however. Is the film uncanny for them because of their own surmounted belief in ghosts? Or is it more likely that they gain access to feelings of the uncanny via an empathy with Eleanor herself as the film's central character? As the next chapter will demonstrate, predicting how any audience will respond to a film is a difficult matter, but what can be stated here with some certainty is that *The Haunting*'s exploration of the internal spaces of Hill House is largely organised around Eleanor's perceptions of them. At the same time, such is Eleanor's eccentricity and gaucherie (especially as played by Julie Harris) that it is hard to see her as a figure with whom an audience is meant uncritically to identify. While Eleanor is at the centre of things then, the film invites us to watch her from a slight distance and, it could be argued, thereby to gain a clearer understanding of her situation than either she or anyone else in the film ever achieves. The film's almost schematic presentation of the parallels between Eleanor's past and the house's past is for the audience's benefit and contemplation alone. In effect, the audience for *The Haunting* is placed in the position of the analyst-critic, someone who can see the film in terms both of symptoms and their causes (although, as above, whether an audience chooses to take up that position is another matter).

Looking at *The Haunting* in this way does not mean that the haunting itself is explained away as a mere projection of Eleanor's precarious mental state. In fact the whole film is predicated on the idea of Hill House being haunted prior to Eleanor's arrival. The nature of and motivations for these earlier hauntings remain unexplained at the end of the film (and perhaps offer a focus for the surmounted-belief version of the uncanny). In contrast, the nature of Eleanor's experience of the house, while not unambiguous, is much clearer. Just as Marc Daly's exploration of the haunted house in *Profondo Rosso* is figured as a kind of self-exploration, so too Eleanor's passage through Hill House is a journey into herself, although, again as with *Profondo Rosso*, the film-makers and the audiences realise this far more than the fictional characters ever do. These films therefore invite us to experience the uncanny via the experience of various characters and perhaps more generally via supernatural or potentially supernatural story events. But they also put us in a position where we can understand the uncanny as a process by which the return of secrets from the past, which are often but not always psychological secrets, is dramatised via the representation of the house. This is not necessarily an understanding couched in explicitly psychoanalytical terms. Rather it involves a realisation that the actions of characters are determined by repressed or forgotten events and experiences, without this ever being spelled out explicitly in the films' dialogue. In other words, these films are structured around a disparity between the way in which their characters see the world and the way in which that world is represented to us.

The Haunting and *Profondo Rosso* are not the only horror films that operate in this manner. In fact, a recurrent feature of the horror genre is the house that contains secrets from the past, with the characters in these films often discovering that a familiar domestic setting is not so familiar after all. (This notion of the house can also be found in some classic Gothic literature – one thinks here of the work of Ann Radcliffe, Nathaniel Hawthorne and Edgar Allan Poe.) For a distinctly Gothic treatment of this, one can turn to Roger Corman's adaptations of some of Poe's short stories, notably *The Fall of the House of Usher* (1960) and *Pit and the Pendulum* (1961) or, from Italian cinema, Mario Bava's *La maschera del demonio* and Riccardo Freda's *L'orribile segreto del Dr Hichcock* (1962).

A good example of a more modern treatment of the theme is *Halloween*. Here the house in question is the Myers house where in 1963 a six-year old Michael Myers murders his older sister. Fifteen years later, the house is boarded up and derelict, an unsightly blot on the landscape of the otherwise utterly normal small town of Haddonfield. Importantly, however, the house is still there, a reminder of a terrible crime from the past, a familial crime redolent of social taboos such as incest and child sexuality, with a young child stabbing his naked, post-coital sister to death with a large and decidedly phallic carving knife. When the adult Michael finally returns, it is as if the darkness associated with the old Myers house reaches out into the town, so that the 'normal' houses, some of which become Michael's killing zones, start to look like extensions of the Myers house.

It is interesting in this respect that the teenagers in the film who become Michael's victims are blissfully unaware of their own town's history. They know that the Myers house is a bad place but no one seems to know precisely why. Accordingly, Michael's attacks are, to them at least, utterly inexplicable, and even Laurie, the film's final girl, never discovers that the person trying to kill her is Michael Myers (although in the sequel *Halloween 2* it is revealed that she is Michael's long-lost sister). One might argue that, because of this, notions of the uncanny do not apply. Laurie is not like Eleanor in *The Haunting* or Marc in *Profondo Rosso*. The events happening around her bear no relation with her past (until we get to the sequel, that is), so consequently she never experiences that weird sense of the familiar-strange associated with the uncanny.

However, the film does rely on a sense of the return of repressed events, albeit events that relate to a community history rather than to an individual one. Arguably what might be seen here as the uncanny effect is focused more on the audience for the film rather than on the characters within it inasmuch as it is only that audience which witnesses both the initial crime and the changes taking place in Haddonfield upon Michael's return. The extent of the uncanny effect will be determined by the extent to which members of that audience grasp the repression-centred relationship between past and present. The film itself, via the psychiatrist Sam Loomis, articulates a discourse of denial by insisting that Michael is utterly evil, a boogeyman who poses an essentially external threat to the community, but running alongside this is another discourse stressing that Michael is very much the product of Haddonfield, and that the town itself has in some unspecified way produced this monstrous figure. If you believe the former, that Michael is evil, you may well experience the uncanny in an Eleanor-like manner as mysterious connections between the evil and the familiar domestic begin to appear. (Note Michael's Halloween mask in this respect. It might seem to denote something utterly inhuman and alienating, but look closer and slowly it becomes familiar, uncannily so perhaps, until eventually you realise that it is a William Shatner/Captain Kirk mask that has been painted white.) If you believe the latter, then you are more likely to be in an analytical position regarding the film – and let us not presume that such a position is the sole preserve of the critic, for audiences can also adopt it – and are viewing it as a kind of critique of the complacency of the Haddonfield community.

Later teen-horror films, notably the *Nightmare on Elm Street* series (beginning in 1984), would further develop this form of teenage-uncanny by making its teenage characters more aware of the historical context of their problems, which in their case derive from their parents murdering child-killer Freddy Krueger who years later returns to take his revenge on the children. Again, much of this is signified through representations of houses as, with increasing frequency in the series, locations associated with Freddy – his boiler room, his own house – begin magically to show up within or attached to the houses of the teenagers. Here the threat is not only close to home; it is also part of the home. What seeing these films in terms of the uncanny helps to clarify is the powerful sense they convey of these teenagers, and perhaps teenagers in the audience for these films, not being fully at home in their own world, with events from a past of which they are initially ignorant having the power to harm them in ways they do not always understand. Admittedly this way of using the uncanny deviates from Freud's usage in its stress both on the community and on the teenager, neither of which were a concern for Freud. Having said this, the mechanism outlined by Freud by which the return of some form of repressed knowledge changes our sense of the world, making us less at ease within it, arguably has some use in understanding how these films function. All that has changed is that the range of material associated with the uncanny has been increased.

SUMMING UP

Different deployments of the concept of the uncanny; different modulations of the idea of sexual difference: it seems that psychoanalytical film criticism has fragmented into different models, different uses. This is probably all for the best for as a general theory of cinema, psychoanalysis is deeply problematic, struggling as it does with notions of the collective, the economic, the technological, the historical, and race and class, to name but a few of its blind spots. However, so far as an understanding of the horror genre is concerned, psychoanalytical approaches, for all the problems that go with them, are still important. In particular, they can produce interpretations of horror films that illuminate them in ways that are both fascinating and provocative (even if you disagree with the interpretation in question). The recent prominence of the slasher film and Italian horror within horror criticism is largely due to critical accounts of them that were informed by the psychoanalytical method.

It is certainly the case that the more useful of these approaches tend to be those that have moved away from general statements about human psychology and which have engaged instead with the aesthetics of horror and which have also displayed some sensitivity to the contexts of film production and reception. Whether this means that ultimately psychoanalytical film criticism of this kind will turn into something else, become an interpretative school completely detached from the distractions provided by other uses of psychoanalysis, is not at all clear. One thing is clear, however. Psychoanalysis is part of the rather messy fabric of the horror genre. It is woven into the films and into the criticism that surrounds the films, and, regardless of whether or not one likes it, it cannot be ignored and it also has its uses.

CHAPTER FOUR

Terror in the aisles:
horror's audiences

Ladies and gentlemen, please do not panic. But scream, scream for your lives!

(*The Tingler*, 1959)

CHAINSAW!

Back in the late 1970s, a story circulated among horror fans about an event that had allegedly taken place somewhere in the United States a short while before. Apparently someone had contrived to smuggle a chainsaw into a cinema that was showing Tobe Hooper's 1974 horror 'classic' *The Texas Chainsaw Massacre*. At an opportune moment, this person started up the chainsaw and proceeded to brandish it from his position near the back of the cinema.

I recall hearing this story from some horror fans and seeing it printed in a couple of horror fanzines. However, none of these renditions was detailed enough to enable anyone to check whether or not the story was true. The location was vague (perhaps Texas, perhaps not), the chainsaw-wielding individual unnamed (although invariably male), the precise date unspecified. While researching this book, I tried to track down further information on this chainsaw-related event but I could find nothing, either in printed sources or on the internet. Of course, this does not mean that someone somewhere has not unleashed a chainsaw in a cinema auditorium, but it does make it seem a little unlikely. (These things tend to get remembered and recorded.) I am inclined, then, to view the event as a kind of urban legend, a story that is believed to be true by particular groups but which is perhaps just too good to be true.

A useful point about urban legends is made in the 1998 horror film *Urban Legend*, namely that these legends always mean something. In the film,

The scarred lady screams: the horror audience in *Circus of Horrors* (1960).

Professor Wexler (played by horror star Robert Englund) recounts to his students the tale of the female babysitter who receives a series of threatening phone calls only to discover that the calls are being made from inside the house, indeed from inside the room of the children she is meant to be looking after. For Wexler, the message carried by this particular urban legend is clear. 'Young women, mind your children or harm will come your way,' he states authoritatively. A female student disagrees, however, and informs the Professor that the real message is 'Don't babysit'. What this disagreement suggests is that while urban legends might well be meaningful, the meaning in question is not always clear and that the legends can be subject to different interpretations from different people. (Given that *Urban Legend* belongs to a 1990s teen-horror cycle characterised by a self-conscious, self-reflexive sense of horror history, it is surprising that neither the Professor nor his students ponder the question of whether the babysitter story inspired or was itself inspired by *When a Stranger Calls*, a 1979 horror film in which a babysitter discovers that threatening phone calls are coming from inside the house in which she is babysitting.)

Similarly, the incident with the chainsaw can be read in a number of ways. What an irresponsible, inconsiderate thing to do, some might say. Not only is wielding a chainsaw in a public place a dangerous and possibly deranged act, it also spoils an audience's enjoyment of the film. Others might see the event in a more positive light, as a creative disruption of an audience's somnolent passivity and in this respect as a gesture that owes more than a passing debt to the Surrealist movement. As noted by Paul Hammond, surrealist artists advocated a disruptive attendance at the cinema, entering and leaving noisily during the screening itself in order to facilitate a new, potentially more active way of experiencing the medium (Hammond, 1978, p.10). Perhaps, then, our chainsaw-wielding spectator is an artist seeking to shock an audience into an awareness of its own situation. Or then again, perhaps not.

Clearly there are competing notions here of what it means to be a good audience. For some, the good audience is the quiet, well-behaved, decorous audience, while for others that audience is a bad audience inasmuch as it is characterised by passivity, meekly submitting to the authoritative demands made by the institution of cinema. Into this mix can be factored the notion of fandom, for another possibility regarding our disruptive spectator of *The Texas Chainsaw Massacre* is that he is a fan of the film performing a tribute to the object of his devotion. As we will see later in this chapter, fans too can be presented negatively and positively in relation to broader notions of the audience, as either weirder than the normal audience (however one defines that audience) or better than it so far as a knowledge of and commitment to particular films are concerned.

There is one other possible explanation for the chainsaw incident, which is that the gentleman in question is what is sometimes known as a plant, a gimmick, someone put there by the film exhibitors as part of the evening's entertainment. This is not as incredible as it might sound for there is a history of this sort of thing in horror film exhibition. For example, some screenings of *Mark of the Vampire*, a Bela Lugosi vehicle from 1935, featured female spectators who had been hired to scream and pretend to faint during the performance (a tactic also used for other horror films from the period). However, the heyday of such horror gimmicks was the late 1950s and the 1960s when film producers and distributors came up with all manner of devices designed to entice audiences away from what by then had become cinema's main rival, television. Some of these simply involved inviting the audience to don various props and disguises, presumably to put them in a 'horror mood'. For an American double-bill from the mid-1960s of Hammer's *The Plague of the Zombies* and *Dracula – Prince of Darkness*, female spectators were issued with cardboard cut-out 'Zombie Eyes' and male spectators with 'Dracula Fangs'. (The slogan on the poster read: 'Boys! Fight Back . . . Bite Back with Dracula Fangs! Girls! Defend Yourself with Zombie Eyes!' Given the charge of misogyny so often levelled against horror, it is interesting to note not only the advertising appeal here to a female audience but also the assumption that these females will defend themselves from zombies and vampires via a powerful gaze and, apparently, without having to rely on the men.) Something similar happens in the opening sequence of *Scream 2* (1997), in which an audience for the horror film *Stab* are presented with 'scream-masks' and plastic knives, although here the audience, male and female, is invited to play the part of the killer rather than the victim.

Other horror gimmicks are more elaborate. A key figure in this respect is producer-director William Castle who started off with the idea of insuring against anyone dying from fright during screenings of his 1958 film *Macabre* and then proceeded to his gimmick 'masterpieces', Emergo and Percepto. Emergo, used for *The House on Haunted Hill* (1959), involved a plastic skeleton suspended on wires being pulled across the front of the auditorium at a climactic moment in the film's narrative. The even more outrageous Percepto was deployed for *The Tingler* (1959). At the end of this film, incidentally one of the first to mention the hallucinatory drug LSD, the tingler, a spine-crushing parasite, escapes into a cinema, and Vincent Price, the star of the film, announces – both to the audience within the film and to the audience watching *The Tingler* – that if anyone feels the 'tingle' of the tingler, the only way to survive is to scream. Percepto involved wiring up selected chairs in the auditorium so that a number of cinema patrons would experience a genuine 'tingle' and, hopefully, scream. Some accounts of Percepto claim that the process delivered real, albeit minor, electric shocks, but the alternative explanation – involving a vibrating buzzer secreted in a chair – seems more likely both for practical and legal reasons. By contrast, exploitation producer-director Ray Steckler preferred a more direct and economical approach, with screenings of his 1963 production *The Incredibly Strange Creatures Who Stopped Living and Became Mixed-Up Zombies* featuring people (including on occasion Steckler himself) dressed as monsters running through the auditorium at key moments in the film. According to one uncon-firmed report, a similar approach was adopted for some screenings of *The Texas Chainsaw Massacre*, hence the possibility of the chainsaw-wielding customer being a stunt of some kind.

These gimmicks, much like horror itself, were usually sold on the basis of a dare: posters would dare a prospective audience to experience the sensational new shocks on offer by whatever gimmick was being advertised. Sometimes, in fact, a gimmick would be comprised entirely of a dare; one thinks here of the ambulances that would be conspicuously parked outside cinemas show-ing horror films during the 1930s and 1940s, ambulances that, according to the publicity at least, were there to convey to hospital those patrons overcome with terror. Inside the cinema itself, gimmicks could serve an instructive function, demonstrating to spectators how they were meant to behave, with the fake screaming and fainting presumably intended to cue in equivalent responses from audiences. For some of the more spectacular gimmicks, this could be combined with an assaultive intrusion into the space occupied by the audience, represented most clearly by the shocks delivered to the audience in *The Tingler* and the monsters on the loose in *The Incredibly Strange Creatures Who Stopped Living and Became Mixed-Up Zombies*.

This suggests that what horror gimmicks, and for that matter horror films in general, offer to their audience is fear, terror, subjection and victimisation; and, moreover, that audiences willingly and happily buy into this. Therein lies a key paradox addressed by virtually all critical accounts of the horror audience as they try to explain why apparently sane people would pay money for experiences that in other circumstances would be unpleasant and to be avoided if at all possible. There are a variety of explanations available as to the peculiar nature of horror's appeal, and this chapter will shortly be inspecting some of them.

Before doing this, it is worth pointing out another feature of the horror gimmick that is of relevance to an understanding of the horror genre, and that is its playfulness. It is hard to find any horror gimmick that is meant to be taken entirely seriously. It is doubtful, for example, that the Emergo skeleton was ever going to scare anyone, and according to some reports, its appearance was usually greeted with derisive laughter and a volley of popcorn. Similarly, the shocks of the tingler or the massed attack of maniacs seem to have inspired as much laughter from audiences as they did screams. The excitable advertising hyberbole that accompanies horror films indicates that even the dare element can often exhibit a joke-like quality. How seriously is one meant to take threats such as 'If this one doesn't make your skin crawl, it's on too tight' (*Black Christmas*, 1974) or 'If this one doesn't scare you, you're already dead' (*Phantasm*, 1979)?

The horror gimmick's combination of the assaultive and the playful invokes two distinct and separate conceptualisations of the horror audience, both of which have had a part to play in critical writings about that audience. The first is the horror audience as victim (albeit a willing victim), as that which is to be terrorised by the horror experience. Here the horror film itself, along with associated gimmicks, apparently has the power to produce in us an automatic Pavlovian response to whatever stimuli it decides to administer. We scream to order, we faint to order, we are afraid to order. It is perhaps significant in this respect that so many of the most memorable horror gimmicks belong to the late 1950s and 1960s, a period in which, according to some film historians, mainstream cinema in general was constructing a more disciplined role for its audiences (see in particular Williams on *Psycho*, 2000). By contrast, the second model of the horror audience is altogether more raucous than the first and less submissive to the machinations of film-makers and exhibitors. We might scream here but we also laugh, shout, throw popcorn (and perhaps even wield chainsaws), and generally behave in a manner in which obedient audiences are not meant to behave, with the auditorium itself transformed into a kind of performance space.

Which of these models is the truer? One might argue that it depends on the audience (and on the film as well). I have attended a screening of *The Exorcist* (1973) where the audience was noisy throughout and applauded and cheered some of the film's more gruesome moments, another screening where the audience sat in respectful silence, and a third where two people were carried unconscious from the auditorium (and I don't think they had been planted there by the exhibitor). While anyone who regularly attends the cinema will be aware that audiences can behave in unpredictable ways, it is very hard to grasp the precise nature of this dynamic. Because of this, film theory and criticism has often tended to shy away from real audiences and concentrated instead on the ways in which films, and the institution of cinema itself, seek to place an audience in a particular position *vis-à-vis* films so that this audience will respond in the desired manner.

In her book on film spectatorship, Judith Mayne usefully distinguishes between a film's addressing, or positioning, its likely audience and that film's actual reception (Mayne, 1993, pp.80–6). The two are clearly distinct, although one presumes that there has to be some kind of relationship between them. Some critical accounts of the horror audience tend to read off the audience and its likely responses from the films themselves, while other accounts are more engaged in the creative activities undertaken by particular audiences (especially fan audiences). When these notions collide, as they do on occasion, the results can be revealing about how enigmatic film audiences can actually be. For example, Robin Wood concludes his lucid textual exegesis of *The Texas Chainsaw Massacre*, in which he convincingly argues for the film as a critique of aspects of American society, with a description of seeing the film in the cinema.

Watching it recently with a large, half-stoned youth audience who cheered and applauded every one of Leatherface's outrages against their representatives on the screen was a terrifying experience . . . it expresses, with unique force and intensity, at least one important aspect of what the horror film has come to signify – the sense of a civilization condemning itself, through its popular culture, to ultimate disintegration, and ambivalently (with the simultaneous horror/wish-fulfilment of nightmare) celebrating the fact.

(Wood, 1986, pp.93–4)

Wood clearly does not consider himself to be an integral part of this audience and indeed finds being in its presence frightening. However, even as he observes the audience from a distance, he seeks to recuperate it through locating its response in relation to his own reading of *The Texas Chainsaw Massacre*. From his perspective, both the film and its audience are symptomatic of a broader cultural malaise specific to 1970s American society.

In response to this reading of this particular audience, one might reasonably argue that it is not, as Wood somewhat apocalyptically and portentously puts it, an audience revelling in the destruction of its own culture but rather an audience that is having fun; and that this fun does not need to be seen as symptomatic of anything, let alone cultural disintegration. What might be happening instead is that the film's highly effective delivery of thrills and shocks, its cheerful iconoclasm and its ruthlessness, are sending the audience on what, in effect, is a roller-coaster ride, a journey of extreme and enjoyable sensations to which the audience responds enthusiastically. And if the notion of the roller-coaster, which is one that appears regularly in critical descriptions of the horror-film experience, suggests too passive a sense of an audience being taken for a ride, one could think about the way in which *The Texas Chainsaw Massacre* has been appropriated by various youth audiences, made part of a subcultural experience in a manner that does not necessarily respect or have any interest in some of the textual intricacies described so well by Wood. And perhaps somewhere in this audience, sitting quietly at the back and waiting patiently for his moment, is a man with a concealed chainsaw.

It is clear from this that it is not just horror films that can be read in different ways and from different perspectives, but that the audiences for those horror films are also subject to a variety of definitions and interpretations. The remainder of this chapter will consider some of these interpretations, beginning with those critics who have preferred to study the horror audience from a safe distance.

AUDIENCE? WHAT AUDIENCE?

It is not uncommon for critical writings about horror, even the more positive or celebratory ones, to view the horror audience from a distance. However, this distancing process is most apparent in the negative perceptions of the horror genre that have accompanied it ever since its inception. One way of denigrating the horror genre is to denigrate its audiences. With this aim in mind, anti-horror critics have often addressed the question of the likely pleasures afforded by horror by arguing that the only people who could actually enjoy this sort of thing are either sick or stupid (or sick and stupid). This criticism of the horror audience tends to be at its most intense at the beginning of cycles of horror production, those moments when the powers of new types of horror to shock and provoke are undulled by repetition and familiarity.

Taking as a representative example the emergence of Hammer horror in Britain during the late 1950s, one finds critics of the time suggesting new certificates for the new horror – SO (for Sadists Only) and M (for Moronic). The new horror films are seen as both the product of a broader cultural degradation and potential instigators of further degradation; their burgeoning popularity indicates, to some at least, that the society that has produced them and helped make them so successful is indeed in poor moral and spiritual health. 'Only a sick society could bear the hoardings, let alone the films,' commented critic Derek Hill in an article from 1958 entitled 'The Face of Horror', but where precisely was that sickness located (Hill, 1958/59, p.6)? For Hill, the answer was clear – it was the audience's fault for accepting the debasement of cultural standards represented by the new horror. The audience here is figured, as it so often is in writings about horror, as vulnerable to commercial exploitation and, in some instances, as child-like as well. Hill compares an adult audience's experience of the new horror with that of a child reading a horror comic (horror comics were another cause for concern for cultural commentators both in Britain and America during the 1950s): 'Perhaps adult cinemagoers should be more resistant than children,' states Hill without much conviction before commenting that 'the corruption of taste is, after all, a pretty insidious business' (Hill, 1958/59, p.10).

This negative sense of an audience being open to the manipulations of mass culture was quite a common one in writings about mass culture up until and during the 1950s, and it still periodically resurfaces in some of the more virulently negative takes on the horror audience (as anyone familiar with the 'video nasties' furore that took place in Britain during the early 1980s could testify: see Barker, 1984, for details.) The fact that the horror genre has always been such an openly exploitative area of film production, one heavily reliant on sequels, cycles and sensational advertising and associated with pleasures that seem decidedly dubious, ensures that even within the context of an apparently degrading mass culture, the horror film tends to be seen as yet worse, as an epitome of cultural degradation.

This negative take on the vulnerable, impressionable and child-like audience is often coupled with a sense, implicit or explicit, of a better and more mature audience, a good audience, that exists elsewhere and to which the anti-horror critic belongs. This audience, well-educated and armed with a higher moral and cultural sensibility, can see horror as either the dreadful thing that it is or, more patronisingly, as the silly thing that it is or should be.

So far as the critical response to Hammer's first horror film, *The Curse of Frankenstein* (1957), was concerned, the 'horror is dreadful' approach was represented most clearly by the review that appeared in *Tribune* which begins 'For all lovers of the cinema only two words describe this film – Depressing, degrading' and which continues 'The whole business of Grand Guignol . . . needs an analyst rather than a critic . . . in the cinema there are those who find it profitable to keep alive in people – (and especially, one feels, in the case of children) – primitive fears and cruelties' (May 10, 1957). Rarely has a film, or anyone who might like the film, been held so firmly at arm's length. A similar distancing is also apparent in the *Financial Times* review of *The Curse of Frankenstein*, although here the overall tone is more benign. 'Only the saddest of simpletons, one feels, could ever get a really satisfying frisson (from horror films). For the rest of us, they have just become a rather eccentric and specialised form of light entertainment' (May 6, 1957). In effect, the *Tribune* review – or, to be more precise, the *Tribune* rant – is the SO (Sadists Only) review while a more sedate *Financial Times* contents itself with the M (Moronic) approach.

It seems that whether a critic adopts the SO or M position depends upon the extent to which he or she feels secure within a particular cultural hierarchy. If there is confidence that horror is safely in its place as a non-threatening, low-cultural form, then one can view it from a superior position, even be amused by it and approach it with an irony that combines a sense of distance (especially distance from what is perceived to be the intended audience for this form of entertainment) with an imaginative mastery over the genre. As for those audiences who appear to take horror seriously, who lack the cultural sensibility that would enable them to recognise its inferior status, they, not to put too fine a point on it, are simpletons or morons. However, if the horror films are perceived as a threat – because of their groundbreaking explicitness, for example, or their apparent degrading power – then the audiences who like the films can also become threatening objects. The precise nature of this threat is not always clear. At its crudest, the apparent impressionability of horror's 'bad' audiences is such that they might be inspired through their viewing of horror films to carry out anti-social or even criminal acts. More usually, the threat is presented in more insidious terms, involving the gradual erosion of cultural standards and hierarchies from beneath.

An interesting feature of this distancing process is that when critics are confronted with a new type of horror that they do not like, they will often refer back nostalgically to earlier forms of horror that in comparison seem altogether safer. Derek Hill, for example, compares unfavourably the shockingly new 1950s horror cinema with the Universal Frankenstein and Dracula films from the 1930s that 'had strong literary origins and relied on stylised fantasy, with often remarkable qualities of atmosphere and suspense' (Hill, 1958/59, p.8). The irony about this is that only a few years after Hill wrote these comments, many critics would be looking back nostalgically to

Hammer horror itself as a safe form of horror in comparison with a new wave of horror films that began to appear from the late 1960s onwards. So when playwright and occasional film reviewer Alan Bennett wrote in 1968 'Of course blood and guts is the stuff of horror films, though, as with Victorian melodramas, what makes them popular and even healthy are the belly laughs which usually punctuate them', the sort of horror clearly on his mind as safe, amusing entertainment is Hammer horror, by that time a familiar unthreatening object. By contrast, the film Bennett is actually reviewing, *Witchfinder General* (now rightly considered something of a horror masterpiece), is clearly not perceived as a safe object at all. Bennett's response to *Witchfinder General*, a film certainly more violent and intense than the Hammer horror product, is remarkably similar to the negative response received by Hammer when it first appeared: 'it is the most persistently sadistic and morally rotten film I have seen. It was a degrading experience by which I mean it made me feel dirty' (*The Listener*, May 23, 1968). What this suggests is that this particular negative way of viewing horror films is very much bound up with the way in which horror film cycles develop, with SO (Sadists Only) negative perceptions to any new horror cycle gradually becoming M (Moronic) perceptions as that cycle becomes more familiar and accepted.

A more recent version of the bad audience is less concerned with cultural hierarchies than it is with ideological and ethical factors. This is the audience for the slasher films of the late 1970s and early 1980s. The slasher films themselves were heavily criticised by feminist critics at the time of their initial release for their portrayal of violence against women. The audience for such films was viewed as predominantly male (why, the assumption went, would women want to see films like this) and potentially or actually misogynist. Potentially misogynist insofar as the films seemed to encourage their audiences to identify with the male slasher-killer through an extensive use of that killer's point of view, actually misogynist inasmuch as this sort of film would only really appeal to those who were already misogynist. As noted in previous chapters, this reading of the slasher and its audiences has since been questioned, not least by feminist critics themselves. The fact that women formed part of the slasher audience, as well as the complexities of the male audience's response to what was going on in the films, has at the very least made it hard to see these films as simply misogynist (although, of course, this is not the same as saying that the films are therefore progressive).

Whatever the difference between these approaches to the horror audience, they all view that audience in terms of an uncompromising Otherness, as something decidedly unsavoury that thankfully exists apart from the critic. In effect, this notion of the bad audience is being used by critics to talk up the perniciousness of the horror films themselves. Not only are these films seen as rooted in an already troubled socio-cultural context (if not, the audience for them would not exist in the first place), they are also making it worse by further degrading their impressionable audience. In other words, this unfortunate horror audience functions in part as cause, in part as symptom and in part as effect of a broader cultural malaise.

The horror audience has not always received such a negative press, and sometimes it has even been viewed in a positive light. Take the psychiatrist Dr Martin Grotjahn, for example, who in 1958 published an article confidently entitled 'Horror – Yes, it can do you good'. For Grotjahn, 'there is, perhaps, a healthy function in the fascination of horror. It keeps us on the task to face our anxieties and to work on them' (Grotjahn, 1958, p.9). This sense of horror as having a therapeutic quality is one that has featured in previous chapters in the context of discussions of psychoanalytical approaches to the genre (with Evans, 1984 and Twitchell, 1985 as representative examples of such an approach). What is striking here, especially in comparison with the 'bad audience' approaches outlined above, is the way in which Grotjahn aligns himself to a certain extent with the horror audience; it is not a question of their anxieties but rather of our anxieties. Having said this, Grotjahn clearly does not identify completely with horror audiences; his attitude towards them is very much that of an analyst to a patient, replacing the demonisation found in the bad-audience approach with sympathetic understanding. The audience here is not irredeemably sick in the way that a bad audience is sick, with its sickness expressing a moral degradation as well as a mental one. Instead the anxieties of Grotjahn's audience are merely indications of how normal that audience actually is. As is generally the case with psychoanalytical understandings of the cinema audience, Grotjahn presumes that horror audiences are not consciously aware of why they go to horror films and that therefore they require an analyst such as himself to explain to them the motivations behind their behaviour.

Other non-condemnatory approaches to the horror audience have been less concerned with that audience's unconscious and more interested in the ways in which it knowingly engages with and makes sense of the horror experience. Hence references to horror as a kind of roller-coaster ride, providing its audiences with thrills via elements of simulated danger. Hence too the stress laid on the knowledge and competences deployed by audience in their understanding of horror films. This way of thinking about horror audiences can be related to what has come to be called the historical poetics approach to cinema, an approach that, according to film scholar Henry Jenkins, 'is more interested in explanation than in interpretation'. As Jenkins puts it, 'Historical poetics forestalls this search for meaning in order to ask other questions about how film narratives are organized, how films structure our visual and auditory experience, how films draw upon the previous knowledge and expectations of spectators' (Jenkins, 1995, p.101). From this perspective, the horror audience is not an audience overwhelmed by terror or, for that matter, susceptible to moral corruption, but rather an audience that is actively working with the film in order to get the 'horror effect', reading in a knowledgeable manner the codes, conventions and cues provided by the film-makers, and performing particular cognitive operations without which the films in question would simply not make sense. The knowledge and skills this involves need not be something that spectators can articulate and reflect upon – i.e. they would probably fail an exam in the historical poetics of horror – but neither is it necessarily hidden away in the unconscious. Horror historian Andrew Tudor makes a useful distinction in this respect (borrowing some terms from sociologist Anthony Giddens) between discursive consciousness – that type of knowledge that can be articulated by audiences – and practical conscious-ness, a term which, according to Tudor, 'invokes the vast area of pragmatic understanding of a genre's functioning, ordinarily left entirely unarticulated by the genre audience, but, in principle, intelligible to it' (Tudor, 1989, p.4).

It is this sense of an audience's consciously adopting certain modes of behaviour that informs Linda Williams' account of the way in which the original marketing for Hitchcock's *Psycho* (1960) 'trained' its audiences to behave in a disciplined manner, showing up punctually for the screening (unusually for the time, no one was admitted into the cinema after the film had started) and not giving away the film's secrets after the screening was over. Williams suggests that this discipline was carried over into the audience's experience of the film which is figured here as a gruelling but enjoyable roller-coaster ride (Williams, 2000). In a different but comparable manner, Noel Carroll's book *The Philosophy of Horror* posits a spectator/audience that seeks out horror in order to experience a particular affective response. In order to achieve this, the audience has to deploy not only a prior knowledge of generic conventions and a 'practical consciousness' about cultural categories of naturalness, but also has to negotiate its way round the issue of the fundamental unbelievability of the images it is viewing (Carroll, 1990).

While Carroll's account of horror lacks the stress on discipline found in Williams' account of *Psycho*, both tend to assume that the audience's response, for all the knowledge and cognition it involves, will be appropriate, that it will be defined, and to a certain extent limited, by the contexts – generic, institutional – within which horror films are encountered. This assumption is stronger in Carroll's book, perhaps because he offers an account of spectatorship based largely on readings of films and what they require of the spectator. By contrast, in the latter part of her essay, Williams does engage, albeit somewhat tentatively, with the behaviour of an actual audience, and here one does get a sense that perhaps audiences do not always behave in a consistently appropriate manner, that is to say the manner elicited by films and their marketing. The audience's response can be heterogeneous, with for example men reacting differently from women (or, for that matter, men reacting differently from other men, and women reacting differently from other women); it can be developmental, with the behaviour of audiences changing over time; and it can also be performative, with an audience response – whether it is organised by the films or spontaneous (and it is sometimes hard to tell which is which) – itself becoming part of the horror experience. As Williams puts it, 'While learning to enjoy the roller-coaster ride of a new kind of thrill, the audience may begin to perceive its own performances of fear as part of the show' (Williams, 2000, p.372). There seems to be an oscillation here between two notions of the audience, both of which we have encountered before in this chapter, with the relation of this to the authority and discipline provided by cinema itself not always clear. On the one hand, there is the decorous audience who correctly interpret the film and respond accordingly; on the other hand, there is the raucous audience who, in part at least, use the film as a prop for their own performative behaviour and do not always do what they are told.

Other ways of thinking about the horror audience accentuate yet further that audience's ability to produce interpretations and find meanings that do not necessarily respect the intentions of film-makers and cinema exhibitors. For one example of this, we can turn to those readings of horror that have emerged from queer theory. In particular, queer theory's sense of gender identity as something that is fluid and unstable has been used by horror critics and historians to explore the ways in which spectators can make sense of horror cinema according to their own complex identities and desires (see in particular Benshoff, 1997; Berenstein, 1996; Doty 1993, 2000). This has sometimes been seen as offering a general explanation for the complexities of an audience's response to horror, one that can involve mobile identification with a range of characters unlike oneself, cross-gender identification, identification with monsters, etc. In this respect, horror, like many other areas of entertainment, functions as a potentially queer space for its audiences, one that offers illicit and transgressive (especially sexually transgressive) identifications and pleasures, if only ultimately to recuperate and contain these.

Often running alongside this claim for the innate queerness of horror, however, is a sense that particular sectors of the audience – notably gays and lesbians – are more alert to this property of the genre, and that they actually have more need to snatch moments that are significant to them from films that in other respects might not be sympathetic to their identity, values or lifestyles. This is not the same as saying that gay and lesbian readings of apparently straight horror films simply manufacture meaning from nothing. Rather, such readings can be seen to focus on tensions and ambiguities present within films (and the horror genre seems especially rich in such elements) and to use these as the basis for their own engagements, affective and interpretative, with the films. Sometimes such readings are so convincing and persuasive that they can take on a wider, canonical status. For example, it is now quite common for horror critics, regardless of sexual orientation, to view *Bride of Frankenstein* (1935) as in some way a gay or queer film, in part because of the gayness of its director James Whale but also because of the film's camp qualities. Whether such a reading was – or, for that matter, still is – available to straight mainstream audiences in precisely these terms is not clear. While it is hard to imagine that an audience for *Bride of Frankenstein* would not pick up on some of these elements – the outrageously camp performance of Ernest Thesiger as Dr Pretorious, for example – it does not necessarily follow that such elements would be central to all audiences' understandings of the film.

What this suggests is that different groups, and different ways of making sense of films, co-exist in the same auditorium at the same time. Social categories and divisions, including not just sexual orientation but also class, race, generational difference, national difference, etc., can be seen in this respect as reaching into, impacting upon and in some instances undermining the apparent collective identity of any audience for any film. In other words, the horror audience, like audiences in general, is comprised of individuals who bring with them into the cinema a wide range of identities, beliefs and values that are not determined or limited by cinema itself. Cinema might be able to call particular audiences into being for its films but it cannot completely isolate spectators from what they are elsewhere.

THE HORROR FAN

A related way of thinking about film audiences, and one that is especially pertinent to an understanding of the horror genre, is in terms of fans. To a certain extent, changes in the evaluation of horror fandom have reproduced, and become intertwined with, a general shift apparent in horror criticism away from the 'bad' audience towards the idea of an audience as active and knowledgeable. From the late 1950s, when horror fandom started to become a noticeable social phenomenon, through to the 1980s, horror fans often received a decidedly negative press. Joli Jenson's comments on fandom in general are particularly relevant for the horror fan. 'The literature of fandom is haunted by images of deviance. The fan is consistently characterized (referencing the term's origins) as a potential fanatic. This means that fandom is seen as excessive, bordering on deranged, behaviour' (Jenson, 1992, p.9). For an early and fairly typical representation of a horror fan, we can turn to 'Bilko's Vampire', a 1958 episode of the US TV sitcom *Bilko*. In this, Ritzik, one of the show's regular characters, has become a regular and committed viewer of the late-night horror films being shown on television. Here horror fandom is associated with childishness (Ritzik is absurdly scared by the films), anti-social behaviour (Ritzik has given up his regular poker game so he can stay in and watch the films) and credulousness, with the latter clearly demonstrated when the unfortunate Ritzik is conned into believing that he has become a vampire. This is one of the more benign versions of the horror fan, but it shares some of its characteristics with the demonised version of the horror fan that shows up in moral panics about horror (for example, the video nasties scare of the early 1980s) – notably an overly close, obsessive, unhealthy relation with horror films that has the potential to lead to imitative behaviour.

More recently, there has been something of a change in the critical fortunes of the fan. His or her activities have increasingly been seen by critics and academics as significant and meaningful in their own right, with the knowledge accumulated by fans about the objects of their fandom deemed to be worthwhile cultural capital rather than worthless cultural detritus. (For a discussion of this, see Fiske, 1992.) It is interesting in this respect that a number of academics, precisely the sort of people who in previous decades would strenuously have objected to being thought of as fans, will now in their writing about various forms of culture, including horror, happily proclaim their own fandom. (See Jenkins 1992 as a key statement of this.)

Thinking about horror-fan audiences draws our attention to yet another way in which an audience, a group of people seated in a cinema watching a film, can be divided into distinct groups. Critic Mark Kermode provides an instance of this when reminiscing about his own horror fandom and what he, with some irony, describes as 'the absolute divide between horror fans and everybody else in the world'. Kermode continues,

> I remember forming a fleeting bond with a fellow movie-goer at a screening of The Fly at the Manchester Oxford Road Odeon in the 1980s when an on-screen doctor preparing to abort Geena Davis' insect foetus turned out to be director David Cronenberg. While everybody else cringed, the two of us chuckled smugly from opposite sides of the auditorium, like ships signalling each other in deep fog.

> (Kermode, 1997, pp.59–60)

The majority-mainstream audience filling the space between Kermode and his fellow horror fan is not presented here as a 'bad' audience but it is certainly seen as a lesser audience so far as its knowledge of and commitment to the horror genre is concerned.

The activities of horror fans are by no means restricted to their membership of cinema audiences. Outside the walls of the cinema, fans will seek to acquire information about the horror genre – via books, magazines and other sources – and will sometimes themselves circulate information in the form of privately published and distributed 'fanzines' or more recently on the internet. (On horror fanzines, see Sanjek, 1990.) In effect, what is happening here is the construction of fan communities that, given that fans tend only rarely to meet (at fan conventions and associated events), necessarily have a virtual or imaginary basis, with the availability of fan-related material helping to reassure each fan that he or she is not alone, that there are other people out there with the same interests and enthusiasms. However, it does not follow that horror fandom is a unitary and cohesive phenomenon. In fact a survey of the material produced by horror fans reveals, perhaps unsurprisingly, a variety of interests and approaches. For example, one can find some quite traditional auteurist devotions to particular horror directors (Italian horror-maestro Dario Argento seems a particular favourite in this respect), historicist approaches concerned to gather as many facts as possible about the production of particular horror films (with, for some reason, Hammer horror being a key focus of activity here), and more ambitious (or, depending on your perspective, pretentious) approaches that view horror as part of a trash counter-culture that can potentially challenge normative standards of good taste. (For a discussion of the latter, see Sconce 1995 and Hawkins, 2000.) One can also readily find instances of fans seeing themselves not just as better (i.e. more knowledgeable and committed) than mainstream audiences, but also as better than other groups of fans. (See Jancovich, 2000 for a discussion of this.) It seems from this that horror fans are, in their own way, just as various and divided a group as horror audiences in general.

Another feature of horror fandom that has some broader relevance relates to the way in which from the 1980s onwards this fandom has largely shifted away from the viewing of films in cinemas to viewing them on video and more recently on DVD. In part, this shift was motivated by the fact that some of the horror films that fans wanted to see were not receiving widespread cinematic distribution in this period, but, more particularly, it offered a means for evading censorship restrictions, especially in Britain where the 1984 Video Recordings Act imposed a draconian censorship regime that did not start noticeably to relax until the late 1990s. In fact, British horror fandom of the 1980s and 1990s seems largely to have been founded on the obtaining, usually by nefarious means, of uncertificated and uncut video versions of banned horror films.

Of course, it was not just fans that were being dispersed away from the cinema auditorium for nowadays most people see films not in the cinema but rather at home on television, video or DVD. It is a matter for debate whether watching a film on television is like watching any other television programme. (The plethora of directors' cuts and wide-screen versions along with home-cinema systems suggests that, for some viewers at least, the viewing of certain films represent special events even within domestic settings.) But it is certainly the case that watching a film on television is different from watching it in the cinema, not just in terms of the size and the quality of the image but also in terms of the conditions of viewing, in being seated in a familiar domestic environment usually in the company of people you know rather than being surrounded by strangers in a darkened public space.

So where does this leave the horror audience? Let us take the audience in the auditorium first. There has been a tendency in writings not just about horror cinema but cinema in general to view the audience as a homogeneous mass, offering a space where the spectator becomes part of a collective entity. In horror criticism, the most extreme form of this was the bad/sadistic/moronic audience, but a sense of the homogeneous mass audience can also be found in some of the more positive accounts of horror. What this chapter has suggested is that horror audiences are more divided and fragmented than this, with different sensibilities and different values being brought into play in different parts of the auditorium. Much the same can probably be said of the viewing of films elsewhere, with spectators treating the films in a variety of ways – as a casual diversion, as a main event in an evening's entertainment – that are appropriate for them and their lifestyles and needs.

It can be argued that a sense of being part of an audience is actually quite a complex and fluid thing. Seeing a film in the cinema, for example, can involve a mixture of audience-related feelings, including annoyance (at those people who talk to each other or use their mobile phones), indifference (when you become totally absorbed in the film or when your mind wanders and you start thinking about something else) and, perhaps, moments of a communal sharing (when everyone laughs or – in a horror film – screams). Once you factor in all the cultural and social differences mentioned above, and the possibilities of different sections of the audience reacting in different ways from other sections (i.e. some laughing at a joke while others, who might consider themselves the butt of the joke, emit a disapproving silence), you have a very complicated picture indeed.

While there are clearly moments of collective response to films, these tend then to be fragile and short-lived rather than involving an extended absorption into some large, collective entity. I suspect many with experience of watching horror films in the cinema will have their own memories of such moments. In my case, it relates to the conclusion of Brian De Palma's 1976 film *Carrie*. In this, the only teenager left alive after Carrie's telekinetic attack on the school prom approaches Carrie's wrecked house (the site earlier in the film of Carrie's death). As she kneels to lay some flowers there, a bloody hand erupts from the wreckage and grabs her. The teenager wakes up screaming. It's just a dream. The film ends.

A contemporary horror audience would probably see this 'shock' coming from a mile away, so accustomed have we become now to horror films having 'unexpected' shock endings (a convention that is constantly mocked throughout the *Scream* trilogy). However, the unsuspecting 1970s audience to which I belonged had no such prior knowledge and consequently was completely unprepared for what was about to happen when our teenage heroine knelt over Carrie's grave. I don't think that the entire audience actually rose up in the air when the bloody hand unexpectedly appeared; it just felt like that. What I do recall is an extraordinary collective screaming and shouting as well as a sense of people all around me jerking backwards away from the screen, with this immediately followed by laughter and cheers from all sides as we realised that we had been well and truly had by the film-makers.

This is a moment of which Hitchcock or gimmick-master William Castle would have been proud; the audience seemed to respond exactly in the way that the film-makers intended. But this was only one moment in the film (albeit a very memorable moment), a few seconds of unity in the context of a more varied, disconnected and fragmented experience of horror. And even this shock moment is likely to have had different effects, some quite extreme, on different people, effects that I, seated in the darkness, could not possibly have perceived. Some might have screamed and shouted more loudly than their neighbours while others would have probably remained totally silent (and I think it is too simplistic to map this entirely on to a gender division, with the women screaming and the men silent). Some might have laughed at the enjoyable thrill of the moment while others might have been upset by an experience that went beyond what to them felt like comfortable entertainment. A friend told me that he had known someone who, as a result of *Carrie*'s shock conclusion, had – how to put this delicately – experienced a sudden, involuntary bowel movement, but we can only hope that this is just another urban legend.

It seems from this that the horror audience, much like cinema audiences in general, is hard to define and understand. At the same time, particular notions of the audience have played an important part in debates about the nature and worth of the horror genre. Key questions posed by horror – especially those to do with the sorts of pleasures it offers – have appeared unanswerable without reference to the people who actually watch and enjoy the films. As we have seen, however, some ideas about the horror audience seem to operate at a distance from the observable behaviour of real audiences. In particular, the idea of the horror audience as a singular entity possessing distinctive properties and exhibiting predictable forms of behaviour has proved rather problematic. Certainly this model of the audience has proved a durable one in horror criticism, especially in those accounts of the genre concerned to establish that either horror is a bad thing or a good thing, with, for example, recent British debates about video censorship focusing almost entirely on the question of whether the horror audience is degraded or potentially corruptible (if you don't like horror) or knowledgeable and capable of exercising appropriate judgements about the films being viewed (if you are defending horror).

Approaches that have engaged with more localised versions of horror's audiences have arguably proved more productive in their ability to highlight and explore the different ways in which various groupings of people watch horror films. This can involve looking at historically specific audiences (for example, Rhona Berenstein's work on 1930s US horror audiences; Berenstein, 1996) or segments of the mainstream audience (work on female spectators, for example, or work from a queer perspective) or fan audiences. Each of these areas of research has raised and sought to answer specific questions about the social and historical locations of the audiences, the viewing practices associated with particular audiences, and the relation of these to the industry's various attempts to position and manipulate audiences.

Even as this critical work has helped develop our understanding of the complex, multifaceted nature of audiences' responses to horror films, its tendency to focus on broad patterns of behaviour has sometimes obscured the sheer unpredictability and contingent nature of any audience's responses to any films. Sometimes the audience screams; sometimes it doesn't (as it didn't on my second trip to see *Carrie*). Sometimes it will respond to the exhibitor's gimmicks in the manner intended by the exhibitor; sometimes it will mock the exhibitor's efforts. And none of this can ever be predicted in advance. This does not mean that we should give up in our attempts to understand the complicated interrelated sets of activities that comprise audience behaviour. It does mean that we need to beware of generalising notions of the audience or models of audience behaviour that discount its contingent, unpredictable aspects as insignificant simply because they are difficult to measure or explain.

Think then of the horror audience not as a static group of individuals, as an object for blame or praise, but rather as a constant and turbulent coalescing of different sensibilities, values and modes of behaviour that in different locations operates somewhere between discipline and performance, passivity and activity, silence and noise, individuality and the collective, the contingent and the (relatively) predictable. Much like the horror genre itself, the horror audience is heterogeneous, mutable and decidedly elusive; just when you think you have it identified and neatly labelled, it has a habit of vanishing mysteriously into the dark.

CHAPTER FIVE

Dealing with difference

There are still the others.

(The Innocents, 1961)

THE OTHER AND BEYOND

It is a commonplace of horror criticism that the horror genre offers us fearful encounters with the Other. What Otherness – with a capital 'O' – designates in this context is not only something that is different from the normal but also something perceived as a threat to the normal. Often underpinning the use of this term in criticism is the sense that Otherness relates, both in psychological and social terms, to notions of repression and projection. As Robin Wood puts it in his account of the American horror film, the Other 'functions not simply as something external to the culture or to the self, but also as what is repressed (though never destroyed) in the self and projected outward in order to be hated and disowned' (Wood, 1986, p.73). For Wood, Otherness is the product of a repressive society, a society in which powerful groups impose or project identities upon subordinate groups in a manner that underlines the 'superiority' and 'normality' of the powerful but which can sometimes render the subordinate groups not just as 'inferior' but also as menacing.

Wood goes on to identify what he sees as significant categories of Otherness for our culture, beginning with the Otherness of other people: 'It is logical and probable that under capitalism all human relations will be characterized by power, dominance, possessiveness, manipulation: the extension into relationships of the property principle' (Wood, 1986, p.73). Wood's list of significant Others also includes women, the proletariat, other cultures, ethnic groups within our culture, alternative ideologies or political systems, deviations from sexual norms, and children. What is left, so far as social categories are concerned, are whites, men, heterosexuals, the bourgeois, and capitalists who, in various combinations, are seen not just by Wood but by many others as forming the dominant and most oppressive groups in western society. For Wood, horror's relationship with Otherness is a complicated one. He argues that some horror films – what he calls the reactionary wing of the genre – seek overtly or covertly to reinforce notions of Otherness, while other films interrogate and attempt to deconstruct categories of the Other and in so doing function as critiques of dominant social ideologies.

Whatever the usefulness of Wood's labelling of horror films as either progressive or reactionary in terms of the way in which they handle Otherness (and his approach has been questioned by other writers on the genre), it is certainly possible to illustrate nearly all his categories of social Otherness with examples from the genre. For women as Other, we can turn to female-monster films such as *Cat People* (1942), *La maschera del demonio* (1960), *The Vampire Lovers* (1970), *Carrie* (1976) and *The Brood* (1979), as well as to what some have seen as the slasher film's transformation of female sexual difference into castrated Otherness; for the proletariat, think of Frankenstein's monster in the 1931 version of *Frankenstein* or the working-class Freddy Krueger murdering middle-class kids in the *Nightmare on Elm Street* series of films; for other cultures, think of any voodoo-zombie film set in the West Indies, or films such as *The Kiss* (1988) or *The Relic* (1997) in which something foreign and nasty makes its murderous way to western 'civilization'; for ethnic groups within our own culture, there are the *Candyman* films (three to date) as well as the accusations of unconscious or institutional racism occasionally levelled at some 1930s horror films that take degeneracy as their main theme – notably *Dr Jekyll and Mr Hyde* (1931) and *Island of Lost Souls* (1932). Alternative political systems as Other (Wood gives Marxism as an example) is not a theme much explored by horror, but it is fairly easy to find horror films that rely on notions of sexual deviation as monstrous and Other: for example, *The Silence of the Lambs* (1991) was heavily criticised at the time of its release for what was perceived as its homophobic representation of serial killer Jame Gumb/ Buffalo Bill (a charge denied by the film-makers), while the iconography of the *Hellraiser* films (six to date) relies heavily on sadomasochistic imagery. As for children, horror films from the 1960s onwards offer so many examples of wicked infants and adolescents, including *Village of the Damned* (1960), *Rosemary's Baby* (1968), *Night of the Living Dead* (1968), *The Other* (1972), *The Exorcist* (1973) and *The Omen* (1976), that one horror historian has entitled a section of his book on the genre 'The Case for Child Abuse' (Paul, 1994).

However, there are problems associated with this approach to horror, with these relating both to the model of society it proposes and to its application to horror films. It is now widely argued that the formation of social identities and the distribution of power within society is more complicated than

Wood's account suggests; in particular, it does not simply involve a structuring opposition between the white male heterosexual bourgeois capitalists and everyone else. Rather identity, whether it be individual identity or more collective types of identity, is seen to arise from complex movements and negotiations across a range of different social categories, to do with gender, class, race, nationality and so on. It follows that we are not merely white or black, male or female, bourgeois or proletariat, straight or gay (or part of any other binary opposition), but instead that we all exist in a variety of ways at the intersections of many social categories. This way of thinking about identity problematises any notion of there being a once-and-for-all distribution of power to one group with disempowerment for everyone else. Robyn Wiegman notes in this respect 'the many instances in which social positioning straddles the strict duality of oppressor/oppressed, where rights and privileges may be accorded along one particular axis but are circumvented and violently denied along others' (Wiegman, 1993, p.174). Wiegman focuses in particular on the position of African-American males who can be seen to have access to some areas of social power and privilege via their masculinity but are in other ways socially disempowered via their racial identity.

Looking back at some of the films cited above, one finds that, so far as the identities of monsters, victims and heroes (or heroines) are concerned, the interrelation of categories of dominance and subordination appears to be the order of the day. For example, while *The Silence of the Lambs* is often seen as a gender-centred story about a lone woman, FBI agent Clarice Starling, attempting to make her way in a male world, notions of class also have an important part to play in defining the film's various characters and do this in a manner that cuts across some of the gender-specific oppositions. For while Clarice is contrasted with a whole series of males – lawmen and criminals – she is also aligned with serial killer Jame Gumb/Buffalo Bill via their shared working-classness, with this rendering Clarice doubly 'inferior' to the cultured professional middle-class male serial killer Dr Hannibal Lecter, both in terms of her gender and in terms of her class (and in their first meeting, it is Clarice's class background that Lecter mocks rather than her gender).

Another interesting example of the complexities entailed in the construction of social Otherness is Daniel Robitaille/Candyman in *Candyman* (1992), the educated son of a slave who is murdered by white thugs after falling in love with a white woman and who returns from death as a murderous urban legend. Robitaille exists in relation to, and is largely defined by, a range of intersecting social categories, namely race, class and gender. Robitaille's education and associated class-based privileges set him apart from the black working-class males, some of whom become his victims in the film, and his masculinity renders him 'superior' to women, regardless of their class. Indeed, he kills a working-class black woman and a middle-class black woman and also makes strenuous attempts to kill the middle-class white woman who is the main female character in the film. Robitaille's victims are therefore those deemed to be beneath him in a social hierarchy of power, either because of their working-class identity or their femaleness (or both). The only group above Robitaille in this social hierarchy would seem to be the white middle-class males who populate the university where the film's main female character works; none of these men is presented sympathetically but Robitaille leaves them alone (until the sequel to *Candyman, Candyman 2: Farewell to the Flesh*, where he starts killing them off as well) and instead it is a white woman who kills one of these men at the film's conclusion.

The question that arises from looking at horror films in this way is – where is the Other now? Where is social domination and where is social oppression? Clearly dominant–subordinate relationships are a significant feature of social structures, and presumably have an important part to play within films, but the nature of these relationships is not always clear or consistent and can alter noticeably from one context to another. It follows that readings of horror films that seek to relate them to ideological projections of Otherness need to be attentive to these complexities rather than simply identifying texts as either unproblematically progressive or unproblematically reactionary.

There are further questions about the role of the Other in horror that need to be addressed. Does horror always rely on multiple and interactive categories of Otherness; if so, how do we recognise the different types of Otherness this involves, both in themselves and in terms of their interactions? Taking what appears to be an especially Other-rich film, *Bride of Frankenstein* (1935), we find a range of interpretations of it that are grounded in different notions of Otherness. For Paul O'Flinn, Universal's Frankenstein films, much like all adaptations of Mary Shelley's original novel, are meditations on the role of the proletariat within capitalism (O'Flinn, 1986). By contrast, Elizabeth Young sees *Bride of Frankenstein* not in terms of class at all but instead as a film organised around issues to do with gender and race (Young, 1996). So far as gender is concerned, the film, according to Young, offers a scenario that in various ways undermines or questions conventional notions of masculinity and femininity through both the homosocial relationship between Frankenstein and Dr Pretorious and the resistance to male definitions of femininity provided by Mary Shelley – as she appears in the film's prologue – and the female monster (with both these characters played by Elsa Lanchester).

Young also argues that the film offers a representation of racial Otherness via the figure of the male monster (played, of course, by Boris Karloff) who, in terms of his role in the narrative and the imagery associated with him, might be viewed in terms of stereotypes associated with African-American masculinity. For Young, the film's engagement with race is incoherent. On the one hand, its presentation of the monster as a sympathetic figure, especially in

The ambiguous Other: Boris Karloff as Frankenstein's Monster in *Frankenstein* (1931). Courtesy of Universal Studios Licensing LLLP.

the scenes where the monster is hounded by torch-carrying mobs (images, according to Young, that are redolent of lynchings) potentially has a progressive tenor. On the other hand, the portrayal in other parts of the film of the monster preying upon white women can be seen to align him with what Young calls 'the myth of the black rapist' (Young, 1996, p.325). Young concludes her analysis of *Bride of Frankenstein* by pointing out that 'gender, sexuality, and race inextricably implicate one another in this film' and 'that bonds between men in the film are located on two axes, sexual and racial, which contradict each other' (Young, 1996, p.327).

Harry Benshoff and Rhona Berenstein offer accounts of *Bride of Frankenstein* that overlap with Young's reading in certain respects but have different emphases (Benshoff, 1997, pp.49–51; Berenstein, 1996, pp.136–47). Both Benshoff and Berenstein focus on what they see as the film's 'queer dynamic' and its fascination with unconventional and transgressive male relationships: '*Bride of Frankenstein* is . . . a narrative of illicit homosocial desire, a film in which conventional masculinity and heterosexuality are under attack by the unrepressible forces of human "nature" . . . and medical science' (Berenstein, 1996, p.146). But while Young gives as much space in her account of the film to racial matters as she does to the representation of gender, neither Benshoff nor Berenstein strays far from the film's gender politics. Berenstein does refer at the end of her analysis of *Bride of Frankenstein* to Young's work and points out that 'the film's explorations of gender ambiguity and homosociality appear alongside and in concert with a racist undercurrent' (Berenstein, 1996, p.147). However, Berenstein does not specify precisely how racial Otherness and gender ambiguity act in concert with each other in the film or to what effect. In fact, if one looks back at Young's account of *Bride of Frankenstein*, one finds that while she does seek to show how race and gender intertwine with each other, her analysis nevertheless places a greater emphasis on race for certain parts of the film – notably those scenes where the male monster takes centre-stage – and on gender for other parts of the film – notably those scenes in which Baron Frankenstein is the centre of attention.

One might be tempted to assume from this that these different interpretations of the film are simply finding what they want to find in it, that whatever area of social oppression and Otherness preoccupies the critic in question determines which aspects of the film he or she will consider important. One could go further and argue that the significance and usefulness of *Bride of Frankenstein* in this respect is that it is sufficiently ambiguous to sustain a range of different interpretations. From this perspective, *Bride of Frankenstein* offers something to every keen interpreter of horror; not only does it have class, it has gender and race as well, plus religious references (if that is your area of interest) and discussions of the morality of science.

Nevertheless, the fact that it seems difficult to relate together the different categories of Otherness – to do with gender, class and race – apparently at work within *Bride of Frankenstein* merits further consideration. Thinking about the film in this way, as a text that is not necessarily cohesive so far as its treatment of Otherness is concerned, leads us to another important question about the role of the Other in horror cinema – namely, why does horror engage with it at all?

Accounts of horror that see it in terms of the Other tend to assume that the presence of the Other is a *sine qua non* of the genre, that a horror film deals with notions of the Other because that is what horror films do, and if a film is not doing this in some way, then it is probably not a horror film at all. Essentially these interpretations of the Other in horror cinema are drawing analogies and making metaphors, arguing that specific elements within films refer to, or stand in for, particular subordinate social groups. Hence Elisabeth Young's claim that Frankenstein's monster functions in terms of racial difference or Amy Taubin's argument that the alien queen in *Aliens* (1986) is a coded representation of the African-American mother as she appeared in right-wing discourses of the 1980s (Young, 1996; Taubin, 1992). There are limits to this, of course. Neither Frankenstein's monster nor the alien queen is literally African-American. Even those representations of Otherness that can be correlated more directly to subordinate social groups – for example, Candyman is literally a black male and Asa in *La maschera del demonio* is literally a female oppressed by men – are far from being realistic representations of the group in question. Candyman might well be black and Asa female but they are also the living dead. Or, to give another example, the monstrous families in *The Texas Chainsaw Massacre* (1974) and *The Hills Have Eyes* (1977) could well represent the degraded proletariat but they are also cannibals – so not that typical then. The space that exists here between the apparent image of the Other in horror and the reality of the social category to which it is being related by the critic is thus a space within which one can both refuse particular interpretations and offer one's own interpretation – so Frankenstein's monster, say, can be 'really' proletarian, 'really' gay or 'really' black.

It does not follow that seeing horror films in terms of Otherness cannot be enlightening, whether one defines Otherness in social or in psychological terms (and, since Wood, many critics often combine the two). But there are problems with viewing horror's function as being essentially to express, confirm or sometimes critique pre-existing notions of the Other. For one thing, such an approach can be very reductive. In its cruder forms, it can lead to interpretations in which the critic simply identifies the social category of Otherness that he or she sees the monster or victim as representing without due regard for the specific narrative and generic contexts within which monsters and victims are being deployed. Even in those Other-centred accounts of horror that are more alert to nuance and complexity, both in the films and in the social context of their production (and I include here all the accounts cited earlier in this chapter), one detects a tendency to think about horror solely or primarily in terms of social oppression or repression. The implication is that in a just world, a world in which no one is oppressed, horror itself would simply cease to exist.

In the face of this, one could argue that it makes sense to see horror's relationship with notions of Otherness, in part at least, as an opportunistic and exploitative one. Returning to *Bride of Frankenstein* in this light, the ambiguous or polysemic nature of the male monster, which has helped to generate such a wide range of interpretations, could derive from the fact that the film-makers are just using the monster in different, sometimes inconsistent, ways throughout the film. So in some scenes he is sympathetic, in other scenes he is menacing; in some scenes – notably the one in which he kidnaps Frankenstein's bride – he is presented in heterosexual terms, while in other scenes – notably his idyll in the forest with the blind hermit – homosocial elements are brought into play. Given that cinema, and the people who work within it, are part of the social fabric, it is perhaps inevitable that horror films will often draw in their creation of the monstrous on discourses of social difference and Otherness which are in circulation in society at the time, but it does seem that in many cases horror's engagement with these discourses is a piecemeal one fitted to suit the multiple dramatic needs of the horror narrative.

Bearing this in mind, it is therefore legitimate to view *Bride of Frankenstein*, along with other horror films of the early 1930s such as *Dr Jekyll and Mr Hyde* and *Island of Lost Souls*, as using, probably unconsciously (if one wishes to be generous to the film-makers concerned), racist tropes of the black rapist in their presentation of stories dealing with degeneracy and sexual violence. Similarly, there are clearly proletarian qualities associated with Frankenstein's monster, especially as shown in his hobo-like costume (which is more contemporary-looking than any other costume in the film). But in neither case do these qualities, racial or class-specific, necessarily represent something consistently worked through in *Bride of Frankenstein*. Rather, they become meaningful only in some scenes while elsewhere they are not particularly significant.

As for the 'queerness' of *Bride of Frankenstein*, this can be assigned both to a narrative in which men attempt to create life together without the presence of women (something similar is apparent in the equally homosocial *Island of Lost Souls*, a film version of H.G. Well's novel, *The Island of Dr Moreau*) and, more particularly, to the queer sensibility of the director James Whale, who in this and other respects was one of the most distinctive horror film-makers of the 1930s. But even Whale's orchestration of this unconventional take on gender relations is not maintained consistently throughout, with not only the conventional restoration of the heterosexual couple at the film's conclusion (admittedly an ending imposed by the studio) but also the class and racial differences intermingled in the body of the male monster getting in the way of any utopian queer understanding of the film as a whole.

Another problem with thinking about horror exclusively in terms of Otherness (especially social Otherness) is that it puts too much emphasis on horror as a regressive form, as a form that constantly and inevitably returns us to our own normality. From this perspective, all of horror's strangeness – its weird happenings, its supernatural and quasi-supernatural monsters – is, when properly interpreted and decoded, an expression of social and/or psychological patterns of domination and subordination. Such an approach sometimes flourishes when dealing with types of horror that offer themselves as social critiques – notably a number of US horror films from the 1970s (see Chapter 8 for a discussion of these) – or which self-consciously deploy psychoanalytical ideas – the gothic horror films of director Roger Corman, for example. However, it falters when confronted with horror films that seem indifferent to or distant from any engagement with social or psychological contexts.

As an illustration of this, one can turn to two gateway-to-hell movies, the Italian horror film *The Beyond* (1981) and the American SF/horror film *Event Horizon* (1997). In *The Beyond*, the opening of a gateway to hell brings about the collapse of conventional notions of space, with locations that were distinct and separate suddenly, and impossibly, joined together, and the breaking down of barriers between past and present and between the living and the dead. In *Event Horizon* a rescue crew board a spaceship that is apparently haunted after its visit to another dimension (a dimension which, the film strongly hints, is hell) and one of the crew members is eventually transformed into a demonic representative of that other dimension. In both cases, hell is figured as 'out there', apparently located in a space that is extra-dimensional and, because of this, difficult to represent: *The Beyond* shows it only in the form of a painting; *Event Horizon* gives us a few glimpses of it via the degraded video recording of the ship's mission that is viewed by the rescue crew. But at the same time hell is also revealed to be 'in here', close to hand, transforming bodies and the spaces through which those bodies move in a most direct and assaultive manner. Hence the stress in both films on scenes of claustrophobic confinement and the pervasiveness and proximity of that which is 'beyond'. Hence, too, the importance of the idea of bodily trans-formation, an idea which clearly has a much broader significance in horror, featuring regularly as it does in films about vampires, werewolves and zombies, to name but a few of horror's transformative monsters.

Each of these 'haunted house' (or, in the case of *Event Horizon*, haunted spaceship) films reworks ideas, themes and scenarios readily apparent else-where in the horror genre, but it is hard to find any significant social or psychological dimension to either of them. This is not the same as saying that neither film contains any reference to social divisions or psychological concepts; it would be hard to imagine any film, horror or otherwise, that is completely free of such things. It is just that here they do not appear to be central to the film's invoking of the monstrous. So, for example, *Event Horizon*'s borrowings from *The Haunting* do not follow through the uncanny-psychological logic of that film (see Chapter 3 for a discussion of *The Haunting* in these terms), while *The Beyond*'s location of its gateway to hell in property owned by one of its characters does not invoke the materialistic preoccupation with property values found, say, in the rather more 'realistic' and socially-minded American gateway-to-hell movie *The Amityville Horror* (1979). It seems from this that neither *The Beyond* nor *Event Horizon* are 'about' anything, i.e. their content does not readily lend itself to being thought of in terms of either psychological or social repression.

This vein of indifference to social/psychological matters runs through those horror films, admittedly few in number, that aspire towards what might be termed a sublime effect, concerned as they are to produce a sense of not just fear but also awe and wonder usually in relation to something imagined as vast and mysterious, something that offers new realms of experience existing beyond what we can currently know and feel. One thinks here in particular of Carl Dreyer's art-horror film *Vampyr* (1932), Dario Argento's *Inferno* (1980), Lucio Fulci's *The Beyond*, Sam Raimi's *The Evil Dead* (1982) and *The Evil Dead 2* (1987), John Carpenter's *Prince of Darkness* (1987) and *In the Mouth of Madness* (1995) and Mariano Baino's *Dark Waters* (1994). (Many of these films show the influence of the horror writings of H.P. Lovecraft, who was the key twentieth-century representative of the visionary school of horror fiction.) But this preoccupation with 'beyondness' also has a more pervasive, albeit low-key, presence within the horror genre, notably in the genre's reliance on the conjuring up of strange realms within or in relation to a world of normality. As already noted, the horror critic's Other-centred task is usually to locate and reveal the symptomatic and the figurative in these realms, to move beyond the surface and in so doing to tame and domesticate the strangeness. But perhaps we should not be in such a hurry to discard or explain away the literal here. In fact it could be argued that to view monsters such as, say, vampires, werewolves or, to give a more modern example, serial killers purely in symptomatic terms, as expressions of something other than what they appear to be, is to miss an important point about them, namely that they are all, in their own ways, entities that speak very directly of something that lies beyond, where that beyondness does not necessarily have a social or psychological dimension. In other words, thinking about such figures in terms of Otherness helps to bring the monsters back home to us while thinking about them in terms of beyondness can potentially take us outside ourselves, engaging our imaginations in creative, speculative and unexpected ways.

Of course, this is a rather vague way of thinking about horror when compared with the detailed and authoritative (and often very convincing) interpretations produced within the terms of Otherness. But it is important to maintain a sense of horror that does not deliver it wholly to being explained away as the product of repression, if only because this repression-centred approach makes the genre appear more straightforward and limited than it actually is. To give an example of this, the male monster in *Bride of Frankenstein* might well be the point of intersection for a range of discourses expressing social difference and Otherness, and seeing this figure in these terms can illuminate our understanding of its cultural and historical significance. But simply thinking about the monster as the sum total of its composite discursive parts fails to engage with the fact that this monster has a life of its own, a life which in various ways exceeds the materials from which it has been fashioned and which, arguably, has helped transform it into a long-lived cultural icon and made it a focus for imaginative responses and creative appropriations. Put another way, this monster exists as something beyond us, something that might well invite our interpretations but which will never be wholly defined or simply explained away by these.

The remainder of this chapter will focus on the roles played by racial and class difference in horror cinema. Up until recently the most influential critical approaches to horror have tended to focus exclusively or mainly on questions relating to sexual difference – with this especially the case for those approaches influenced by psychoanalysis – and this has led to other forms of social difference being marginalised or overlooked. It follows that a consideration of race and class can develop an understanding of horror by clarifying the complexities of social difference and Otherness as they are articulated within particular groups of films. However, looking at horror in this way does not provide us with a master key with which we can unlock all of horror's secrets. As a critical approach it can move our understanding on but it cannot complete that understanding because its attempts to close the circle between film and society (i.e. social designations of Otherness enable horror to come into being while decoding horror films in terms of Otherness leads us back to those social designations) tend to downgrade, or view as transparently illusory, the imaginary and fantasy-based elements that are present within, and arguably fundamental to, the horror genre. What follows then will seek to highlight the explanatory power of certain concepts of social difference and Otherness in a way that opens up the films being discussed rather than closing them down.

BLACK ZOMBIE TO BLACK VAMPIRE

Discussions of negative and prejudicial portrayals of particular social groups often focus on the question of stereotypes. It is the function of the stereotype in this instance to exemplify the way in which subordinate groups in society can be represented in a manner that is both reductive and demeaning. One possible reaction against being typed like this is to manufacture representations of the group in question that aspire to be either more positive or more 'realistic' (or both) than the stereotype. However, such an approach does raise the considerable question of whether cohesive social identities actually exist in a way that can adequately be captured by specific representations. In other words, is there an unproblematic 'real' out there against which stereotypes can be judged and found wanting? Related to this is the question of whether stereotypes are as stable and consistent as some critics have made them out to be. To what extent can stereotypes be inflected and reworked by cultural texts, and how, if at all, can the creative work this involves change the meanings associated with stereotypes? Can a stereotype be negative or insulting in one context and progressive in another?

Consider in this respect the representation of blackness in the American horror film. One might reasonably argue that stereotypes abound here, but which stereotypes and how are they being used? A useful starting point is the Val Lewton production *I Walked with a Zombie* (1943), a horror film that contains a number of representations of black characters that might be considered as stereotypical. For example, Carrefour, a black male 'zombie', could be seen in terms of a stereotype already mentioned in this chapter in respect of Frankenstein's monster – the black male as a figure who menaces white women, with that menace often having a sexual component. Certainly the film contains one scene in which Carrefour enters the home of the white characters and advances threateningly upon the white female nurse, a scene decidedly reminiscent of the moment in *Bride of Frankenstein* where the male monster abducts the Baron's bride. In contrast, the black calypso singer (played by 'Sir Lancelot') – who, when he thinks the white characters are not present, sings a scurrilous song about their activities but, on discovering their presence, makes an abject, fawning apology – might be seen as a subservient 'Uncle Tom' figure. From this perspective, the film acquires a racist tenor, objectifying the black male either as excessively sexual and threatening or, in a more patronising way, as a child-like servant in need of white authority and leadership.

Before writing off *I Walked with a Zombie* as racist (and, as this chapter will show, the film is considerably more complex than the above account of it suggests), it is worth comparing its use of particular black characterisations with their use elsewhere. For example, picture this scene from *Vampire in Brooklyn* (1995), a horror film directed by genre specialist Wes Craven. The setting is a city park at night. A white woman out walking her dog is assaulted by a black male. A potentially racist scenario no doubt, of the kind in which Carrefour was involved in *I Walked with a Zombie*. But let us add some details.

It is not just any black male here or even a black zombie but instead a black male vampire. And not just any black male vampire but rather the main character in the film, a character played by Eddie Murphy, a major movie star since the early 1980s, especially in comic roles. As for the female victim (a cameo appearance by Jerry Hall), she too is offered to us in comic terms as a caricatural portrayal of an insecure, guilt-ridden white liberal. 'I have pepper spray and I swear I'll use it,' she exclaims on first seeing the Murphy character, but then as he approaches, 'But I want you to know I understand the negro people. I understand how you've been chained down by the oppression of white capitalist society.' Add to this the fact that the assault is being carried out for the benefit of a black female neophyte vampire being trained in the ways of vampirism by Murphy and who looks on as Murphy launches his attack on the hapless victim, and this scene becomes less straightforward than might originally have been supposed, both in its racial and gendered dimensions.

Take another example, this time involving the passive 'Uncle Tom' stereotype. Here a white male dismisses a black male to his face as weak and subservient, as – and the white man does use this term – an 'Uncle Tom' at the beck and call of others. The film is *Blade* (1998), the white male is arch-vampire villain Deacon Frost (played by Stephen Dorff) and the black male is arch-vampire hunter Blade (as played by Wesley Snipes). The interesting feature of this scene is that while Frost is using a term that has undeniable racist associations, he is not apparently using it to refer to Blade's blackness. Instead he is criticising Blade, who is part vampire, part human, for protecting humans rather than embracing his vampire identity. Complicating this further is the fact that Frost himself is a 'half-blood', someone made a vampire by another vampire rather than being born that way. Within the film, the half-blood designation clearly has a racial element – with the racial purity of the 'full-blood' vampire contrasted unfavourably with the impurity of the half-blood/half-breed – and a class dimension as well, with Frost figured in this respect as an insurrectionary figure from the lower ranks of an intensely hierarchical and conservative vampiric social order. What seems to be happening in this sequence then is that references to racial difference (and the fact that Frost, as he delivers his insult, is holding as hostage a young Chinese-American girl implies that this does not just mean a white/black difference) are being displaced on to fantasy-based divisions between humans and vampires and between one set of vampires and another set of vampires.

It might be possible to view both *Vampire in Brooklyn* and *Blade* as more 'progressive' than the likes of *I Walked with a Zombie*, if only because they offer scenarios in which black characters are central either as the hero (in *Blade*) or as the charming and amusing anti-hero (in *Vampire in Brooklyn*). It follows that the movement apparent here from the black zombiedom of *I Walked with a Zombie* (and it is worth noting that zombiedom is the customary role for the few black characters figured as monsters in horror films of the 1930s and 1940s) to the black vampirism of the 1990s is also a movement from subjection – with zombies in the 1930s and 1940s usually defined as the mindless slaves of others – to realms of vampiric activity and desire, with vampires (or, in *Blade's* case, half-vampires) not really subject to anyone. This shift in the way in which black characters are being represented might also be related to the fact that both Eddie Murphy and Wesley Snipes are producers of the films in which they are starring, and that, like the characters they play, they too are powerful figures.

However, it can also be argued that to see the transition from *I Walked with a Zombie* to *Vampire in Brooklyn* and *Blade* as simply an emancipatory one so far as the representation of racial difference is concerned is doing an injustice to all these films. It has already been suggested of both *Vampire in Brooklyn* and *Blade* that they are appropriating pre-existing stereotypes in ways that are provocative and mocking but which do not necessarily involve the stereotypes being rejected out of hand and replaced with more 'realistic' or positive representations. In *Vampire in Brooklyn*, for instance, the stereotypical and potentially racist scenario of a white woman being attacked by a black male is both invoked and then ironised through the scene's comic inflections, but this is not done in a way that totally disperses all of the aggression and violence associated with that scenario, i.e. the victim might be a caricature and the assailant might be a vampire but a violent attack is still taking place. So far as *Blade* is concerned, it is hard to think of Blade himself in kowtowing 'Uncle Tom' terms, such is the extreme violence he directs against vampires. Nevertheless, his devotion to Whistler, a white male father surrogate (Blade's biological father is never mentioned) does potentially suggest a servile relation to white paternalism that the film acknowledges but never really explores.

Similarly, if we look back at *I Walked with a Zombie*, we find that all is not as it seems. For example, while Carrefour might have a menacing appearance, it is never clear whether he actually poses a threat. White characters – and especially the nurse – might see him in these terms but that could, and probably does, say more about white people than it does about black people. In fact, Carrefour remains something of a cipher throughout the film. He seems to be acting on behalf of the practitioners of voodoo based at the home fort, the centre of voodoo activity on the island of St Sebastian, but their motivations – and by extension Carrefour's motivations – remain, like so much else in the film, shrouded in mystery. And, to complicate matters further, in the film's opening sequence, Carrefour is shown walking in an apparently non-threatening manner along a beach in the company of the nurse who later in the film will be so scared of him.

The calypso singer also turns out to be decidedly ambiguous. For one thing, how do we know for certain that his apology to the whites is a sincere one? This is especially so given that in the very next scene the singer is shown slowly advancing through the darkness towards the nurse – in this respect not unlike Carrefour as he appears later in the film – while he sings the remainder of the song that caused so much offence in the first place. As is the case with Carrefour, the extent to which the menace apparent here in the shadowy lighting and in the nurse's fearful reaction is something that emanates from the singer or instead from the nurse's perceptions of him remains unresolved (and we do not see this character again in the film).

I Walked with a Zombie belongs to a period in the history of the horror genre in which blackness tended to be shown in terms of primitivism and exoticism. One instance of this, already mentioned earlier in this chapter, is the way in which certain 1930s horror films figured a white descent into animalistic degradation via stereotypical imagery associated with the representation of blackness, with examples here including *Dr Jekyll and Mr Hyde*, *Island of Lost Souls* and *Bride of Frankenstein*. So far as representations of black people themselves in horror cinema were concerned (as opposed to 'blackness' as a state into which white characters can fall), the stress, especially in American horror of the 1930s and 1940s, tended to be on non-American blacks, with African-American characters making only occasional appearances in minor roles as comic relief. As initially seemed the case with *I Walked with a Zombie*, white encounters with black people in foreign climes were organised around a threat/subservience dichotomy, with the black natives in question either one thing or the other and in any event defined entirely via their relationship with the white characters who provided the main focus of the drama. So, for example, in *King Kong* (1933), aggressive natives kidnap the white heroine and attempt to sacrifice her to the great ape Kong (and Kong himself has been seen by some critics as a coded representation of blackness) while in *White Zombie* (1932) black characters are either servants to whites or zombie-slaves controlled by the white villain Murder Legendre (played by Bela Lugosi). This pattern of subjection prevails in various forms right up to the 1960s, and not just in American horror cinema. The British Hammer horror film *The Plague of the Zombies* (1966), for example, has as its villain an evil squire who, in the manner of Murder Legendre, has mastered voodoo skills while on a visit to the West Indies and uses them to his own advantage on his return to England. The few black characters that appear in this film are simply given us as the squire's servants or slaves. By contrast, Hammer's *The Reptile* (1966) features a sinister Asian villain who spends most of the film tormenting the white characters that have fallen into his control. The fact that *The Plague of the Zombies* and *The Reptile*, shot back-to-back on the same sets by the same director and crew, share a similar set of stylistic and thematic preoccupations (and have often been linked together by horror historians) suggests that these two ways of presenting non-white characters, while apparently diametrically opposed, are actually very close to each other, equally structured as they are around a certain white-centredness.

It is not uncommon for films to contain representations of both aggressor-black and subservient-black characters. What makes *I Walked with a Zombie* distinctive is the extent to which it problematises this way of thinking about blackness, albeit in a manner that does not necessarily reject it. Certainly black characters that appear to be threatening in some scenes are shown as non-threatening in other scenes, and black stereotypes in general are thrown into some disarray. But ultimately this difficulty in placing black people according to pre-existing stereotypical definitions of them leads the film back to the psychological problems of white people rather than to any under-standing of or engagement with the black characters in question. The 1940s horror films produced by Val Lewton – and especially the ones directed by Jacques Tourneur (*Cat People*, *I Walked with a Zombie* and *The Leopard Man*) – often featured characters motivated by unconscious drives. Accordingly, in the case of *I Walked with a Zombie*, virtually all of the white characters are compromised in some way or other by desires and impulses of which they are either not consciously aware or ashamed. In particular, the nurse's suggestion that her patient, the wife of the man loved by the nurse, should undergo a dangerous and potentially fatal insulin-shock treatment can be read in two ways, either as an expression of concern for her patient's well-being or as an unconscious desire to get rid of the wife.

Seen like this, the main role of the black characters in *I Walked with a Zombie* seems to be to convey how screwed up these white people are. Showing that white people do not really understand black people becomes a way of showing that white people do not understand themselves and their own problems. While it is implied in some scenes – notably in the calypso song sequence – that the black characters do have some kind of perspective on the whites, this is never explored in any detail. Instead throughout much of the film black men and women and their culture remain mysterious, enigmatic and shadowy (quite literally shadowy in a film which, like Val Lewton's other productions, makes extensive use of chiaroscuro lighting). We never really know for certain or in any detail what these characters are thinking or feeling because we only ever see them through the confused eyes of the film's white protagonists. It is interesting in this respect to compare the film's treatment of Carrefour, the black zombie, with Jessica, the white zombie. While Carrefour remains an ambiguous figure throughout the narrative, Jessica turns out to be a much more straightforward sort of zombie. There might be some unresolved issues about the cause of her zombiedom – was it the result of a fever or the outcome of a voodoo ritual initiated by her mother-in-law – but her narrative function within *I Walked with a Zombie* is clear. She forms part of two romantic triangles, the first involving her husband and her husband's half-brother, the second involving her husband and the newly-arrived nurse; and her death at the end of the film (along with the death of the half-brother) effectively dissolves both triangles and enables the formation of the white heterosexual couple of her husband and the nurse. Jessica also has a fairly obvious symbolic function, with her deathly whiteness – i.e. her blondeness, the paleness of her skin, her white clothes – standing for a broader emotional paralysis experienced by all the principal white characters in the film. (For an interesting discussion of the association of whiteness with death, especially in horror cinema, see Richard Dyer, 1997, pp.207–23; for a relevant discussion of *I Walked with a Zombie*, see Robin Wood, 1976, pp.209–23.) In a sense, the film seems to be suggesting that all of these people are, in emotional terms at least, zombies. And throughout all this, Carrefour remains as enigmatic as ever. *I Walked with a Zombie* thus emerges as a kind of limit-case for this period in horror history, lamenting in a very masochistic way the shortcomings of a particular kind of colonial whiteness but not really replacing this with anything else.

Things do not start to change in the horror genre until the late 1960s, and in particular the release of George Romero's seminal *Night of the Living Dead* (1968), a film featuring an African-American man as its hero. Gone is the primitive tribalism of *King Kong*. Instead we are presented with a personable and articulate young black man by the name of Ben. The fact that the hero's racial identity is never referred to by any of the characters in the film, even the bigoted ones, suggests a certain liberal egalitarianism, but at the same time the film is replete with covert race-specific imagery, especially at its conclusion. In this, the hero is mistaken for a zombie by a posse and shot dead and his body then burned. More than one critic has seen references here to lynching, an impression encouraged by the fact that the posse seems comprised entirely of gun-toting, trigger-happy rednecks. At the same time, however, Ben is hardly offered as an unproblematically positive representation of heroic leadership. In a film that sets out to confound as many of our expectations as it possibly can, this is a hero, after all, who consistently gets things wrong, whose every decision leads to death and disaster for those around him, and who ends up himself getting shot.

In the midst of this general cynicism about authority and the ability (or rather inability) of humans – black and white – to defeat the monster, Ben's blackness seems, ostensibly at least, a non-issue. Consequently, his role as hero, albeit a compromised hero, might be seen as quietly working to dispel some of the Otherness associated with the black male in earlier American horror films. However, *Night of the Living Dead*'s avoidance of any explicit engagement with his racial identity betrays a surprising reticence on the film's part, surprising because in many other respects the film is absolutely ruthless in its broaching of difficult subject matter. What other film from the 1960s, for example, depicts a little girl stabbing her mother to death with a trowel and then eating the body of her own dead father? One can speculate as to the reasons for this reticence – perhaps at the time of *Night of the Living Dead's* production the issue of race relations did not lend itself to fantasy in the way that other issues to do with the institution of the family obviously did – but the outcome is that the undoubtedly provocative casting of a black male in a prominent role is not really explored (or exploited) by the film. Consequently, for all his being centre-stage, Ben remains, in his own way, as much an enigma as does Carrefour in *I Walked with a Zombie*.

Times change, and four years after *Night of the Living Dead* tiptoed around the race issue, *Blacula* (1972) engaged with it in a much more direct fashion. In this blaxploitation horror film, an African prince is vampirised by Count Dracula and, centuries later, is revived in the contemporary United States. *Blacula* was part of a 1970s vogue for 'black horror' that also included *Scream Blacula Scream* (1973), *Blackenstein* (1973), *Abby* (1974, marketed as a black version of *The Exorcist*) and *Dr Black, Mr Hyde* (1976). Blaxploitation films of the 1970s have tended to be viewed ambivalently within black film history. On the one hand, they provided new opportunities for black film-makers and black performers, and they also arguably offered a space in which oppositional and socially critical ideas could be expressed. But on the other hand, this black-centred material could also be co-opted and exploited by a predominantly white film industry (by no means all blaxploitation films were made by black film-makers). The fact that most blaxploitation films were genre pieces raised especially the question of how precisely they were different from more standardised (i.e. white-centred) genre fare. Did this difference simply involve having black actors in roles usually reserved for white actors (as might be the case with *Night of the Living Dead*), or was a more fundamental reworking of genre conventions involved?

Harry Benshoff has argued that 'many blaxploitation horror films reappropriated the mainstream cinema's monstrous figures for black goals, turning vampires, Frankenstein monsters, and transformation monsters into agents of black pride and black power' (Benshoff, 2000, p.37). From this perspective, Prince Mamuwalde (renamed – in slave-like fashion – as Blacula by Count Dracula) has the potential to become a metaphor both for black enslavement and, as a powerful black male, for black resistance to that enslavement. In contrast, horror historian David J. Skal has offered a less positive reading of the film. For Skal, '*Blacula* is just a formula vampire movie with a mostly black cast, proving only that white fangs are indeed effective when displayed against dark skin' (Skal, 1996, pp.30–1). So where does this leave Prince Mamuwalde/Blacula? Is he (and the film in which he appears) different from the generic norm to the extent that he acquires an oppositional force, or is he just one modern-day vampire among many?

Blacula certainly fits into a broader transition apparent in vampire films of the early 1970s from period settings to contemporary ones. One thinks here of American productions *Count Yorga – Vampire* (1970), *House of Dark Shadows* (1970, a film version of the cult television series *Dark Shadows*), *The Night Stalker* (1971, a highly successful television film that spawned the TV series *Kolchack – the Night Stalker*), *The Return of Count Yorga* (1971), *The Velvet Vampire* (1971) and *Grave of the Vampire* (1972) as well, from Britain, Hammer's *Dracula AD 1972* (1972) and *The Satanic Rites of Dracula* (1973) and, from Belgium, *Le Rouge aux lèvres/Daughters of Darkness* (1971), all of which place their vampires firmly in the modern world. In fact, from this point onwards in the history of vampire films, period vampire stories (such as the 1979 and 1992 American film versions of *Dracula* directed, respectively, by John Badham and Francis Ford Coppola) would often have a nostalgic tinge to them as they yearned for an older form of horror cinema. Similarly, while Benshoff is right to identify *Blacula*'s romanticising of the figure of the vampire as a distinctive and important innovation in movie-vampirism, this quality too fits into broader patterns of development in horror's treatment of the vampire, for it is also the case that a certain mournfulness was beginning to attach itself to other film vampires at this time. One thinks here in particular of *House of Dark Shadows* and *Daughters of Darkness* as well as some of the vampire films directed by French film-maker Jean Rollin in the late 1960s and early 1970s (Benshoff, 2000, p.37).

This difference of critical opinion between Benshoff and Skal can be related to the contexts within which each of them forms their reading of *Blacula*. Benshoff is concerned to evaluate blaxploitation horror as a distinctive horror cycle in its own right while Skal's engagement with *Blacula* is just a small part of a book dealing in broader terms with vampirism in general. Both these critics do have something interesting to say, but what arguably emerges from comparing their different takes on the film is a certain indeterminacy or open-endedness in *Blacula* itself. Ultimately the question of whether the race-specific elements undoubtedly present in the film are politically significant (as Benshoff suggests) or merely minor variations on established generic norms (as Skal suggests) is probably not answerable by reference to the film itself but instead by reference to the various contexts within which *Blacula* was received and interpreted. While one should beware of assuming that the 'black audience' and the 'white audience' exist as distinct and separate entities that read films in different ways, there is something to be said for the idea that *Blacula*, like many blaxploitation films, is structured in such a manner that it can reasonably be read either as a critique of white-centred generic norms or as a more straightforward, if slightly *outré*, genre project.

Clearly blaxploitation horror is an important reference point for later horror films such as *Vampire in Brooklyn* and *Blade*. But the transition it seems to mark from the subjection of black characters in horror films from the 1930s–1960s period to the more active and independent black characters that start showing up in horror from the late 1960s onwards is far from straightforward. In particular, one has constantly to attend to the complexities and nuances of individual films' treatment of blackness and be aware of the ambiguities that often gather around black characters in horror films, ambiguities that enable these characters to be interpreted in a range of different ways. Having said this, it is also the case that blackness, especially in American horror films, is nearly always an issue for the films concerned, something with which they have to negotiate (even if that negotiation involves an awkward silence, as it does in *Night of the Living Dead*). To a certain extent, this is true for mainstream cinema's treatment of blackness in general, but horror's terms of engagement are distinctive if only because they are so much based in fantasy. One might argue that, far from leading to the inflexible marking of blackness as Other/monstrous, horror's fantastical quality has produced more imaginative, innovative and provocative (as well as tortuous and confused) approaches than is sometimes apparent in those areas of representation more bound by the demands of realism.

Complicating matters further is the fact that what has been discussed here thus far is not blackness in its totality but more specifically the representation of black males in American cinema (and even within this limited aim, a large number of relevant films have been omitted). Other categories of social difference that intersect with blackness – notably those to do with gender, class and nationhood – and inflect the meanings of racial difference, as well as being meaningful in their own right, have not featured at all. In the case of *I Walked with a Zombie*, for example, the division of its black female characters into two groups, one the dutiful servants of the whites and the other the voodoo worshippers engaged in sensual and abandoned dances, is comparable in some ways with the film's division of black males into subservient and threatening groups, but it is not the same. And in the case of *Blacula* and *Blade* – and for that matter many blaxploitation or blaxploitation-influenced films, horror and otherwise, as well – what might be seen as progressive representations of black men as powerful figures are often coupled with images of considerably less powerful, if not powerless, black women.

THE HAVES AND THE HAVE-NOTS OF HORROR

All the complexities and ambiguities involved in horror's representation of racial difference suggest that looking at horror in terms of Otherness is a challenging enterprise. This is confirmed when we consider the role played in the genre by class difference – and in particular by the proletariat. As already noted in this chapter, some critics have viewed 1930s US horror cinema's version of Frankenstein's monster as a representation of the proletariat. He dresses like someone from the proletariat, he seems to share in a proletarian social disempowerment, and his acts of violence can be seen as a covert expression of the anger of the socially disenfranchised, especially during a time of economic depression. (Something similar can and has been said for that other classic 1930s monster movie *King Kong*: see in particular Carroll, 1984.) However, if he is a representation of the proletariat – and, as we have seen, there are other ways of thinking about him – then it is a representation couched in terms of individuality rather than in any notion of the collective. As Mark Jancovich has noted, when 1930s US horror does offer image of collective actions emanating from the 'lower' social orders, it tends to view them negatively (Jancovich, 1992, p.58). One thinks here of the torch-carrying peasants who show up in many Universal horror films. At best, these peasants are shown as a superstitious lot, easily frightened, prone to child-like behaviour and in need of strong leadership (see *Son of Frankenstein* in this respect); at worst, they are a cruel and vengeful mob rampaging through the countryside and victimising people who are not always guilty of the crimes of which they are accused (see here especially *Bride of Frankenstein* and the non-Universal horror *The Vampire Bat*, 1933). Much the same can be said of the zombies in *White Zombie*. Clearly a narrative in which a white man uses zombified black men as slaves to run his mill lends itself to some kind of class analysis (as well as, of course, a racial-colonial analysis). As one critic has bluntly put it, 'the film provides the Marxist a casebook in which to view the horrors of Adam Smith; here capitalism literally grinds up the lives of the workers' (Twitchell, 1985, p.264). Yet those zombies never acquire a voice of their own and remain instead just a mindless, threatening force.

This way of thinking about horror might seem to confirm an idea that we have encountered before in this book, namely that the true significance of horror is not to be found in its ostensible subject matter but instead lies hidden beneath its surface. So while one might find in various 1930s US horror films – although by no means all films from this period – feudal settings replete with aristocrats in their castles and humble peasants in the village below, an altogether more modern drama is apparently taking place here, one in which various characters, regardless of their ostensible social position, enact a proletarian disempowerment that corresponds in some way to the experiences of the original audiences for these films.

Thinking about 1930s US horror in this way might well cast an interesting light on some of the films, but as an approach to the period in general it has its shortcomings. It is not just that many 1930s horror films do not seem even remotely interested, either in literal or in figurative terms, in social class divisions. Nor is it solely the fact that many of the proletarian figures can also be viewed in terms of gender, race, etc. It also, and perhaps more importantly, has something to do with the reasons that are offered – or implied – for why horror films should be engaging with notions of class at all. What often happens here is that a 'monster as metaphor' approach is deployed in a manner implying that these films are either simply reflecting a social truth or functioning as an ideological response to a social problem (with in each case the film-makers themselves not necessarily consciously aware of the full significance of what they are doing).

In response to this, it is important to stress both the creative agency of the film-makers and a sense of the films themselves as constructions designed to elicit certain emotional responses from audiences. From this perspective, it can be argued that when 1930s horror films invoke notions of the proletarian, they are doing so for dramatic reasons, especially to create moments of pathos. One thinks here of the famous scene in *Frankenstein* (1931) in which Frankenstein's monster meets a little girl by a lake and which culminates in his accidentally drowning her. Here we are clearly not meant to see him as a figure of horror but rather as someone to be pitied, a sad and isolated social outcast. Similarly, in the concluding scenes of *King Kong* – when the giant ape is being machine-gunned by biplanes as he clings to the top of the Empire State Building – the audience is encouraged to sympathise with Kong, another isolated, bewildered and victimised individual trapped in a hostile landscape. In both cases, these figures are characterised by a physical strength that is poignantly combined with a verbal inarticulacy, and it is arguably the association of these qualities with stereotypical notions of the proletariat that helps to bestow upon Frankenstein's monster and Kong a certain working-class character. However, one can further argue that this 'working-classness' is not in itself the point of these representations; in other words, such moments in horror films do not necessarily have much to say about the proletariat. Instead these sequences are more concerned with invoking our sympathy and perhaps our tears as well. It is undoubtedly the case that the gestural performances offered both by Karloff's monster and by special-effects expert Willis O'Brien's animated Kong borrow more in this respect from melodrama than they do from other expressive types of acting (notably the extreme performance style of German Expressionist cinema which has often been seen as an influence on 1930s US horror), and that the films themselves are as much tales of sentiment as they are tales of terror.

Seen in this way, horror's references to the proletariat, whether they are intended or incidental, lose the metaphorical or symbolic status accorded them by some critics and become instead just one of the ways in which the films direct the audience's perceptions of the monster. A sympathetically portrayed disempowerment can be conveyed via images associated with the proletariat; by contrast, a monster's empowerment is altogether more dangerous and, in the case of Frankenstein's monster and some other 1930s monsters as well, can involve the deployment of potentially racist imagery. This way of thinking about 1930s horror has the advantage of focusing our attention on the films themselves rather than seeing them as simple expressions or reflections of a broader social reality. It can also help to explain both why and how films deploy various notions of difference and Otherness in a way that does not assume that horror's prime function is to express the Other.

This does not mean that these films were not influenced by and make sense in relation to the social context of their production. It is highly likely that those moments of pathos in 1930s American horror that assumed, in part at least, a proletarian quality would have had a particular resonance for audiences suffering under the effects of the Depression. However, such moments seem in some form or other to have maintained their effectiveness well beyond the immediate context of production, working for other audiences in subsequent decades and in very different socio-economic circumstances. It is also the case that post-1930s horror films too sometimes invoke notions of the proletarian as a way of creating sympathy for certain characters. One thinks here especially of Universal's Wolf Man films of the 1940s. In the first of these, *The Wolf Man* (1941), Larry Talbot/the Wolf Man (as played by Lon Chaney Junior) is introduced as the son of a Welsh squire but he quickly takes on a working-class aura. In part, this is down to the fact that the character is largely defined through the manual skills he has acquired while working in America. In part, it has to do with Lon Chaney Junior himself who, as the son of star Lon Chaney, could be seen as part of Hollywood's 'aristocracy' but whose screen persona was firmly associated with working-class performances, notably as Lennie Small in the 1939 film version of John Steinbeck's *Of Mice and Men*. (This made his subsequent casting – or perhaps miscasting – as Dracula in *Son of Dracula* in 1943 decidedly bizarre, and his version of the Count does turn out to be considerably less aristocratic in demeanour than the earlier Bela Lugosi version.) As a figure subject to terrifying forces beyond its control, the werewolf itself, much like Frankenstein's monster, might also be seen as potentially a metaphor for the plight of the proletariat, and indeed there are a few werewolf stories that explore this particular aspect of this monster – notably Guy Endore's 1933 novel *The Werewolf of Paris* (subsequently filmed, shorn of its political elements, in 1961 by Hammer as *The Curse of the Werewolf*). However, so far as understanding Universal's version of the werewolf is concerned, it is probably more useful to see Talbot's proletarian qualities as serving another function, namely to signify a pathos-ridden powerlessness.

While Universal horror of the 1930s and 1940s was especially reliant on pathos as a key element, other types of horror too sometimes adopted similar strategies. For example Hammer horror of the 1950s and 1960s offers images of subjection involving some sense of the proletariat. A good example here is *The Revenge of Frankenstein* (1958) in which Frankenstein's 'monster', one of Hammer's most sympathetically presented creations, has been constructed from the bodies of the poor and lives in the poor hospital run by Frankenstein. In the manner of the Universal Frankenstein films of the 1930s, *The Revenge of Frankenstein* is, in part, the story of the monster's suffering at the hands of those more powerful than itself, with the association of the monster with society's lower reaches an indispensable part of this. At the same time, again like Universal, Hammer's film-makers distance this monster from the much less sympathetically presented poor patients in the hospital, for while the monster represents a humanity that is threatened by Frankenstein's experiments, the poor themselves are offered as degraded, animalistic and cruel, especially at the film's conclusion when, transformed into a vengeful mob, they brutally beat Frankenstein to death.

It seems from this that the attitude of the film-makers at both Universal and Hammer to the working class is an ambivalent one. On the one hand, the working class provides a source of humanity, especially as defined through suffering; on the other hand, it is also a source of degradation and violence. One way of interpreting this is to see it in terms of ideological containment. The working class in the audience can empathise with characters in film who in some way or other have characteristics associated with the working class but only in a proscribed, limited way, i.e. you can share in the suffering of the proletariat but you are not permitted to identify with it as an organised, collective social force because that would be far too threatening to the powers that be. The problem with such an approach is that it tends to be rather reductive and insufficiently attentive to the different tone and emphases of particular films. For instance, while Universal's representation of mob rule often entailed a shying away from anything that might resemble a political uprising, Hammer's sideswiping of the poor tended to be just a subsidiary part of its single-minded promotion of a bourgeois patriarchal individualism, most clearly embodied by Van Helsing in its *Dracula* films. (For more on Hammer in these terms, see Hutchings, 1993a.)

The appeals frequently made by Hammer horror to bourgeois male authority do not feature much in 1970s US horror but nevertheless a sense of the working class as a source of danger, degradation and violence, as potentially a source of Otherness, is maintained in various forms. The key difference between Hammer and 1970s US horror lies in what the American film-makers do with this. Many accounts of 1970s American horror see it as a period in which young ambitious film-makers set out to say something significant and critical about their society and its values, with this reflected in the films' contemporary settings and 'realist' qualities. (For more on this period in these terms, see Chapter 8 of this book.) One of the ways of doing this and thereby establishing some counter-cultural credentials was to attack dominant social groups, and especially the middle class. The ensuing assaults upon well-off but ultimately hapless middle-class characters might emanate from abroad – Iraq in *The Exorcist*, Europe in *The Omen* – but, more disturbingly, they could also come from within US society itself, with this sometimes taking the form of what might be described as a proletarian uprising. Key films here are Tobe Hooper's *The Texas Chainsaw Massacre* and Wes Craven's *The Hills Have Eyes*, in both of which monstrous cannibalistic families of poor people stalk and attempt to kill (and eat) some of their social 'betters'.

The idea that 1970s horror has in some way a political or even oppositional subtext has proved influential in histories of the genre, but there is a danger here – as, in a different way, there is elsewhere in the horror genre – of rushing too quickly through the literal in these films in the search for what might be hidden beneath their surface. There is actually very little explicit engagement with the political issues of the day in 1970s US horror; for example, Vietnam, a key focus of political debate, is mentioned in passing in only a few films, with Bob Clark's *Dead of Night* (1972) – in which an American soldier returns from Vietnam as a zombie – probably the only one that engages with the subject at any length. The assumption made by some critics writing about the 1970s that there are 'progressive' horror films, i.e. films which dwell upon the injustice involved in various social categories of Otherness, and 'reaction-ary' horror films – films which seek to support those same categories of Otherness – is especially problematic in this respect as it can lead to a neglect of the ways in which horror films actually deploy notions of social difference and Otherness. The reliance of all of these films on fantasy-based scenarios, even those films that aspire to some kind of realism, tends to produce a series of ambiguities *vis-à-vis* Otherness that cannot readily be translated into a cohesive political message, progressive or reactionary.

For example, cases can be made for both *The Texas Chainsaw Massacre* and *The Hills Have Eyes* as social critiques. They both give us proletarian monsters that are a product of US society, they share an iconoclastic take on sacred social institutions such as the family, and generally they offer a powerful sense of a society tearing itself apart. One might go further and argue that their disturbing quality can be traced back to, and in part is an expression of, the turmoil within 1970s American society that was associated in particular with protests against the Vietnam War. By contrast, *The Exorcist* and *The Omen* might be seen as reactionary because of their insistence that the source of the threat to American values is foreign. However, matters become more complicated when one looks in more detail at *The Texas Chainsaw Massacre* and *The Hills Have Eyes* (and, for that matter, at *The Exorcist* and *The Omen* as well), with this especially applying to their representation of the socially dispossessed monsters.

For one thing, neither the monstrous family in *The Texas Chainsaw Massacre* nor the one in *The Hills Have Eyes* is portrayed in a positive or sympathetic light. For another, while their victims might have more money and possessions, and a higher social position, than the cannibals, they tend to be offered to us as 'ordinary' people undeserving of their fate. Neither of the films shies away from their shortcomings but the remarkable violence directed against them (which includes crucifixion, being burned alive, death by chainsaw, and being impaled on a hook) seems, to put it mildly, a disproportionate response to these faults. It follows therefore that it is through identification or empathy with these characters that we enter into the nightmarish worlds conjured up by both films. However, at the same time the spectacle of their torture and death is clearly meant to be thrilling. There is an apparent paradox here that was already evident in earlier horror films but which becomes an increasingly prominent feature in the horror genre from the 1970s onwards, namely horror's invitation to its audience to take pleasure from the traumatising and violating of those characters with whom the audience is simultaneously being invited to identify or empathise.

One way of viewing this is in terms of the audience's self-immolating and nihilistic despair (as Robin Wood does in the account of an audience response to *The Texas Chainsaw Massacre*: Wood, 1986, pp.93–4), but it is also worth thinking about it as a pleasurable experience that, in certain respects at least, is distant from the real world outside the cinema. Here notions of reversibility can help to explain what might be going on. Most horror films – and indeed most films featuring conflict between the forces of good and evil – rely on some kind of reversal of fortunes; a standard narrative structure in horror involves the monster appearing and prospering for a while before the forces of normality rally and destroy it. However, this sense of tables being turned arguably becomes more important in horror from the 1970s onwards. The reversal of fortune here is given in more detail, takes up more screen time, and is mediated via more extreme violence than ever before.

The initial reversal in *The Texas Chainsaw Massacre* and *The Hills Have Eyes* (as well as *The Exorcist, The Omen* and numerous other horrors from this period) is predicated in part on the softness and vulnerability of the relatively well-off – the urban dwellers out for a drive in *Chainsaw* and *Hills*, the film star played by Ellen Burstyn in *The Exorcist*, and the American ambassador to London in *The Omen* – but also, perhaps more importantly, on their slowness in responding appropriately to the situations in which they find themselves. Hitchcock once said of *The Birds* (1963), itself a film that anticipated a number of important trends in horror, that it was an attack upon complacency,

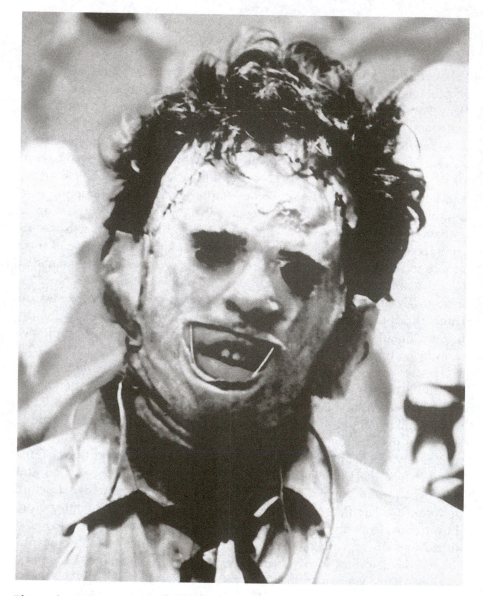

The proletariat strikes back: Leatherface (Gunnar Hansen) in *The Texas Chainsaw Massacre* (1974).

and clearly these later films also rely on a disparity between how the unsuspecting victims complacently react to the environment through which they are moving and how a genre-conscious audience, much more alert to the possibility of attack, reads that environment. In the case of *Chainsaw*, for example, would any of us really go into that astonishingly sinister house, or, in *Hills*, cross that astonishingly sinister desert? It is likely that such a disparity between us (the audience) and them (the characters in the film) causes our empathy with the victims to become attenuated. The eventual 'comeuppance' of the unfortunate characters who do venture into the sinister house or cross the desert thus vindicates our own superior knowledge in a manner that, for all the violence involved, is – potentially at least – pleasurable.

But it is not just a question of witnessing the complacent middle-class subjected to attack. While this becomes a notable feature of horror from the 1970s onwards (think of the *Nightmare on Elm Street* series of films from the 1980s, for example), it is often coupled with yet another reversal as the victims turn the tables back on their proletarian attackers. In *The Hills Have Eyes*, for example, the family terrorised by the cannibals eventually defeat the cannibals by becoming equally ruthless, notably in one scene where family members use their dead mother's body as bait to trap the cannibal's leader. (Wes Craven, *Hills'* director, had done something similar for his first film, the controversial and much-banned *Last House on the Left*, in which a 'nice' bourgeois couple carry out an appallingly violent revenge on the low-life gang of delinquents who have murdered their daughter.)

One can see this series of fearful and pleasurable reversals as inviting a masochistic/sadistic response from the audience. We suffer with the 'normal' middle-class victims and then glean sadistic pleasure from their revenge on the poor white trash that had attacked them in the first place. At the same time, and a little more perversely, we might also be getting sadistic pleasure from the initial terrorising of the well off. How we negotiate our way through this would depend on a range of factors, with one of these being our own class position. For some, no doubt, an incidental pleasure of certain 1970s and 1980s horror films is seeing people better off than they are suffering horrible deaths.

There is something to be said both for the approach that seeks to politicise these films and the approach that engages with them as a kind of thrilling rollercoaster ride. Certainly *The Texas Chainsaw Massacre* and *The Hills Have Eyes*, for all their low budgets and modest production values, do set out to say something about American society in the 1970s. Their shared emphasis on monstrous families, and on savage violence erupting from within American society, becomes in this respect a way of bringing into question a whole set of American values and ideals. But these films are not, as some critics would have it, political manifestos bearing a cohesive ideological message; they are horror films designed to provoke emotional responses from audiences, and whatever social-critical elements they might contain tend to get mixed up, often in a very messy way, with the sadistic-masochistic thrills that the films are also offering. This suggests that readings of 1970s horror that move too quickly to a judgement of the films in political or ideological terms necessarily miss some of the integral thrills of horror, thrills which for many audiences provide the main reason for going to see horror films. Conversely, readings that focus exclusively on the emotional or affective responses generated by these films risk missing some of the qualities that make this type of horror so distinctive, particularly its iconoclastic take on various social institutions.

This has implications for our understanding of how and why the proletariat is figured as Other. On the one hand, the monstrous, cannibalistic families in *The Texas Chainsaw Massacre* and *The Hills Have Eyes* can be seen as representing the return of the socially repressed and dispossessed. What might be termed the revenge-of-the-poor format recurs in horror and horror-related projects from the 1970s onwards, in the *Nightmare on Elm Street* films where a murderous undead janitor attacks rich kids, in various rape-revenge films (notably the infamous *I Spit On Your Grave*), and in 'yuppie nightmare' films such as *Breakdown* (1997). But at the same time, one should not underestimate the 'bogeyman' function served by the various proletarian characters in these films. Certainly both *The Texas Chainsaw Massacre* and *The Hills Have Eyes* put considerable efforts into making their cannibal families as appalling, grotesque and nasty as possible, with this all in the interests of delivering a series of shocks, thrills and anxiety-inducing moments to the films' audiences.

In fact, it could be argued that what underpins these representations of the proletariat is the objectification they involve, and that generally, and regardless of whether they are of domestic or foreign origin, these figures are presented as something 'out there' which threatens us, with the 'us' often involving a middle-class perspective. Seen in this way, the cannibals in both *The Texas Chainsaw Massacre* and *The Hills Have Eyes* (and any number of implicitly working-class monsters in other horror films) serve a similar function to that served by the black characters in *I Walked with a Zombie*; they help to reveal the shortcomings of the middle classes (or whites), their values and their lifestyles, but not in a manner that encourages much sympathy with or understanding of the oppressed ones themselves.

It is interesting that the vicious proletarian monster assumes a prominence in horror in the 1970s, precisely the time when the objectification of black characters in horror (and, of course, in other types of film as well) is increasingly being brought into question. One of the achievements of the civil rights movement in the United States, especially from the 1960s onwards, had been to politicise representations of black people in such a way that American film-makers generally became much more conscious of the need to deal carefully with this particular area of representation and the issues it raised. For horror, this involved in some instances film-makers dodging round some of those issues (as is arguably the case with *Night of the Living Dead*), and in other instances engaging with them more directly, albeit not unproblematically (in *Blacula* or *Blade*, for example). By contrast, class divisions have not acquired a comparable political significance or resonance, at least not so far as their status in popular fictions is concerned. It follows that it is still easier, i.e. more socially acceptable, for film-makers to have demonised working-class characters as villains or monsters than it is to have black people in those roles.

However, this has made for considerable awkwardness when, in recent years, horror film-makers have sought to engage with the experiences of the African-American working-class. Notable in this respect are two films from the 1990s, Wes Craven's *The People Under the Stairs* (1991) and Bernard Rose's *Candyman* (1992). Both of these contain elements of social critique in their representations of a contemporary America in which black people form a disproportionately large sector of the economically disadvantaged, but the narratives of each film, for all their attempts to be socially aware, tend to lead us away from any explicit political engagement with social issues. This is, perhaps surprisingly, most apparent in the moments when each film invokes very explicitly the idea of the working-class black community as an oppositional force. In *The People Under the Stairs*, one of the villainous white slum landlords (or in this case landlady) opens the door of her suburban house to be confronted by a large group of her black tenants, while in *Candyman*, a procession of black inhabitants from the Cabrini Green housing project unexpectedly appear at the funeral of Helen, the film's white heroine. In both instances, the white characters – the white landlady, the white mourners at the funeral – are silenced in the face of this collective black action. At the same time, however, the films do not offer any explanation of how this collectivity has come into being. All that we have been shown of the black 'ghettos' from which these groups have sprung has suggested a dysfunctional world beset by drug taking and violence, a world completely devoid of the will or the means to organise itself politically or in any other way. Because of this, the sudden appearance, apparently from nowhere, of a functional and cohesive black community feels strained and overly rhetorical, a gesture towards political significance and social relevance rather than a systematic and politically aware engagement with issues to do with racial and class divisions. In line with this, the dramatic function of these 'communal' moments within both *The People Under the Stairs* and *Candyman* seems, as it has been before in horror, to signify in a rather moralistic manner the oppressiveness or complacent arrogance of the well-off white characters, but with this criticism delivered primarily through the presence of a group of the 'oppressed' poor and black who themselves have little or nothing to say about their own situation.

As is the case elsewhere in the horror genre, one finds here that the films' attitudes to socially repressed groups is ambivalent and shifting, with much of this stemming from the instabilities inherent in the narrative process, whereby the status of characters and our attitudes to them is constantly being reworked as we move through the story. What this often entails is a vacillation between what might be termed a register of Otherness, of scariness and monstrosity, and a more open-minded exploration of notions of social difference. It is actually very difficult to think of many horror films that are so completely bound up with Otherness that they are unable to contemplate, even if only intermittently, the challenge posed by notions of the Other to the legitimacy of social norms and social institutions, or, for that matter, to think of any horror films which, for all their socially critical ambitions, do not appeal to Otherness.

So far as the meaning of these films is concerned, one also needs to think about how different audiences – and, for that matter, critics – make sense of all these uncertainties. Clearly there are numerous ways of illuminating horror films through focusing upon a particular category of social difference and Otherness and interpreting particular films from this perspective, and to a certain extent the history of horror is the history of such interpretations. However, problems arise when Other-centred interpretations suppress or marginalise elements within films that do not neatly fit into the interpretation in question. This might involve concentrating on one type of Otherness – gender, say – at the expense of others rather than considering how (and why) they are interacting within whatever horror films are being discussed. But it could also involve not paying enough attention to some of the limitations of Otherness itself as an explanatory concept, and especially the way in which it tends to direct our attention away from what is going on in horror films to some pre-existing social truth lurking behind the films in question. There is no doubt that many horror films can fairly convincingly be translated into a discourse of Otherness; given that horror is so reliant on dramas involving power and subjection, it is perhaps inevitable that its films, which like all films are social artefacts, will draw upon socially specific notions of the Other. But, equally inevitably, something gets lost in the translation, namely the distinctive character of horror itself as a set of imaginative fictions that often takes those elements of Otherness in unexpected, unpredictable directions. Ultimately, looking at horror in terms of Otherness can alert us to some of the ambiguities, ambivalences, contradictions and mysteries at the heart of horror but it does not fully explain (or explain away) the genre. In other words, recognising Otherness marks the beginning of our understanding of this thing called horror, not its completion.

CHAPTER SIX

The sounds of horror

It's only a noise.

(The Haunting, 1963)

KNOCK KNOCK

In 'The Door Ajar', a 1982 article on the horror film, W.H. Rockett claims that, in his words, 'one of the most terrifying stories in fiction is one of the shortest', namely 'The last man on earth sat reading in his library. Something knocked at the door' (Rockett, 1982, p.131). Nuances of language aside (surely 'the last person' would be better than 'the last man' if one wanted to avoid the possibility that the 'something' beyond the door was a woman), the prospect of fear here is bound up with the fact that some entity that is not human but which is capable of knocking on a door is waiting outside the library. If this were a scene from a horror film rather than a self-contained little story, presumably the tension would mount as the man fearfully approaches the door. Slowly he turns the door knob, opens the door and *either* the monster springs, scaring us or – if the monster is too obviously an actor in a tatty monster suit – making us laugh, *or* nothing is there, with the mystery of the initial knock at the door remaining unsolved and the tension continuing to mount as our hero explores the rest of the house or else retreats into the library to await the next unexplained sound.

As Rockett notes in his article, this little story highlights a crucial issue for horror film-makers – to show or not to show. Do you show your monster in all its gory detail and thereby run the risk of that monster not living up to the demands made of it by the narrative? Or do you not show it at all, either keeping the library door firmly closed or not having anything there when the door is finally opened? Many critics writing about horror have preferred the latter option; it is seen as more effective because it allows the imagination of the spectator to go to work, to dream up monsters of his or her own that, because they are not bounded by the limitations of film budgets and special-effects technology, will always be more effective than those horrific entities conjured up by the film-makers. Any horror fan can in this respect readily provide a list of movie monsters that have not made the grade, either because of an inadequate visual realisation (the man in a leotard and papier-mâché mask pretending to be a giant moth in *The Blood Beast Terror* (1967) springs to mind here) or because of problems with the conceptualisation of the monster itself (for example, it is hard to believe that the marauding giant rabbits who feature in *Night of the Lepus* (1972) were ever going to frighten anyone, regardless of how well they were presented to us by the film-makers; rabbits are just not that frightening). However, it is equally true that certain monsters – ranging from Boris Karloff's Frankenstein-monster to Christopher Lee's Dracula and Anthony Hopkins' Hannibal Lecter – have successfully provoked responses of fear and of fascination that are all the more powerful for these creatures being shown to us in unsparing confrontational detail. Ultimately, perhaps, the question of whether explicit horror is more effective than implicit horror depends both on the skills of the film-makers in conveying that which is monstrous and on the imaginative abilities of whoever is watching the film.

But Rockett's little story raises another issue about horror, one that connects with the question of how the monster should – or should not – be shown but which, strangely, Rockett himself does not consider in his article. That issue is the importance of sound to horror. For all its antecedents in silent cinema, horror is primarily a sound-based medium. It first emerged as a significant commercial generic category in the early 1930s, only a few years after the widespread introduction of sound into cinema, and from its beginnings it offered film-makers opportunities to explore some of the possibilities of new sound technologies. This often involved the use of sound to create a particular mood or atmosphere, with the distant howling of wolves, the sinister creaking of doors, and the eerie wind passing through some desolate landscape, all helping to signify a mysterious world existing apart from everyday reality. Sound has also been used by horror film-makers to underline or augment moments of shock and violence – for example, the scene in *The Texas Chainsaw Massacre* (1974) in which Leatherface strikes an unfortunate victim on the head with a sledge hammer is all the more effectively horrible because of the awful squelching noise that has been added to the soundtrack – and sometimes, primarily for reasons of censorship, sound can also stand in for an act of violence that is not represented visually. A good example of this can be found in the Val Lewton production *The Leopard Man* (1943) where the murder of a young woman, apparently by a leopard, takes place unseen on the other side of a door. We hear the scream and what sounds like an animal snarling but all we see is blood seeping under the door.

But Rockett's story about the knocking on the library door suggests another use of sound (albeit one that does relate to our *Leopard Man* example). Our hero (or potential victim) does not realise that something is wrong until he hears an unexpected sound, a sound that denotes the unseen presence of something that should not be there. Seen (and heard) from this perspective, the tension in the scene is dependent on anticipation – by the person in the library, by the film's audience – of the moment where the sound made by this thing and the thing itself will be put together in our field of vision. It is worth thinking a bit more about this sound because, if this were a scene in a movie, the quality of the sound too would be highly significant. Is it a violent, powerful knocking, in which case the tension is racked up? Or is it a comic rat-a-tat, in which case the tension probably dissipates? Or is it a polite unobtrusive knock, with the disparity apparent here between a mundane sound and the impossibility of its source perhaps making this the creepiest rendition of all? In each case, the sound is disconnected from the object that is making the sound. We hear the sound, we do not – initially at least – see the thing that is knocking on the door. Some film historians have used the term 'off-screen sound' to describe such moments, although, as Christian Metz has pointed out, 'we tend to forget that a sound in itself is never "off": either it is audible or it doesn't exist' (Metz, 1985, p.157).

The idea of sound as a kind of presence – within the film, within the cinema auditorium – which can draw an audience's attention to that which is not visible within the frame, that can in other words make that audience acutely aware of the space which exists beyond the edges of the cinema screen, is a vital element in the creation of cinematic suspense. As John Belton has noted of such sound effects, 'their separation from their source can produce suspense that ranges from the familiar off-screen footsteps that stalk central characters, such as the helpless L.B. Jeffries trapped in his darkened apartment at the end of *Rear Window* (1954), to the mysterious noises and screeches throughout *The Haunting* (1963)' (Belton, 1985, p.65). As Belton also points out, it is standard practice in mainstream cinema, as part of a more general self-effacement so far as the techniques of film-making are concerned, for sounds initially separated from their source to be reunited with that source at some point (with *The Haunting*, which never shows us what is making all those eerie noises in Hill House, untypical in this respect). The more radical separation of sound from image that one finds in some avant-garde film-making, and which invites an audience to think about the materials out of which films are fashioned, is alien to a commercial mainstream use of sound which, while not necessarily realistic in itself, is committed to sound's seamless integration into our experience of particular narratives.

While there are numerous examples of mainstream cinema transgressing its own standard practices, these tend to be licensed transgressions, bendings of the rules that are motivated more often than not by particular generic requirements. For example, the musical permits a blurring of the distinction between diegetic sound (the sound produced within the world conjured up by the film, i.e. the sounds that can be heard by the characters within the film) and non-diegetic sound (sound external to the film-world, for example the incidental music that characters in the film cannot hear) that would be unacceptable in other film genres. Similarly, it can be argued that part of the horror film's distinctiveness lies in the way that its use of sound deviates in certain respects from more standardised uses of sound in mainstream cinema. In particular, horror film-makers will often set up disparities between sound and image, with the sounds in question not always matched exactly to their apparent sources. The best way of grasping how this works, and what its function is within horror, is to consider specific instances where the sounds of horror take on a peculiar character of their own.

It is worth returning here to that knock on the library door. As already noted, one option available to film-makers in such a situation involves not opening the door at all. Perhaps the best-known example of such an approach is *The Haunting*, and particularly a scene in the film in which Eleanor and Theodora are terrorised by the sound of something knocking on the wall and door of their room. We are never shown, either in the scene or anywhere else in the film, the object that makes that noise. One might deduce from this that *The Haunting* is one of those critically acclaimed horror films that leave things to the viewer's imagination rather than confronting him or her with an all-too-visible monster (in comparison, say, with the poorly-received, special-effects laden 1999 remake of *The Haunting*). However, while the 1963 version of *The Haunting* is undoubtedly a distinguished piece of film-making, this way of thinking about it arguably misses the point, for the film is very insistently directing its audiences to think about the supernatural events in a certain way. Consider the quality of the sound itself, for instance. Eleanor describes it as the sound of someone knocking on the door with a cannon ball, but in fact it is not the sound of knocking at all. Instead it is a booming noise which has very obviously been distorted electronically and which does not match the acoustics of the corridor from which the noise appears to be coming. In addition to this, the characters themselves observe that the room door itself is conspicuously unmarked by the apparent assault that has taken place on it. From this perspective, the knocking noise is an impossible noise, a noise that not only has no obvious source within the world of the film but which also itself as a sound does not seem to exist in the same space as the film's characters.

The impossibility of the sound becomes part of a broader ambiguity within *The Haunting* to do with whether such spectral manifestations are meant to be seen as external to the characters in Hill House or as an expression of those characters' inner psychological turmoil. Certainly the film entertains the possibility that Eleanor, one of the characters trapped in the room, is in some way (and the film does briefly raise the prospect of Eleanor being telekinetic) causing the knocking sound, a sound which recreates in a monstrously distorted fashion the sound made by Eleanor's now dead mother as she banged on her bedroom wall to summon her daughter. It is significant in this respect that the scene opens with Eleanor, who is guilt-ridden over her mother's death, mistaking the apparently supernatural noise for her mother's summons. (See Chapter 3 for a fuller discussion of the film in these terms.) It seems then that *The Haunting* uses a particular type of sound to signify the presence of a dimension that reaches into the space through which the characters move but which at the same time is not wholly reducible to or defined by that space. Whether this dimension is of a supernatural or psychological nature (or a combination thereof) is provocatively left open for the viewer's consideration.

While *The Haunting* chooses not to present us with any monsters (other than, perhaps, the house itself), most horror films do open the library door, so to speak, and show us what has been knocking on it. However, they often do not do this until near the end of the narrative. A recurrent narrative structure in the horror genre involves keeping the monster hidden away either in shadows or in off-screen space, glimpsed briefly if at all, until such time as the final confrontation with it is to take place, at which point the monster is finally revealed in all its ugly glory. In effect, there is a dynamic at work here organised around notions of power and subjection, with the monster much more powerful (and its victims weaker) so long as it lurks in off-screen space or, to use Pascal Bonitzer's evocative phrase, 'blind space' (Bonitzer, 1981, p.58). With visibility, of course, comes the possibility that the monster will not be as impressively frightening as the film-makers hoped. But in addition to this, visibility imposes limits upon the monster that render it vulnerable. So long as you are unable to see the shark in *Jaws* (1975), the creature in *The Relic* (1997) or the giant insects in *Mimic* (1997), they can be everywhere and anywhere and consequently you are constantly vulnerable to attack; once they are in full sight, you can protect yourself more effectively and get on with the task of killing them.

What sound can do here is signal the presence of a monster that is absent from a film's visuals within a narrative trajectory that will, in what is a fairly conventional way for mainstream cinema, eventually reunite the sound with the object that produced it. One thinks here, to give just a few examples, of the whistling noises that signal the presence of the giant ants in the classic SF/horror *Them!* (1954), the eerie whispers and sighs surrounding the witch in *Suspiria* (1977), and the metallic sounds associated with the ghostly Sadako in *Ring* (1998). (Clearly music too has a part to play here, one which will be discussed at the end of this chapter.) However, while the sounds of monsters and the monsters themselves might ultimately be joined together in a conventional manner, there is often something rather odd about the relation of sound to image when this does occur.

Generally this is manifested in what might be termed a ventriloquistic manner, where the sound or voice of the monster seems mismatched either with the monster's physique – i.e. the voice is too loud, the wrong pitch, too masculine/feminine, etc. – or with the acoustics of the monster's environment. For instance, the voices of the entombed monster in *The Keep* (1983) and of Candyman/Robitaille in *Candyman* (1992) are characterised by deep and echoing reverberations (especially when one sees these films in cinemas with good sound systems; the effect is lost or weakened on television) which, much like the sound of knocking in *The Haunting*, have no basis in any conventional sense of verisimilitude. Similarly, the voice of the possessed child in *The Exorcist* (1973) is not her voice; it is another voice, bass and guttural, which the child herself should not be able to produce. This type of monstrous ventriloquism, which can involve both elaborate special effects technology and extravagant voice performances (notably Mercedes McCambridge's performance of the demon's voice in *The Exorcist*), applies as much to non-verbal monstrous noises. Most notable here is Hitchcock's *The Birds* (1963) which contains virtually no natural bird sounds and instead uses, to considerable eerie effect, electronic re-workings of bird sound, but one can also point to any number of horror films that use distorted animal noise to construct the sounds made by their monsters.

The established conventions of sound in mainstream cinema dictate that sounds be appropriate to their source. Horror's departure from this in certain circumstances – and the more realistic the presentation of the monster, the less likely the deviation from standard practice – enables films to signify the monster as an entity not fully bound by the 'natural' order. In other words, the dimension of sound can be inflected by horror film-makers in ways that bestow a supernatural quality upon particular images of monstrosity and deviance.

There is one other important example of a ventriloquistic device that recurs in horror. It relates not to the monster but rather to the monster's victim, and in certain respects it is the defining sound of horror. It is, of course, the scream. The next chapter in this book will explore some of the ways in which fear can be performed by actors, and clearly screaming is one of these, but it also needs to be noted that screaming is often a sound effect as well. It has not been uncommon in the history of horror for screams to be dubbed in after the film has been shot, and not always by the actor who delivered the scream in the film. (For a typically sour and mordant take on this practice, see Brian De

Palma's 1981 thriller *Blow Out*, in which a sound recordist dubs the dying scream of the woman he loves into the horror film on which he is working.) This is very apparent if one compares a scene of Barbara Shelley screaming in Hammer's *Dracula – Prince of Darkness* (1965) as it appears in the trailer for that film (available on the 1995 Lumiere video release of the film) with the scene in the film itself. In the trailer version, it seems to be Shelley herself delivering the scream; the sound of the scream as it develops matches Shelley's changing expression and its pitch matches Shelley's low-pitched voice. When we get to the film version, however, this scream has been dubbed over with another scream, one that is higher-pitched and more piercing and which does not even remotely match the expression on the actor's face.

One could argue here with some justice that this change entails the imposition of a more conventionally 'feminine' expression of fear upon Shelley's altogether huskier performance of the scream. (One could probably go further and relate this to the more general ways in which the film seeks to contain a sense of Shelley's imposing physical presence, most notably in the controversial scene where a group of monks hold her character down while another monk drives a stake through her.) But at the same time, the disconnection between the performance of the sound and the sound itself also gives a sense of how difficult it can be to represent abject terror in a way that links the sound of fear and the visualisation of fear. As will be shown in the next chapter, putting the body in a position where it can deliver the sort of scream that might denote extreme fear is not always consistent with a visual performance of terror. One solution to this problem is to develop a performance style that can accommodate shifts back and forth between visual fear and aural fear; another is to produce the sound of fear separately and dub it into the film later on.

It is interesting to compare *Dracula – Prince of Darkness* with Roger Corman's Poe adaptation *Pit and the Pendulum* (1961) so far as the problem of the terrified scream is concerned. At one point in Corman's film, Elizabeth (played by horror icon Barbara Steele) is supposed to see some vaguely specified supernatural thing so horrible that it causes her to die of fright. However, we do not get to witness this event which takes place off-screen, we only hear a scream that is described by Nicholas, Elizabeth's husband (played by Vincent Price) as 'the most hideous, blood-chilling scream I have ever heard in my life'. Later in the film, we discover that Elizabeth is still alive and that her 'death' was part of a plan to drive her husband mad. In narrative terms, this explains why this death took place off-screen; it helped to disguise the fact that it was faked. But it also suggests that the most effective scream – so far as the conveying of fear is concerned – is the one that is disembodied, which does not have a visual source. *Pit and the Pendulum* concludes with Elizabeth trapped in an iron maiden device and, because she has been gagged, unable to stop those people unaware of her presence from sealing her in forever. Here we are given another image of terror but this time it is a silent one, a close-up of Barbara Steele's face trapped behind bars, her eyes widened, with the camera irising in on those eyes before the screen fades to black. There then follows a quote from Edgar Allan Poe: 'the agony of my soul found vent in one loud, long, and final scream of despair,' with these words clearly standing in for the scream that cannot actually be uttered by the unfortunate Elizabeth. Extreme terror can be represented by a sound or by a facial expression, *Pit and the Pendulum* suggests, but both cannot represent it at once.

It seems from this that sound in horror is far from being meekly subservient to the image. Particular sounds do not just underline or augment images but can also anticipate them and sometimes stand in for them altogether. Even when sounds are connected to their sources within horror films, there is still sometimes a sense that sound and image are operating in relation to different registers. The frequent mismatching of sound to image in horror clearly offers film-makers opportunities not only to denote the beyondness or otherness of its monsters but also to dramatise extreme emotional states – especially that of terror – in ways not bounded by the limitations of any particular performance. More generally, one might argue that just as literary horror fiction sometimes seems to be straining to capture something beyond words (with the tortured and tortuous prose of American horror writer H.P. Lovecraft a good example here), horror cinema too sometimes strains to give a sense of extreme or perhaps even sublime dimensions and states of being that are difficult to represent visually, and that one of the ways in which it projects a sense of the limitations of images is through its use of sound.

BOO!

There is another area in which horror's use of sound is important. Not to put too fine a point on it, sound can make you jump. Clearly the horror genre does not have a monopoly on what is sometimes called 'the startle effect'; examples of well-known 'startles' from non-horror films include Magwitch's sudden appearance in *Great Expectations* (1946) and Alan Arkin's climactic attack on a blind Audrey Hepburn in the thriller *Wait Until Dark* (1967). However, horror does deploy more 'startles' than any other film genre, and there are certain moments in horror history where the startle effect is very important indeed.

Robert Baird, one of the few writers to explore at any length the role of the startle effect within horror, defines the conditions necessary for a startle to occur: 'The core elements of a film startle effect are (1) a character presence, (2) an implied offscreen threat, and (3) a disturbing intrusion into the character's immediate space.' He goes on to note that 'most startle effects rely on a sound bump, a sudden burst of sound effects, dialogue and/or music' (Baird, 2000, pp.15, 24). In order to illustrate this, we can turn to what has often been seen by horror historians as the horror genre's first startle effect – the bus scene in *Cat People* (1942). In this night-time scene, a woman is being stalked by Irina, the 'cat person'. There is no dialogue or music, just the sound of echoing footsteps. At a certain point, this sound ceases, leading an audience to suspect that Irina has just transformed into a murderous panther. The other woman, and potential victim, becomes alarmed. Suddenly we hear what sounds like an animal's snarl. A fraction of a second later a bus pulls up in front of the woman, and the apparent animal sound becomes the sound made by the brakes of the bus. The woman gets onto the bus and the scene then cuts away to images of dead sheep presumably savaged by whatever Irina has become (in a film which is considerably less ambiguous over the question of whether Irina actually does turn into a big cat than some critics have made it out to be). Here, as it nearly always is with startle moments, sound is crucial, as much as if not more so than the image. It is the sound of the snarl (and it does sound like a snarl, not like a bus braking) that initiates the startle, with the sudden appearance of the bus possibly augmenting the startle but only for the fraction of a second it takes for an audience to realise that this object speeding into frame from off-screen space does not actually pose a threat to the woman.

As is apparent from this moment in *Cat People*, one of the functions of the startle effect in horror is to punctuate or conclude scenes of suspense. Film critics (although not necessarily audiences) have tended to favour suspense over shock effects, preferring the artfulness of a sustained suspense sequence to what is sometimes perceived as the mechanistic device of the shock. This is perhaps because suspense implies an intense involvement with the characters and their situation over a period of time whereas by contrast shocks in themselves seem to involve a primitive or child-like credulity on the part of audiences as the film-makers shout 'boo!' at them in order to elicit the desired response. It follows that the deployment of a shock moment as a flourish at the end of a suspense sequence – note not just *Cat People*'s bus sequence but also, for example, Ellen Burstyn's exploration of the attic in *The Exorcist* or Jane Asher's exploration of the castle dungeon in *The Masque of the Red Death* (1964), both of which are concluded by sudden, unexpected sounds and events – is more likely to be acceptable to critics than an apparently more artless and suspense-free invoking of the shock effect.

Horror from the late 1970s onwards has tended to use far more shock effects than before, especially in the slasher films and *Nightmare on Elm Street* films of the 1970s and 1980s and the slasher revival films of the 1990s, and it is fair to say that the more mechanistic quality of the shock – involving the film-makers saying 'boo' and the audience being startled to order – is far more apparent in these films than it is in earlier horrors. Take as an example a short scene from near the beginning of *Urban Legend* (1998). Two female college students are investigating what is reported to be a haunted building on campus. As they stand outside the building and hear some mysterious spooky sounds coming from within, there is a loud burst of music as someone – who turns out just to be a classmate – appears behind them, with this appearance making the women and (the film-makers hope) us jump as well. This is clearly not a suspense scene in the manner of *Cat People*. The scene is very short so there is no time for a build-up of suspense, and in any event we barely know the characters at this stage nor have any particular sense that there is much danger here. As if to confirm the mechanistic nature of this shock, less than a minute later one of these women walks into a college hall – again no sense of danger, no suspense – and suddenly we have yet another loud outburst of music as she unexpectedly comes face to face with the janitor.

One way of interpreting this rapid, helter-skelter movement from one shock effect to the next is to mourn the decline of horror since *Cat People* and its ilk, with their apparently more measured deployment of shocks in relation to suspense replaced in recent films by an altogether more artless and mechanical attitude to story telling, one that seems dependent on the gullibility of the teenagers who have formed an increasingly large part of the horror audience since the 1970s. This does not mean that films like *Urban Legend*, or any of the earlier slasher films (notably *Halloween* and *Friday the 13th*), do not feature suspense sequences – they all do – but that in general terms they are overly reliant on shocks that the films in question have not earned through inventive staging and use of sound. Instead you tend to have scenes where someone just wanders into a dark room and – suddenly, unexpectedly – something jumps out at them. Loud crash of music. Boo!

There are a number of questions raised by thinking about horror in these terms. For one thing, and regardless of how one values it, the startle effect clearly has a part to play in horror history, especially in relation to the growing importance within that history of off-screen space. There are moments of suspense in 1930s US horror and also moments that, for audiences of the time, might have been shocking – for example, the first appearance of Frankenstein's monster in *Frankenstein* (1931) or the scene in *Mystery of the Wax Museum* (1933) in which Fay Wray smashes Lionel Atwill's mask and we see the monstrous face beneath (or, if one wants to go back into horror's prehistory, the unmasking of Lon Chaney's Phantom in the 1925 production of *The Phantom of the Opera*). However, there is little or nothing in the way of objects launching an assault, or potential assault, upon characters from the realm of off-screen space in a manner designed to startle an audience. In fact,

THE SOUNDS OF HORROR

there is very little dramatic sense of off-screen space at all in 1930s US horror other than that apparent in the conjuring up via 'off-screen sound' of a certain brooding atmosphere (for example, the sounds of wolves howling in the Lugosi *Dracula* or the sounds that are heard emanating from the House of Pain in *Island of Lost Souls* long before we get to see what is actually contained in the House). This is quite surprising given that, as Robert Baird notes, the theatrical sources for a number of 1930s films made extensive use of off-stage sound to startle their audience, and it suggests that these films' interests were elsewhere, in constructing dramas of pathos and subjection rather than in fashioning moments designed to make us jump (Baird, 2000, p.14).

Cat People's deployment of off-screen space as a potential source of danger, a quality also apparent in other films by producer Val Lewton during the 1940s (including *I Walked with a Zombie, The Leopard Man, The Seventh Victim* and several others, all of which contained notable sound effects in this respect), therefore represented a significant innovation in the history of horror cinema, albeit an innovation that was not immediately taken up. Unlike the horror film-makers of the 1930s, the makers of many of the American SF/horror hybrids from the 1950s, including *The Thing from Another World* (1951) and *It! The Terror from Beyond Space* (1958), often kept their monsters mainly in off-screen space, using sound to suggest their presence, until the end of the film when the monster would be revealed in all its shocking and ugly glory, but they tended not to feature startle effects. Similarly, Hammer horror films of the 1950s and 1960s, the Poe adaptations directed by American film-maker Roger Corman in the early 1960s, and the Italian gothic horrors from the same period (including films directed by Mario Bava and Riccardo Freda) used off-screen space primarily for atmospheric reasons – with weird sounds emanating from either outside or deep within the castles within which these films were usually located – with startle moments featuring only occasionally.

It seems from this that it was not until the late 1970s, and the advent of the American slasher film, that shock became a central part of horror's operations rather than just a marginal technique. The phrase 'a machine for saying boo', reportedly coined to describe *Halloween* (1978), one of the first slashers, describes in this respect both a narrative structure in which a series of teenage victims are dispatched by the killer in an impersonally efficient manner and an audience experience consisting of repeated shocks and startles, virtually all of which involve sound in some way. Within a context where the vast majority of characters are expendable victims, and where the narratives themselves are structured around a succession of death scenes, suspense, while not absent, becomes attenuated.

To a certain extent, the concluding sequence of Brian De Palma's *Carrie* (1976) (already discussed in Chapter 4) anticipates the shift in the horror genre that occurs in the late 1970s. For much of its running length, *Carrie* exhibits many of the thematic features that characterise other 1970s US horror films, notably an exploration of repressive social norms coupled with a sympathetic portrayal of 'deviant' characters. It is qualities such as these, which lend themselves to being seen in terms of oppositional social critique, that have often led to this type of horror being valued positively by critics. However, for its conclusion, *Carrie* abandons this social consciousness and sets out to startle us, doing this in a decidedly unconventional manner. Robert Baird, in his article on the startle effect, indicates that there has to be an element of implied off-screen threat for a startle effect to work, otherwise we could all end up being startled by, for example, sudden entrances in comedies. But in the concluding scene of *Carrie* there is no sense of threat at all, not for the woman who approaches the scene of Carrie's death and not for the audience either (and it is worth remembering that *Carrie* precedes the now standard convention – popularised by *Halloween* – whereby the killer-monster inevitably returns just when you think it has been killed). The scene, cunningly designed to resemble a rather sentimental coda with its soft-focus photography and lush romantic score, lulls us into a false sense of security, and then, with a crash of loud music, Carrie's bloody hand reaches out from the grave. It's a quality 'boo' – certainly the most effective I have ever experienced – but it can also be seen as an irresponsible 'boo', a jettisoning of all that prior social criticism in favour of a base and primitive effect. Similarly, the slasher format itself has been interpreted negatively, not only for its apparent misogyny but also for its apparent betrayal of all the good works done in horror throughout the 1970s in its replacing complex social understanding with simple reactive shock effects.

This view of 1970s horror, which – to put it mildly – is a questionable one, will be discussed in more detail in Chapters 8 and 9 of this book. What is useful here is to think about the startle effect itself as a particular conjoining of sound and image and consider the extent to which it might have changed its meaning, if at all, from its introduction in *Cat People* to its popularisation in the slasher format. Both Robert Baird and film theorist Noel Carroll have made the case for the startle effect consisting of an instinctive physiological response to particular stimuli, especially loud noises. If we hear a loud noise, our response is to jump, and this is so regardless of whether we are in the street or sitting in a cinema. The response is immediate and involuntary; we do not have time to think about it, to assess whether the noise – or whatever else has startled us – actually poses a threat, we just jump and then, once the startle has dissipated, work out what it was that made us jump. As Baird puts it, 'It seems an obstinate and defensive rationalism that would deny our experience of film space and film objects any of the phenomenological depth we bring to reality' (Baird, 2000, p.18; see also Carroll, 1996, p.50). From this perspective, any difference between the bus startle in *Cat People* and various startle moments in, say, *Halloween* or *Friday the 13th* (1980) has to do with the quality of the execution of the startle – some startles might work better than others because of the skill with which they are staged – rather than with any change in the nature of the startle effect itself. A good 1940s startle will make you jump in the same way as a good 1980s startle, and both will make you jump in the same way as a good real-life startle outside the cinema.

Before completely abandoning the startle effect to the world of the reflex action, we should consider the phenomenon of the startle that does not work, or rather does not work for everyone. An example from my own viewing experience is the moment at the conclusion of the thriller *Fatal Attraction* (1987) where the Glenn Close character, who has apparently been drowned by Michael Douglas, suddenly and noisily springs up from the bath tub and recommences her attack. It is a *Carrie*-like moment in that, if the scene works as it was apparently intended, neither the Michael Douglas character nor the audience sense any threat and are beginning to relax as the movie comes to its end. Thus the shock comes completely out of the blue. Judging by the response of the people with whom I saw the movie, the shock worked for them. However, it did not work for me, primarily, I think, because I saw the shock coming. I was confidently expecting the Glenn Close character to return; I had noticed that the scene had become too protracted and too quiet (to accentuate the noise of Close's return when it came). This suggests to me that I, along with others in the audience who perhaps sat quietly while around them were screams and gasps, were familiar with the by then well-established conventions of the slasher film, and especially the one that dictated that the monster needed to be 'killed' several times before the film was over (and even then it might not finally be killed off). By contrast, I can only presume that those for whom the shock worked were not horror fans and were therefore unprepared for this importation of a horror-based technique into the thriller genre.

Of course, one could argue that simply being able to neutralise the startle effect through prior knowledge of some of the techniques associated with it does not change the essential nature of the startle itself. To give a comparison, a loud noise is much less likely to startle you if you are witnessing whatever it is that is causing the noise; but the person standing with his back to the source of the noise is still likely to jump. However, there is a paradox here. The film genre most dependent on the startle effect during the 1980s is horror, and yet the people in the audience most likely to be familiar with the conventions of the startle, and consequently least likely to be affected by it, are the horror fans. In fact, the knowledge acquired through the cumulative viewing of horror films, and especially the slasher variant, encourages the horror audi- ence to be constantly aware of off-screen space as a potential source of threat.

The slasher emerges from this, so far as its reliance on the startle is concerned at least (and, as we will see in a later chapter, there is more to the slasher than this), as a kind of game being played between film-makers and genre-conscious audiences. (For a discussion of this, see Dika, 1990.) In going to a slasher film, we are not only expecting to be startled but expecting to be startled in particular ways (as the *Scream* films, with their exhaustive setting out of those slasher conventions which are presumably already familiar to their audience, demonstrate). We know that off-screen space is dangerous and that if a character moves towards that space – and it is usually a sound that lures them there – we should tense ourselves in order to resist an anticipated startle. And, of course, the film-makers know that we know this, and they will do whatever they can to get past our defences, either using areas of off-screen space that we might not have thought of as dangerous (above and below the frame, for example, rather than at the sides) or through increasing the volume of sound associated with the startle (a startle experience on video with the sound turned down is usually no startle at all). And when the startle works in this context, then the audience's physiological response to the startle yields pleasure that is potentially twofold: on a general level, as Robert Baird suggests, it can 'prove to us, in the very maw of virtual death, how very much alive we are'; but on a more genre-specific level it can involve an appreciation of a film-making skill that, even with our prior knowledge of its aims, has managed to confound us (Baird, 2000, p.22).

This is probably the case for all horror startles. As I indicated in a previous chapter, I recall that my immediate response to the conclusion of *Carrie* was a mixture of exhilaration at having 'survived' the experience and of admiration of the film's ability to do what it had just done to me. But it seems to me that this twofold response is much more central to those types of horror film that rely on the startle as a key device than it is for those moments of startle elsewhere in horror, especially in pre-1970s horror, which because they were genuinely unexpected and, in the case of *Cat People*, unprecedented, were more likely to be overwhelming events functioning in the manner of 'real-life' startles. It follows that the movement from *Cat People* to the slasher film is not necessarily, as some accounts would have it, a movement away from skilful and suspenseful film-making to an impoverished and mechanical delivery of shocks to an undiscerning audience. Rather it entails a transition from one model of the audience, the audience that allows itself to be drawn into a particular drama, to another model of an altogether more suspicious and canny audience, an audience that spends most of its time trying to second guess whatever the film-makers are attempting to do to it. One should not use this distinction to argue against the idea that our response to films has a physiological dimension. Clearly they do, and it is certainly the case that this aspect of audience behaviour has been sadly neglected in the study of cinema.

However, this type of physiological response never exists in isolation and, as I hope I have shown for the startle effect, is likely to mean something quite different for different audiences at different moments in the history of the horror genre.

HORROR'S MUSIC

This chapter has already touched upon some of the roles played by music in horror cinema. But it is worth exploring in more detail the question of whether there is something special and distinctive about horror music, something that makes it stand apart from other film music either in the inherent quality of the music itself or in the uses to which it is put by horror film-makers. In her book on film music, Claudia Gorbman identifies what she sees as the key functions of film music in mainstream cinema. These include the signifying of moods and emotions, the establishing of settings and characters, and the interpreting of narrative events. Music can also 'via repetition and variation of musical material and instrumentation' aid in 'the construction of formal and narrative unity' (Gorbman, 1987, p.73). Clearly all these standard uses of music apply as much to horror as they do to any other mainstream film genre. Alongside these, however, one can find other musical functions that are arguably more specific to horror (although not necessarily unique to the genre), including the use of music to signal the off-screen presence of the monster (in the opening sequence of Hammer's 1958 version of *Dracula*, for example, where the three-note main theme, which is structured around the word 'Drac-u-la' itself, stands in for the unseen vampire) and to underline, and sometimes to produce, a startle effect. The extent and significance of these and other genre-specific musical cues and devices are perhaps best illustrated through an overview of the historical development of horror film music.

The musical accompaniment for what we think of now as the early horror films (although they were often not thought of as that at the time of their initial release) was limited in scope. The 1931 *Dracula*, for example, simply used an excerpt from Tchaikovsky's *Swan Lake* over its opening credits and also included excerpts from the work of Schubert and Wagner as diegetic source music during its concert hall scene. The doomed romanticism of Tchaikovsky's work clearly appealed to horror film-makers for *Swan Lake* showed up yet again as accompaniment to *The Mummy* (1932) and the gothic thriller *Secret of the Blue Room* (1933). However, as the genre developed in the 1930s, music became an ever more important feature, with an increasing number of scores penned especially for films. In particular, Max Steiner's music for *King Kong* (1933, not widely thought of as a horror film when first released but since claimed for the genre by numerous horror historians) and Franz Waxman's music for *Bride of Frankenstein* (1935) stand as important milestones in the development of the dramatic film score. Both scores made extensive use of leitmotifs, themes associated with specific characters that via their repetition throughout the narratives helped to bring some formal cohesion to the films. The music also emphasised or underlined particular dramatic moments, with Steiner's score matched at certain points with Kong's movements and with the bridal march penned by Waxman for the female monster's entrance functioning as a quirky commentary – perfectly in line with the film's tongue-in-cheek tone – on the forthcoming 'marriage' between Frankenstein's two monsters.

For all the undoubted quality of Steiner's and Waxman's work on *King Kong* and *Bride of Frankenstein* (and both composers would go on to become major contributors to Hollywood film music), it has to be said that there is little about the music itself, or its use within the films, which separates it out from film music elsewhere in Hollywood. As if to underline this, elements from both scores would be re-used repeatedly during the 1930s as music for a range of non-horror projects. The idea that music for horror films tended to be fairly conventional arguably holds true throughout the 1930s and 1940s. While one can quite easily find quality music in these decades – some of Roy Webb's work for horror producer Val Lewton springs to mind – and moments of genuine innovation – for example, the use of spirituals in *White Zombie* (1932) and *I Walked with a Zombie* (1943) – there is nothing here that sub-stantially challenges the general conventions of film music, nothing that could not easily be recycled as music for films in other genres.

Things change during the 1950s, however. This does not mean that horror film music in that decade and afterwards suddenly separated itself out com-pletely from all other types of film music. It does mean that in various ways horror music from the 1950s onwards acquired some distinctive qualities that in certain circumstances, and to a greater or lesser degree, set it apart from the more mainstream uses of film music. That this shift in the identity of horror music occurs at a time when the traditional Hollywood studio system was starting to fragment, and when horror production itself was becoming more internationalised, is probably no coincidence for this was a period which saw a reworking of many of the aesthetic practices associated with the horror genre.

One thing that quickly becomes apparent from a survey of post-1950 horror music is that it is extremely varied, and that it is hard to capture this variety in any conventional chronological survey. Therefore I have instead identified a number of categories which, I hope, will enable a sense to be given both of the different ways in which innovative musical work took place within the genre and of the range of that work.

Electronic music

Electronic music produced by unconventional instruments like the theremin and the novachord quickly became part of many scores for 1950s SF/horror monster movies. While it was not restricted to the genre – Miklos Rozsa, for one, used the theremin very effectively to suggest mental imbalance both in Hitchcock's psychological thriller *Spellbound* (1945) and Billy Wilder's harrowing tale of alcoholism *The Lost Weekend* (1945) – odd, eerie music of this kind seemed most suited to illustrating the presence of aliens, most notably in Jack Arnold's *It Came from Outer Space* (1953), or futuristic worlds. This particular use of electronic music, much like the SF/horror monster movies themselves, did not carry over into the 1960s, but its blurring of the distinction between music and sound effects was later developed in an interesting direction in composer Bernard Herrmann's collaboration with Remi Gassman and Oscar Sala on the electronically-generated bird sounds, produced on an instrument called the Studio Trautonium, for Hitchcock's *The Birds* in 1963.

Horror's next significant engagement with electronic music occurred in the 1970s. Bernard Herrmann incorporated synthesizer music into his score for Brian De Palma's *Sisters* (1973) in a manner reminiscent of the use of the theremin in *Spellbound*, that is to say as a way of denoting extreme mental instability. By contrast, *The Texas Chainsaw Massacre* took everyday sounds and, in the style of musique concrete, distorted them electronically to produce discordant noises that, as had been the case with some 1950s electronic music, hovered disconcertingly between music and sound effect. (Apparently one of the sounds for *The Texas Chainsaw Massacre* was produced by the director striking a pitchfork and then running it along the edge of a table.)

By the end of the 1970s, synthesizer-based scores were becoming a much more noticeable feature of film music, and especially horror film music. One thinks here especially of Delia Derbyshire's and Brian Hodgson's atonal music for *The Legend of Hell House* (1973) and John Carpenter's more melodic scores for *Halloween* in 1978 and *The Fog* in 1980. But this occurred in a broader musical context in which electronic music, which for so long had been an *outré* and decidedly avant-garde enterprise, was starting to become an acceptable part of the popular musical scene. The success during the 1970s of bands such as Kraftwerk and Tangerine Dream (who would go on to write the score for Michael Mann's horror film *The Keep*) and musicians such as Bryan Eno had helped to promote, and to a certain extent 'normalise', electronically produced music, with this having implications for the use of such music in horror films. In particular, the association of electronic sound with images of Otherness and insanity made by horror films from the 1940s through to the early 1970s became much less noticeable from the late 1970s onwards.

Instead electronic music started to operate in a more straightforward way as an extension of or replacement for orchestral musical sources. As the electronic-music technology itself became much better known, its role as a significant producer of oddity and weirdness came to an end.

Voices

Up until the 1950s the only film genre that had made much of the human voice as a source of music was, unsurprisingly, the musical. During the 1950s, films from a range of genres acquired theme songs (Frankie Laine's rendition of the theme for *High Noon* (1952) is probably the best known of these) and yet vocals only made a limited inroad into incidental or non-diegetic film music, principally in blockbuster biblical dramas such as *Ben Hur* (1959) and *King of Kings* (1961) where massed choruses helped both to underline the films' epic qualities and to give a sense of heavenly realms existing above and beyond the world of the drama.

More daring and innovatory uses of the voice appeared during the 1960s and 1970s, with the horror film very much in the vanguard. The Italian influence was especially important in this respect. In the early 1960s Italian film composer Ennio Morricone had helped to establish the distinctiveness of the new spaghetti western through scores that made pioneering use of voices as, in effect, musical instruments. Later on the same composer would develop this approach further for the Italian horror film. For example, his score for Dario Argento's *giallo The Bird with the Crystal Plumage* (1970) featured both a lullaby-like theme tune firmly at odds with the film's violent subject matter and the sound of female sighs meant, presumably, to convey the terror of the killer's victims (and perhaps also the psychosis of the killer, who at the end of the film is revealed to be a woman). The Italian prog-rock group Goblin's work with Argento from the mid-1970s onwards would take this approach yet further; in particular, their groundbreaking score for *Suspiria* contained sighs, whispers and shrieks as well as occasional shouts of 'Witch!' In part this music was clearly meant to convey the presence of a monster, the witch Eleanor Markos, who for most of the film lurked unseen in off-screen space. But the music's extremity – its aggressive vocal and percussive elements, its reliance on highly repetitive phrases, and (especially if you were fortunate enough to see the film in a cinema with a good sound system) its extraordinary volume – also made it an indispensable part of *Suspiria*'s assaultive approach to its audience.

The association in the 1950s between choral music and biblical subject matter was given a new twist in the 1970s when the satanic thriller became an important part of horror production. Most notable here was Jerry Goldsmith's Oscar-winning score for *The Omen* (1976) which featured a chorus of male and female voices singing, in an appropriately portentous Gregorian-chant style, such Latin phrases as 'Ave versus cristus, Ave santani' (translated: Hail the Antichrist, Hail Satan). As with Goblin's score for *Suspiria*, the music here represented a villain who remained firmly off-screen, namely Satan himself. But it was also an important vehicle for the film's systematic counter-pointing of a contemporary world's rational scepticism with pre-modern beliefs in such things as heaven-sent visions and biblical prophecies. As an extension of this, a more lyrical use of the chorus – apparent in Goldsmith's score for the third Omen film *The Final Conflict* (1981), in which the Antichrist is finally defeated, as well as in the Ennio Morricone scores for the satanic thrillers *Holocaust 2000* (1977) and *Exorcist 2: The Heretic* (1977) – suggested, very much in the style of 1950s biblical epics, those heavenly realms which could not be represented directly but from which positive moral values emanated. Thus the choral music, both in its heavenly and its satanic variants, helped to give a sense of an ages-old conflict between good and evil that predated the drama of the films and which gave narrative events a portentous resonance they might otherwise have lacked. Interestingly, some more recent devil-related horror movies, including *End of Days* (1999) and *Bless the Child* (2000), have used *Omen*-style choruses in exactly the same way, suggesting that this particular type of horror scoring has now become something of a genre convention.

Undoubtedly some of the thrills provided by the *Omen* films and subsequent satanic thrillers lay in the dramatic disjunction between the films' modern settings and the apparently pre-modern music that would suddenly invade that modernity, with this usually prefacing a spectacular Satanic intervention into the narrative. This idea of music existing at odds with, or in counterpoint to, the drama has been taken up elsewhere in the horror genre, albeit in different ways. Morricone's lullaby theme for serial-killer film *The Bird with the Crystal Plumage* has already been mentioned in this respect, and to this can be added the lullaby (written by Polish composer Krzysztof Komeda and sung by Mia Farrow) that opens and concludes *Rosemary's Baby* (1968) and the jaunty whistling tune that opens *Horror Express* (1972). Innocuous and quite charming themes in themselves, they suddenly become a source of eeriness when placed in the context of a horror scenario. Similarly, the use of children's voices – conventionally associated with innocence – can become, via incongruous juxtapositions with horrifying screen events, decidedly unsettling. Examples here include the children's choruses that feature in Lalo Schifrin's score for *The Amityville Horror* (1979) and Jerry Goldsmith's score for *Poltergeist* (1982) as well as the children's song that cues the ultra-violent murders in Goblin's music for *Profondo Rosso* (1975). (Horror film-makers can also use innocuous pre-existing songs in this way. Note for example, the appearance of the Chordette's 1950s hit

'Mr Sandman' in *Halloween 2* or Type O Negative's splendidly gothic cover of the early 1970s hit 'Summer Breeze' featured in the opening sequence of *I Know What You Did Last Summer*.)

Using voices in incidental film music is still sufficiently unusual to be considered as a deviation from the norm. Of course, horror is not the only film genre to deploy vocals, but it can be seen as a centre for both innovation and significant work in this area. While some of the functions of this music are fairly conventional ones for which other forms of music will also serve – notably, having the music stand in for the unseen monster, using music as a counterpoint to the drama – the sound of the human voice can also be used in a manner that exceeds the particular dramatic demands of a narrative, conveying instead a sense of some unrepresentable realm or dimension that lies beyond the world conjured up by the narrative. If, as noted above, sound in horror cinema can express or compensate for an inadequacy apparent in a film's visuals, vocal music too, it seems, can serve a similar function.

Dissonance

A reliance on dissonance and atonality, on awkward and jarring musical sounds and combinations of notes, is perhaps the most characteristic and also the most straightforward aspect of horror film music from the 1950s onwards. From the weird electronic sounds found in 1950s SF/horror films, through Bernard Herrmann's Schoenberg-influenced music for Hitchcock's *Psycho* (1960) and Humphrey Searle's unnerving score for *The Haunting*, to any of the horror work of James Bernard (the main composer for Hammer horror), Ennio Morricone (to the titles listed above add John Carpenter's 1982 version of *The Thing*), Jerry Goldsmith (to the already mentioned *Omen* trilogy and *Poltergeist* add *Alien*) or Goblin (all their Argento scores), to name but a few of the significant horror composers, the music of horror is, to a greater or lesser extent, a discordant music. This is even the case with those few horror films that utilise pre-existing music, notably *The Exorcist* and *The Shining* (1980), both of which turn to the rather stern work of Polish composer Krzysztof Penderecki. And let us not forget the 'stingers' (short bursts of music designed to make us jump) that litter the films of John Carpenter and a whole range of slasher movies. If, as seems likely, horror's main preoccupation is to do with the limitations of normality, the type of music which perhaps best character- ises the genre (and it is worth remembering that much horror music is conventional and indistinguishable from other forms of film music) is that which in some way or other departs from the general norms of film music, which deviates from what would be appropriate elsewhere in cinema either because of the weirdness of the sounds or the incongruity of their use. Given that the atonal, the discordant and the dissonant tend to be linked with experimental music and have not featured much in any popular musical idiom, their presence within horror entails a flaunting of musical oddness that both correlates to and augments a sense of normality itself being brought into question. That this process has involved a vulgar commercial form such as horror co-opting musical techniques more associated with the avant-garde is just one of the many paradoxes of the genre.

Most film theory and film criticism has concerned itself with images rather than with sound. When it has been discussed at all, sound has tended to be subsumed into the visual rather than considered as a significant element in its own right. This has been especially damaging to an understanding of how horror films operate, for, as this chapter has demonstrated, sound and music in horror can in some circumstances change very fundamentally the way in which an audience interprets what it is seeing. If we go back to the little scene in the library with which this chapter began, it should be clear how much this scene, if in a horror film, would be dependent on sound for its effectiveness, in the creation of an ominous atmosphere, in the construction of off-screen space both for the purpose of suspense and (if it is that type of horror film) for the projection of a sense of dimensions lurking beyond the real, and in helping to produce the monstrous itself.

Another use of sound available to horror film-makers might also be deployed in the scene – namely quietness or even total silence. In horror's world of sounds dissociated from their sources, of startling bangs and bumps, of dissonant and atonal music, sometimes the most unnerving sound is no sound at all, because if it is quiet, it usually means that something unpleasant – and noisy – is about to happen. Consider, for example, the bus scene from *Cat People*: quiet echoing footsteps, no music at all, and suddenly the loud snarl/hiss of a bus. It is perhaps the most obvious sign of sound's importance to horror that its mere absence can provoke anxiety. Think then, when you open that library door, that it is not just what you see (or don't see) that might unnerve you, it is what you hear (or don't hear) as well.

CHAPTER SEVEN

Performing horror

She's no Jamie Lee Curtis

(Urban Legends: Final Cut, 2000)

THE SCENE

The monster advances upon the terrified woman. She backs away screaming. It's an archetypal horror scene, one that has provoked all manner of negative criticism, especially from those who view horror as a genre dependent on the terrorising of women. Some of the issues arising from this way of thinking about horror have already been discussed in this book and they will also feature later on. Here, however, we engage with the 'monster versus victim' scenario in a different way, in terms of how the actors involved play the scene and how their performances affect our response to the drama. It could reasonably be argued that a good deal of the acting found in horror is like acting elsewhere in mainstream cinema. It might be worse, it might be better, but fundamentally it involves the same sort of dramatic techniques and practices. But is it possible to identify specific types of performance that, if not unique to the horror genre, are located there more than they are anywhere else?

We begin with the victim.

BEING SCARED

Horror films abound with images of terrified people. People cowering, trembling, screaming as they confront whatever monstrous entity the film-makers have unleashed upon them. Given that many of these terrified people are women (and that the majority of movie monsters who are terrorising them are male), this would seem to lend some support to those criticisms of horror that view it as an irredeemably misogynist area of culture. However, whether audiences – and especially male audiences – experience an essentially sadistic or misogynist pleasure from seeing female victims suffer on screen is far from clear. Critics writing about the slasher film in particular have made a great deal of what they see as the masochistic nature of the horror experience and the way in which this can in certain circumstances involve forms of cross-gender identification.

A related way of thinking about horror's terrified characters is to see the signs of fear they exhibit as cueing in our own responses as spectators to whatever is going on in the film in question. As Noel Carroll, who is concerned in his book *The Philosophy of Horror* to establish the nature of an audience's cognitive response to horror, puts it, 'the emotional reactions of characters, then, provide a set of instructions or, rather, examples about the way in which the audience is to respond to the monsters in the fiction – that is, about the way we are meant to react to its monstrous properties' (Carroll, 1990, p.17). From a different, more psychoanalytically inclined perspective, Linda Williams notes that a distinguishing feature of what she terms 'body genres' (i.e. horror, melodrama, porn) is 'the perception that the body of the spectator is caught up in an almost involuntary mimicry of the emotion or sensation of the body on screen, along with the fact that the body displayed is female' (Williams, 1995, p.143). Both critics here stress the physiological component of an audience's fearful response to horror fictions but are also, in their own distinct ways, interested in the complexities of this response and how it is not just defined through an automatic physical mimicry of the behaviour of frightened characters on screen.

One question that arises from this involves how we as an audience recognise that a character is frightened. Presumably we all have a sense, no matter how subjective, of what the emotion of fear is, and will no doubt have experienced that emotion at some point or other in our lives; less of us, perhaps, will have experienced extreme fear or terror but even here we can probably imagine what that sensation might entail. But how do you know fear when you see it, either in real life or, more particularly, on the cinema screen? What are the visible signs of fear? Noel Carroll lists some of the sensations which he associates with the fearful responses conjured up by horror cinema for both characters within films and the audiences for those films, namely 'muscular contractions, tension, cringing, shrinking, shudder-ing, recoiling, tingling, frozenness, momentary arrests, chilling (hence "spine-chilling") paralysis, trembling, nausea, a reflex of apprehension or physically heightened alertness (a danger response), perhaps involuntary screaming, and so on' (Carroll, 1990, p.24). Carol Clover, in her study of the slasher film, also lists what she sees as some of the signs of abject terror, 'crying, cowering, screaming, fainting, trembling, begging for mercy' (Clover, 1992, p.51).

But it is not clear how precisely these qualities or feelings can be translated into something that is visibly fearful on the screen. One can easily think of situations where, for example, trembling or screaming might not be expressions of fear at all but instead responses to other stimuli. People tremble when they are cold, they (or at least some of them) scream when in the presence of the latest pop idol. Of course, one might argue that it is the context within which particular types of behaviour occur which determines how an audience interprets that behaviour: if a character in a film who is standing in a dark haunted house on a warm night starts to tremble, it is probably a sign that she or he is frightened. However, it is still the case that even though the portrayal of terror is central to horror's identity, the critical language used to describe this portrayal is often very vague. Where are the terms that could enable us to make qualitative distinctions between different expressions of fear and terror in the horror genre? It is all very well to say that a character is trembling and is therefore frightened, but how is that character trembling and what does this convey about the nature or intensity of the emotion being conveyed? Is it simply a question of a big tremble equalling lots of fear and a little tremble signalling only apprehension, or are there subtleties present that need to be teased out?

What would be useful here is some sense of performance and of how the actors concerned are working to produce signs of fear. Yet, surprisingly, film theory and film criticism offers only a few accounts of performance in the cinema. A preoccupation with the film director as source of meaning has often led to actors being seen simply as one of the elements at the director's disposal. Similarly, genre-based criticism has rarely engaged with performance style (with the exception of work on the musical). By contrast, studies of particular film stars have sometimes explored issues relating to performance, but the extent to which ideas about stars can contribute to a more general understanding about how performance functions within cinema – obviously not all performers are stars – is not clear. So far as some of the more recent critical work on the horror film is concerned, the idea that the terrorised female body on screen acts as a conduit through which essentially male fears and anxieties are dramatised has proved influential. Carol Clover, for example, has argued that the female hero of the slasher film is 'on reflection, a congenial double for the adolescent male. She is feminine enough to act out in a gratifying way, a way unapproved for adult males, the terrors and masochistic pleasures of the underlying fantasy, but not so feminine as to disturb the structures of male competence and sexuality' (Clover, 1992, p.51). But this work has not really engaged with the process of acting out itself nor considered how an appreciation of an actor's skills and abilities (and especially female actors) might cause us to modify our understanding of the significance of gender in horror.

To illustrate some of the issues that arise from looking at horror films in this way, let us focus initially on two particular performances of fear. The first, and perhaps the best known, is from *King Kong* (1933). It is the scene from near the beginning of the film in which film-maker Carl Denham photographs Ann Darrow (played by Fay Wray) while instructing her to act scared. For Noel Carroll, the scene is exemplary of the way in which horror films show us as an audience how to respond to fearful scenes; in this sense, the instructions provided by Carl Denham are instructions to us as much as they are to Ann Darrow (Carroll, 1990, pp.17–18). Carol Clover discusses the scene in a similar way (and quotes approvingly Carroll's account) although this time within the context of a more gender-oriented approach to the way that (male) audiences respond to (female) terror (Clover, 1992, p.167). But what is striking about both accounts of the scene is that they do not even attempt to describe what Ann Darrow is actually doing in the scene. Instead they just quote Carl Denham's excitable instructions to Ann as if this were a fully adequate account of what is happening. In effect, this privileging of Denham's words over the acting out of terror on screen renders the details of Fay Wray's performance invisible, something not worthy of discussion in their own right. It also, perhaps erroneously, gives a sense that the female in this scene is simply doing what she is told, and that the terrified response she produces has nothing to do with her but is instead just a male-centred emotion being expressed through her body. It is certainly the case that the scene is dealing in part with Denham's authority over Ann. After all, he is in charge of the expedition to Skull Island and Ann is just his employee. But it should also be clear from looking at the scene itself that there is more to Ann's performance than Denham's instructions to her.

These instructions are quite straightforward but also rather vague in detail: 'It's horrible, Ann, but you can't look away . . . Scream, Ann . . . Throw your arms across your eyes and scream, Ann, scream for your life.' Yet Wray's performance is structured in a way that belies the crudity of Denham's words. This is particularly apparent in the way that Wray uses her hands. Just before the dramatisation of fear begins, she is holding them in front of her at the level of her midriff. Denham instructs her to look up – she does so – and react as if she is seeing something amazing, terrifying. Unprompted by any direct command from the director, Wray then raises her hands, the left hand to the side of her face, the right to the side of her throat. As Denham instructs her to convey helplessness, Wray moves her hands nervously and also, more delicately, makes her fingers tremble. Then comes the command 'Try to scream' and immediately Wray's hands become tense, the fingers momentarily outstretched before they begin to tremble again. Finally we hear Denham's

Performing fear: Fay Wray in *King Kong* © 1933 RKO Pictures, Inc. All Rights Reserved.

authoritative command to throw her arms across her face and scream. Interestingly Wray does not actually do this but instead offers something more elegant. The right arm is brought up across her eyes and the right hand, previously at the level of her throat, clasps the left hand on the left side of her face.

It is clear from this that Wray's performance of fear is structured around the movement of her hands from a relaxed position directly in front of her up either side of her body to a tense clasped position on the left side of her face. No doubt there is some truth both to Carroll's claim that the scene demonstrates to an audience what its own fearful responses might be and to Clover's suggestion that it highlights the importance of vision to horror (although in suggesting this Clover is almost totally reliant on Denham's words rather than on Wray's performance). But at the same time the scene should also be viewed as a bravura display of acting. The fact that Ann's fearful reaction is shot in medium shot in an uninterrupted take means that Fay Wray's performance skills remain the centre of attention throughout as a kind of spectacle in themselves. In line with this, one can argue that the performance is deliberately exaggerated and excessive, especially when compared with Fay Wray's earlier performances of fear in *Mystery of the Wax Museum* (1933) and *The Vampire Bat* (1933), although some details – especially the trembling fingers (which seem to be one of Wray's signature movements) – are present, albeit in a toned-down form. This excess is motivated ostensibly by the fact that the character of Ann Darrow does not have any acting experience but more particularly, one feels, by the pleasurable opportunity this affords to display an actor showing off her control of her own body and her sense of dramatic timing as she poses for the camera.

Our second example of a performance of fear comes from earlier in cinema history and, in fact, not from a horror film at all, although one could argue that it helped to establish within cinema a way of showing fear that would be of some importance in the subsequent development of the horror genre. The film is D.W. Griffith's melodrama *Broken Blossoms* (1919), a climactic scene which involves the heroine (played by Lillian Gish) being menaced by her brutal, drunkard father. To get away from him, Gish locks herself in a cupboard whereupon her father proceeds to break down the cupboard door with a hatchet. Gish's performance of fear here is altogether wilder than that offered by Fay Wray in *King Kong* (although in its own way it is an equally bravura display of actorly technique). Initially she presses herself against one of the cupboard walls with her back to the door, her hands in restless movement as she glances fearfully over her shoulder. When the hatchet assault on the door commences, she becomes panic-stricken, first running back and forth within the tiny confines of the cupboard and then turning frantically in circles. Finally, as her father breaks through the door, she collapses into a corner. Here we have a portrayal of abject terror that combines defensive movements (holding one's arms up before the body, seeking to make the body small by hunching down) with 'excessive', non-defensive actions (such as Gish's turning in circles) that signify a panicked loss of control over the body. What is perhaps most striking about Gish's performance is its extravagant intensity as the actor shifts rapidly and energetically between controlled defensive gestures and out-of-control panicked ones.

It is this form of screen terror rather than the more controlled and self-possessed version practised by Fay Wray in her *King Kong* 'screen test' that seems most important to subsequent horror films, especially in the 1970s and 1980s when images of female terror are especially prevalent. One thinks in particular of two horror films that offer what are in effect reworkings of the *Broken Blossoms* hatchet scene. In *Halloween* (1978), the masked killer breaks down the door of a wardrobe in which Laurie (Jamie Lee Curtis) is hiding, while in *The Shining* (1980), Jack Torrance (Jack Nicholson) attacks with an axe the door of the bathroom inside which his wife Wendy (Shelley Duvall) is trapped. In both cases, there is a strong sense of claustrophobic confinement much like that offered in *Broken Blossoms*, and the performances of Curtis and

Duvall reproduce many of the features of Lillian Gish's earlier performance. Bodies are hunched defensively, eyes are opened wide in terror, eyes are shut and faces turned away from the attacker as if to deny his presence, hands are pressed up against walls or are raised in front of the face, and generally there is a visible expenditure of energy as the actors involved enact the apparent contradiction between self-defence and helpless panic.

A similar pattern is evident elsewhere in horror of the 1960s–1980s period. Note, for example, the performances given by British actor Suzy Kendall in two Italian horrors, *The Bird with the Crystal Plumage* (1970) and *Torso* (1973). In the former, she is trapped in her flat as the killer attempts to break through the front door. In the latter she has to hide from the man who has murdered several of her friends and who is unaware that she is in the same house as he is. Her proactive defence manoeuvres include trying (unsuccessfully) to phone for help, in *Bird* blocking the doorway with furniture and grabbing a knife, in *Torso* quickly effacing all signs of her occupancy in the house before the killer sees them. But she also at certain points lapses into a child-like helplessness – cowering against walls, covering her face, whimpering. Another fairly representative example comes from the opening sequence of the influential slasher film *Friday the 13th* (1980), in which the killer's first female victim, although clearly frightened, makes energetic attempts to get past the killer until, finally realising that there is no escape, she brings her hands up to her face (where, obviously, they are no use in defensive terms) and screams.

What all these performances have in common is physicality, with fear being expressed through an intense physical agitation of the body. Linda Williams has discussed 'the spectacle of a body caught in the grips of intense sensation or emotion' (in horror films, porn and melodrama) in terms of ecstasy and rapture and has also pointed out that 'in each of these genres the bodies of women figured on the screen have functioned traditionally as the primary embodiments of pleasure, fear, and pain' (Williams, 1995, pp.142–3). However, it is worth pointing out that not all performances of fear (or, for that matter, of pleasure or of pain) are the same, and that, for all their common elements, the performances of fear given by Fay Wray and Lillian Gish are in certain respects distinct from later performances by Jamie Lee Curtis, Shelley Duvall and others.

This is most evident in the way that performances construct (or sometimes obscure) the relationship between fear and violence. The potential for such a relationship is always there. The thrashing about of limbs and the other rapid and energetic body movements involved in the performance of fear could quite easily lead to damage being done – if only inadvertently – to anyone straying too close. In pre-1970s horror, this rarely happens. Nevertheless, the reliance of female performances of extreme fear on a display of physical energy has, at the very least, the potential to counter or undermine those notions of female passivity or helplessness that might in other ways inform the films in question. An example that springs to mind here is the memorable moment from *Mystery of the Max Museum* when a panicked Fay Wray strikes the face of Lionel Atwill with her clenched fists only to see the face, actually a wax mask, crack open. The shock this induces marks the end of her resistance and she subsequently has to rely on the film's bland and rather dull hero, along with the opportune arrival of the local police, to save her from being encased in hot wax. However, lodged within the conventional narrative trajectory that involves the boy saving the girl from the monster is a sense of Wray's power. After all, she does smash the monster's face in.

By contrast, in horror from the late 1970s onwards, it is quite rare for the performance of abject female terror not to involve elements of female violence, with this all held together by a particular type of physical performance. So, in *Halloween*'s wardrobe scene, there is a continuity between Laurie's panicked expressions of helpless fear and her equally frantic grabbing of a clothes hanger quickly transformed into a stabbing implement which she then uses to defend herself against the killer. And in *The Shining*, Wendy's increasingly frantic movements include the one where she brings the carving knife down on to the hand of her husband as he tries to open the door. Central to this shift is, of course, the introduction into the genre of the 'final girl', the female hero of the slasher film, but this is not restricted to her, for more and more in horror when victims (female and male) get a chance to react to the monster (sometimes they are killed before having a chance to register anything other than surprise), they do so aggressively. In the opening of *Friday the 13th*, for example, the female victim initially looks and acts as if she is playing a particularly competitive game of net ball, and by the time we get to the 'neo-slashers' of the 1990s, including *Scream* (1996), *I Know What You Did Last Summer* (1997) and *Urban Legend* (1998), an energetic fighting back has become the order of the day. It seems from this that at a certain point in the history of the horror genre abject or helpless terror goes out of fashion, to the extent that an audience's response today to Suzy Kendall's climactic collapse into whimpering passivity in *The Bird with the Crystal Plumage* is likely to be impatience or irritation. After all, she's got a knife so why isn't she using it? Compare this with the moment in *Halloween: H20* (1998) where Laurie Strode (still played by Jamie Lee Curtis), now a grown-up mother and school principal, realises that she is about to be trapped by the masked killer in a cupboard just like the one she was trapped in two decades earlier. 'Oh fuck,' she says with some annoyance before turning on her assailant and hitting him on the head with a fire extinguisher.

It is interesting to consider the scream in this respect. Usually thought of as the essential expression of female terror, it turns out (as the previous chapter hinted) to be something of a problem for performers and film-makers, if only

155

for the practical reason that if you are physically exerting yourself to show fear in the energetic manner of, say, Jamie Lee Curtis or Shelley Duvall, it is difficult to adopt a position where you can then fill your lungs with air and deliver a piercing scream (hence the practice of dubbing in screams). Fay Wray can do it in *King Kong* because she is immobile as can Hilary Dwyer at the end of *Witchfinder General* (1968) or Daria Nicolodi at the end of *Tenebrae* (1982) (*Witchfinder General* and *Tenebrae* are the only two horror films I know where the sound of the scream functions as a kind of performative event in its own right which carries on over the end credits) but for the more active final girls of the slasher film, a kind of breathless whimpering is more common and, ironically, by the time we get to the *Scream* films, where the imperative to fight back is strongest of all, screaming is very rare indeed.

While the movement from Fay Wray's helpless scream to Jamie Lee Curtis's exasperated 'Oh fuck' has been explored by horror film criticism in terms of the genre's promotion of the female hero from the 1980s onwards, it has not been thought about much in terms of performance. This is a shame because paying attention to the performance (by females and males) of fear can arguably lead to a more nuanced understanding of how fear has operated within the horror genre. For one thing, it would be helpful for us to be more alert to the different levels and types of fear apparent in the genre throughout its history. In this respect, simply listing, as some critics have done, the emotional or physical responses associated with fear and then assigning these a particular generic function represents a decidedly crude way of thinking about what can be a detailed, complex and varied set of performances, ranging from some of the more extreme 'show-stopping' performances discussed above to somewhat quieter performances of fearful apprehension (such as that found, say, in *Cat People*'s bus sequence).

Perhaps male performances of fear should also be re-considered here. Carol Clover is not alone in arguing that 'abject terror . . . is gendered feminine, and the more concerned a given film is with that condition – and it is the essence of modern horror – the more likely the femaleness of the victim' and yet it is quite easy to find frightened men in horror films (Clover, 1992, p.51). It is true that relatively few of these are at the extreme abject end of the spectrum of fear (but then one might argue that this also applies to female perform-ances of fear), and those that are particularly extreme are usually offered as grotesque or comic – one thinks here especially of performances by Dwight Frye in *Frankenstein* (1931) and *The Vampire Bat* and by Bruce Campbell in the *Evil Dead* films. Yet in the 1940s horror films of Val Lewton, in British and Italian horror of the 1950s, 1960s and 1970s, in Roger Corman's Poe adaptations from the early 1960s, or in many 1970s US horrors, situations abound in which male characters are shown to be apprehensive, scared or helplessly afraid, with this conveyed performance-wise in much the same way as it would be with female characters. It is also the case that the major male horror stars, notably Boris Karloff, Bela Lugosi, Peter Cushing, Christopher Lee, Vincent Price, are all as adept and as experienced at playing terrified as they are at playing terrifying. It seems from this that in its focusing so much on female terror rather than on the male version, the slasher film is not typical of the genre as a whole, and even with the slasher, as we have seen, the situation is not as straightforward as it might initially seem.

What this suggests is that horror's palette of fear is considerably richer and more varied than is sometimes supposed, and that until we have a fuller account than we have at present of the contributions made by actors – some well-known, others obscure – to this particular aspect of the genre, then our appreciation of how horror actually achieves its effects will necessarily be limited.

BEING SCARY

If the performance of victimhood does not always necessitate being passive and helpless, neither does the performance of monstrousness invariably involve being consistently active and powerful. In part, this has to do with the fact that most horror films end up delivering their monsters to victimhood as those monsters are defeated and/or destroyed by the forces of good. Consider here, for example, the inevitable fate of arch-fiend Dracula. While the 1931 Universal *Dracula* offered us only a rather peremptory off-screen groan as Dracula was staked unseen by Van Helsing, Dracula films from the 1950s onwards nearly always made the vampire's destruction a scene of spectacle reliant not just on special effects but also on the physical agitation or contortion of the body of the actor concerned. So in Hammer's 1958 version of *Dracula*, the Count (played by Christopher Lee) virtually bends over backwards as he is forced into the sunlight by the cross-wielding Van Helsing, while in Hammer's later *Dracula Has Risen From the Grave* (1968), after being staked with a huge ornamental cross, the vampire cries tears of blood, and in *The Satanic Rites of Dracula* (1973) he thrashes about helplessly in a hawthorn bush before finally expiring. The conclusion of the 1979 version of *Dracula* – in which the Count (played this time by Frank Langella) is impaled on a hook by which he is then pulled up into the daylight and from which he frantically tries to escape – clearly fits into the by then well-established horror convention that the monster has to be seen to suffer before its destruction (although, as noted in a previous chapter, Dracula's apparent death at the end of the 1979 version is more than a little ambiguous).

While it is all very well to suggest that performing the monster often entails the projection not just of menacing power but also of weakness, subjection and vulnerability, this begs the important question of how this is actually achieved by the actors in question. This chapter has already discussed some of the performance practices associated with conveying various types of terror – and we see them in action yet again in the scenes of Dracula's victimisation – but what does one have to do to project menace and power? Clearly certain physical attributes help, with height and bulk often proving useful qualifications for getting the role of the monster (although anyone startled or disturbed by the murderous dwarf who appears at the end of *Don't Look Now* will realise that, when it comes to the delivery of shocks, size does not always matter). The question remains, however, of what actors bring to their monstrous roles other than their own physique. This is complicated by the fact that the fearful impact of many of horror's monsters and villains is dependent, in part at least, on make-up, costume and special effects (along with, of course, the contributions made by directors, screenwriters, cinematographers, composers, etc.), with the input of actors, whose faces or bodies will sometimes be obscured or completely concealed, sometimes hard to ascertain. Having said this, there are many examples within the horror genre of performances that contribute in a very significant way to our sense of what horror monsters are.

Rather than just running through a series of distinguished horror performances, which would, I think, be easier to establish than some critics of the genre might suppose, the remainder of this section instead identifies some of the ways in which actors generally have sought, to greater or sometimes lesser effect, to act out the monstrous. As was the case with the earlier discussion of the performance of victimhood, looking at monsters in this way will enable us to put some flesh, so to speak, on the more abstract theoretical conceptualisations of the monster that we have already encountered in this book.

Stillness and energy

Given that the most basic definition of the monster is predicated on action – on the monster being an entity that attacks or threatens to attack us – it is perhaps surprising how many performances of the monstrous rely upon a sense of stillness, with this ranging from physical immobility to more subtle expressions of calmness or pensiveness. This quality can have different, sometimes interrelated functions within horror. It can be associated with suspense, for example. The monster in question might be inactive but we know that it could, and probably will, attack at any moment. Think here of Dr Hannibal Lecter (an Oscar-winning performance by Anthony Hopkins) in *The Silence of the Lambs* (1991) and *Hannibal* (2001) whose periods of intent stillness are punctuated by outbursts of extreme violence. Other such figures include Christopher Lee's Dracula, especially in Hammer's 1958 film where he combines a watchfulness with sudden and explosive bursts of action, and Doug Bradley's Pinhead in the *Hellraiser* films who, despite his menacing appearance, moves slowly and only occasionally resorts to actual violence.

But the stillness, in these and other instances, is not just about extending that suspenseful moment before the monster lunges at you. Stillness can also in itself signify power and dominance, essential prerequisites for any self-respecting monster. This is apparent in one of the first key encounters in the history of the horror film, the meeting of Dracula (played by Bela Lugosi) and Renfield (played by Dwight Frye) in the hallway of Castle Dracula in the 1931 Universal *Dracula*. The composition of the scene – with Dracula standing above Renfield on the grand staircase – helps to give us a sense of who the powerful figure is here, but the differing performance styles of Lugosi and Frye also have a part to play. In particular, Lugosi's self-possession, with his movements and the words he utters both slow and considered in comparison with Frye's much more nervous performance, indicates that it is Dracula who is in charge not only of himself but of the whole situation. Nowadays many audiences find Lugosi's much-parodied performance, which involved the Hungarian actor learning his lines phonetically rather than worrying about learning to speak English, ponderous to the point of risibility, but in its day it was effective enough, and it certainly helped to establish within horror cinema a way of performing dominance that was particularly appropriate for monsters and villains.

If we return to Lee's Dracula and Hannibal Lecter in this light, we can see how, in their initial encounters with respectively Jonathan Harker (John van Eyssen) and Clarice Starling (Jodie Foster), it is the even tone of their voices, their articulacy, and their calmness that mark them as figures in control in contrast to their visibly and audibly nervous interlocutors. In both instances, the movements they make are decisive and considered movements towards the camera (which in both *Dracula* and *The Silence of the Lambs* is often placed so that we are witnessing this advance through the eyes of Harker and Starling), and a great deal is made of their mesmeric gaze and their ability to determine the flow of conversation. Such is their dominance, it seems, that they do not need constantly to resort to violence or to the threat of violence. Something similar could be said of other articulate horror monsters such as Pinhead, Candyman (played by Tony Todd), Molasar (played, with the aid of a considerable amount of make-up and special effects, by Michael Carter) in *The Keep* (1983), or any of the post-Christopher Lee screen Draculas (including Frank Langella, Gary Oldman and Gerard Butler).

A yet more extreme form of stillness, one that this time remains uninterrupted by outbursts of action, is apparent in the performances given by Barbara Steele as Asa in *La maschera del demonio* (1960) and Samantha Eggar as Nola in *The Brood* (1979). In the first of these, the witch Asa remains in her coffin throughout much of the film (although Steele also plays the more mobile Katia), while Nola, whose rage has been externalised in the form of murderous parthenogenetically conceived children, is only ever shown kneeling on the floor of her cabin at the institute where she is a patient. In critical accounts of both films, the power of these female monsters has been seen as inextricably connected with their biological difference from men, with this relating in particular to their reproductive abilities. These women are frightening, it seems, not for what they do or might do (they actually do very little) but rather for what they are (Creed, 1993). But at the same time the performances of the actors involved help – much in the manner of the male performances noted above, although here in a more focused form – to give a sense of an intense self-control and dominance over others (with this arguably qualifying those accounts of *The Brood* which see Nola as a wild, out-of-control figure). Given that neither actor is in a situation where they can move their body freely, the emphasis is placed instead on their facial expressions and voices (although Steele's performance is hampered in this respect by the dubbing in of another voice). The widening of their eyes – conventionally a sign of terror – when coupled with their intense, unblinking stares at those individuals with whom they come into contact, their largely unchanging facial expressions, and the low pitch and evenness of their voices, mark them out as figures of power even in situations where they themselves are clearly incapable of doing physical harm to others.

In a different way, the physical slowness of monsters such as zombies, the mummy or Michael Myers in *Halloween* as they shuffle or walk (never run) towards their prospective victims can be seen as augmenting the threat they pose. Of course, this is somewhat paradoxical inasmuch as these monsters are often moving so slowly that it should be easy to escape from them, and consequently film-makers have been compelled to contrive, with varying degrees of credibility, scenarios in which characters don't just do the sensible thing and make a run for it. Performances of this kind, which usually involve no dialogue and for which the actor's face is hidden beneath either make up (in the case of the mummy) or a mask (Michael Myers or his *Friday the 13th* counterpart Jason Voorhees), are often viewed as demanding less from an actor than some of the more verbal roles discussed above. It is reported, for example, that when Nick Castle, who played Michael Myers in the first *Halloween* film, asked the director John Carpenter what he had to do, Carpenter's reply was 'Just walk'. One might well say that 'just walking' hardly poses much of an acting challenge. However, this way of thinking about performance perhaps overvalues dialogue at the expense of an understanding of the importance of mime-based and gestural forms of expression to horror cinema. As we will soon see, some horror actors have managed to conjure up distinctive performances out of mute, heavily made-up roles; but even in what might be more basic roles, notably that of the zombie, demands are still being made on the actors involved.

Consider in this respect the walk associated with the mummy – especially as performed by Tom Tyler in *The Mummy's Hand* (1940), Lon Chaney Junior in *The Mummy's Tomb* (1942), *The Mummy's Ghost* (1944) and *The Mummy's Curse* (1944), Christopher Lee in *The Mummy* (1959), Dickie Owen in *The Curse of the Mummy's Tomb* (1964), and Eddie Powell in *The Mummy's Shroud* (1967) (Karloff's performance in the 1932 production of *The Mummy* is different given that he only appears in what would later become the familiar cloth-wrapped guise in one scene) – and the zombies featured in, among others, *White Zombie* (1932), *The Plague of the Zombies* (1966) and *Night of the Living Dead* (1968). Here the lack of physical co-ordination, with feet dragged along the ground and arms hanging loosely (or in Chaney's case one arm hanging loosely, the other, apparently withered, held close to the chest) helps to convey the mindlessness upon which the threat posed by these monsters is predicated. At the same time, these performances should not all be lumped together as if they are exactly the same. Chaney's mummy is slower, more hunched over and generally more decrepit than Lee's mummy who, characteristically for this actor, is more dynamic and purposeful in his movements. Similarly, while the zombies in both *White Zombie* and Hammer's *The Plague of the Zombies* (played in most cases by unnamed extras) adopt what to us today seem extremely mannered and somewhat melodramatic gestures, the zombies who populate *Night of the Living Dead* operate in a less stylised or elegant way, in some scenes moving much like the 'ordinary' people in the film, in others (especially those gruesome moments where they are shown eating their victims) moving in an animalistic fashion.

Compare this with the better co-ordinated Michael Myers as he calmly strolls in pursuit of the terrified Laurie in the concluding section of *Halloween*. To a certain extent, Michael resembles monsters such as Hannibal Lecter or Candyman, with his apparent imperturbability and composure underlining his control of the situation. However, the non-verbal quality of Michael's dominance sets him apart from these altogether more articulate monsters, with his muteness rendering him an especially implacable foe with whom it is impossible to have any kind of dialogue (which is clearly not the case with either Lecter or Candyman). This is counter-pointed in Castle's performance by an occasional child-like gesture – for example, when, head cocked to one side, he curiously inspects the body of a victim he has just pinned to a wall with a large carving knife as if it is an accidentally broken toy – which serves to remind us that the roots of Michael's psychosis or evil lie in his childhood (at the age of six, he killed one of his sisters; a later *Halloween* film, *Halloween: H20*, makes a lot of the conflict between Michael and Laurie as a particularly violent brother/sister spat) and which arguably bestows a degree of complexity on what might otherwise have been a very straightforward rendition of the boogey man.

It seems from this that stillness, calmness, quietness, self-control and composure are all important qualities in the performance of horror monsterdom, be they manifested verbally or physically, and that thinking about monsters in these terms can alert us to all kinds of subtleties and nuances that might otherwise go unnoticed. Of course, stillness sits at one end of a continuum of monstrous behaviour, with more energetic and violent behaviour existing at the other end. It is rare to find monsters who do not at some point launch a physical attack on an unfortunate victim (although, as noted above, Asa in *La maschera del demonio* and Nola in *The Brood* do spring to mind as examples of monsters who do not themselves do anything physically to their victims), but it is equally rare to find monsters defined entirely through such activity. Even horror's more manic monsters – one thinks here of Leatherface (played by Gunnar Hansen) in *The Texas Chainsaw Massacre* (1974), Freddy Krueger (played by Robert Englund) in the *Nightmare on Elm Street* films, Buffalo Bill/Jame Gumb (played by Ted Levine) in *The Silence of the Lambs* or the killers (played by numerous actors) in the *Scream* films – will sometimes slow down or lapse into stillness, with this in various ways helping to augment or modulate their power and menace. Horror's monsters emerge from this as entities that, so far as performance is concerned, lead a dynamic existence, constantly caught up as they are in processes of change, moving back and forth between dominance and subordination, activity and stillness. And the main vehicles by which this changeability is articulated, and in large part the distinctive of each monster defined, are the actors involved as they work to bring to life creations that are frightening but not always frightening in the same way and that are sometimes sympathetic and vulnerable as well.

Pathos

Despite the fact that horror films rely on their monsters generally behaving in an unpleasant manner, there are numerous instances where monsters acquire a certain pathos, where we are meant to view them, despite all the bad things they have done, with a degree of sympathy. Clearly this applies more to some monsters than others, and notably those monsters who, for all their threatening qualities, have about them a certain victim-like helplessness as well as an ability to experience suffering. Of particular interest here are Frankenstein's monster and the werewolf, both of whom, especially in their incarnations in Universal horror of the 1930s and 1940s, are defined as much through the pain they themselves experience as the pain they cause others. But by what means can pity for these creatures be elicited from an audience? In part, it can be done through the creation of scenarios in which the monsters are isolated figures hunted down by cruel or ignorant mobs of torch-wielding peasants. In part, it is done via the way in which the monsters in question are presented to us in performance.

The classic horror paradigm of monstrous pathos is, of course, Frankenstein's monster as portrayed by Boris Karloff in Universal's *Frankenstein* (1931), *Bride of Frankenstein* (1935) and *Son of Frankenstein* (1939). While there are important differences between these three performances, with the monster temporarily acquiring speech in *Bride of Frankenstein* and becoming more ruthless than before in *Son of Frankenstein*, there is a consistency throughout in the means used by Karloff to make the monster appear sympathetic. In part, this has to do with the actor's ability to express the monster's emotional states via changes in facial expression. But also important in the creation of pathos are Karloff's repeated deployment of two particular gestures, one denoting a plea for help, the other signalling fear. The first of these involves Karloff making a gentle, non-threatening begging movement with both hands, with this usually accompanied by the monster's inarticulate production of some high-pitched and again non-threatening sounds. One example from the first Frankenstein film occurs when, shortly after his creation, the monster sees daylight for the first time through a trap door opened by Frankenstein. The monster reaches up towards the light, his hands attempting to grasp something that we know cannot be grasped. Then, after the trap door has been closed and the light shut off, the monster repeats the gesture, this time directing it at Frankenstein as a request for the light to be restored (a request ignored by the monster's creator). Or in the second film, *Bride of Frankenstein*, we see it again when the monster stumbles into the home of the blind hermit seeking assistance. In each case – and for all those other moments where this gesture is featured – the pathos derives from the contrast between the delicacy of the gesture and the bulk of the character that is making it. The effect is accentuated by the deliberately shortened sleeves of the monster's jacket (done presumably to make the arms appear longer) which aid the impression that the hands exist almost in a separate space from that occupied by the rest of the monster's body.

The second gesture deployed by Karloff signifies fear or frustration that sometimes shades into anger. It involves moving the arm downwards in a forceful manner, with this often accompanied by a low-pitched growl. We see it for the first time in *Frankenstein* when the monster is threatened by Fritz, Frankenstein's torch-wielding assistant, and we see it again, in a rather more dramatic form, at that film's conclusion, when the monster is trapped in the burning mill. It also shows up on numerous occasions in *Bride of Frankenstein*, for example, in the scene where the shepherdess whom the monster is trying to help starts to scream, or the scene where the blind hermit strikes a match in front of the monster (who, perhaps understandably, has by this stage become somewhat chary of fire). As with the begging gesture, the pathos here derives from the way in which the monster's desperate attempts to communicate with others are constantly thwarted or misunderstood, with this in turn leading to frustration and anger.

The situation is different so far as the Wolf Man, that other great pathos-ridden monster, is concerned, especially as played by Lon Chaney Junior in *The Wolf Man* (1941), *Frankenstein Meets the Wolf Man* (1943), *House of Frankenstein* (1944), *House of Dracula* (1945) and *Abbott and Costello Meet Frankenstein* (1948). Here the werewolf itself is a bundle of animalistic fury that never seeks our sympathy. This is reserved instead for Larry Talbot, the man who against his will is transformed into the werewolf when the moon is full. The hapless Talbot spends most of his time in all of the films listed above either begging other people for help or lapsing into lachrymose self-pity. Chaney gives us a sense of a depressive Talbot's lack of control over his own body through performances in which small nervous gestures mingle with moments of physical lassitude and sudden, volatile movements. A good example of this can be found in the tavern scene in *Frankenstein Meets the Wolf Man*. Talbot and his female companion are being serenaded by a local balladeer. Talbot is not paying much attention to the song but instead is looking nervously around him and generally giving the impression of being tense and uncomfortable (for no apparent reason; no one present – other than himself, of course – poses any threat). Then the singer delivers the line 'May they live eternally' and immediately Talbot reacts, looking aghast with eyes widened. A few second later, he is on his feet and grabbing the singer, screaming at him 'I don't want to live eternally'. Here, as he does elsewhere in Universal's cycle of werewolf films, Chaney gives us a sense of a body never at rest, never in full control of itself.

What is going on here is that some of the attributes of victimhood – to do with loss of bodily control and a physical subjection to forces more powerful than oneself – are also present within the performance of the monstrous. This is not just apparent in Universal horror (although arguably it is more central there than it is elsewhere). For example, the actors playing the 'monsters' in several of Hammer's Frankenstein films are given repeated opportunities to perform sadness, pain and loss, and generally do so through a Chaney-like lassitude and constriction of the body, with this often contrasted with the supreme self-control of Baron Frankenstein (as played by Peter Cushing). One thinks here in particular of Michael Gwynne in *The Revenge of Frankenstein* (1958), Susan Denberg in *Frankenstein Created Woman* (1967) and Freddie Jones in *Frankenstein Must Be Destroyed* (1969). The werewolf too continues, in its human form at least, to demand performances that combine a mournful self-pity with a lack of self-control, for example, Michael Landon's rendition of the man-wolf in *I Was a Teenage Werewolf* (1957) or Oliver Reed in Hammer's *The Curse of the Werewolf* (1961). And let us not forget Count Dracula who, in more recent adaptations such as *Bram Stoker's Dracula* (1992) and *Dracula 2000* (2000), has also been presented to us as an anguished, doom-laden protagonist, someone who, much like Karloff's monster and Chaney's werewolf, has little apparent control over his own destiny and on some level knows it.

Since the 1960s pathos has become a less significant feature of horror than it was beforehand, with this probably having something to do with an ever-increasing ruthlessness and cynicism within the genre. With a few notable exceptions (such as, for example, Carrie White in *Carrie*), monsters just do not ask for our sympathy much anymore. However, in earlier periods of horror history they often did. For all their monstrous qualities, their violence and their destructiveness, they were also, if only partially or temporarily, victims as well. One can argue that the ability of such monsters to affect us emotionally is in large part down to the people who were playing them, who through gesture, expression and movement, managed to convey to us how sad it is sometimes to be a monster.

Transformation

Scenes featuring the transformation of an apparently normal character into a monster have always been showstoppers in the history of the horror film. In part this is because they provide an opportunity for film-makers to impress us with their cinematographic and special-effects skills: think, for example, of the spectacular body-horror special effects in the man-into-werewolf scene in *An American Werewolf in London* (1981). But such scenes have also provided actors with an opportunity to display their own skills, often to disturbing effect. It is not just cinema that does this, of course. In 1888, the actor Richard Mansfield's performance of Jekyll's transformation into Hyde in a West End stage adaptation of Robert Louis Stevenson's *The Strange Case of Dr Jekyll and Mr Hyde* was so shocking that some members of the audience suspected Mansfield of being Jack the Ripper, who at that time was terrorising London. However, horror cinema does seem especially reliant on spectacular transformations that are focused in various ways upon the actor's body.

Having said this, there are not many performances of transformation quite like the one given by John Barrymore in the 1920 silent film version of *Dr Jekyll and Mr Hyde*. Completely eschewing special effects or make-up, Barrymore relies entirely on his own physical contortions to project a sense of the good Jekyll becoming the evil Hyde (although, once the transformation is complete, make-up is applied to underline Hyde's bestial nature). In contrast, later Jekyll/Hyde transformations – notably those given by Fredric March (in an Oscar-winning performance) in the 1931 version, Spencer Tracy in the 1941 version, and John Malkovich in *Mary Reilly* (1996) – deploy a frenzied mix of optical and make-up effects, although here too the contortions of the actor's body have a part to play in bestowing upon the transformation a sense of physical helplessness and abandonment. Much the same could be said of any number of transformations in werewolf movies. One thinks especially of the scene in Hammer's *The Curse of the Werewolf*, in which Leon (Oliver Reed) begins to turn into a werewolf while trapped in a prison cell. As with other werewolf films, make-up and special effects are involved but Reed's own performance, and the impression he manages to give of someone gradually and unwillingly losing control of his own body, is central to the scene's dramatisation of the transformation.

Contortion, shivering and shaking, tensing up, rapid nervous movement: all of these physical responses help to signify a subjection to forces outside one's control. As is also the case with pathos, such transformation scenes enable us, if only temporarily or intermittently, to see the putative monster as itself a victim of some kind. Sometimes horror films will extend the process of transformation in order to develop the idea of the monster as victim. Perhaps the best-known example of this is David Cronenberg's version of *The Fly* (1986), in which Seth Brundle (played by Jeff Goldblum) spends most of the narrative slowly mutating into a human-fly hybrid. While the film relies heavily on extreme (and decidedly gross) make-up effects, and in the concluding scene replaces Goldblum entirely with a special-effects monster, it is principally through Goldblum's own agitated performance, which comes replete with the nervous physical tics and verbal mannerisms apparent elsewhere in that actor's *œuvre*, that the film conveys a sense of the pain and emotional trauma involved in this particular transformation. Of course, the relative importance of the contributions made by special effects and by performance to transformation scenes will vary from one film to the next. For example, Linda Blair's transformation into a possessed, demonic child in *The Exorcist* (1973) arguably owes more to the combined efforts of make-up designers and special effects teams than it does to Blair herself (although she is obviously a very capable actor), while, in contrast, it is hard to imagine anyone playing Brundle/Fly quite like Goldblum.

Transformation can also be seen as having a significance in horror that goes well beyond those moments in horror films where apparently normal people turn into monsters. To a certain extent, one might argue that inasmuch as transformation, in terms of horror at least, denotes a state of extreme physical agitation and lack of self-control, then it is a state in which both monsters and victims can find themselves. It is worth thinking here about one of the great 1970s monster-victims, Carrie White (played by Sissy Spacek) in *Carrie* (1976) and how much her various transformations are conveyed through the

Being scary: Sissy Spacek in *Carrie* (1976). Courtesy of MGM CLIP+STILL.

actor's stance and movements. For example, Carrie's terror in the shower scene that opens the film and in the scene not long after in which she is locked in a cupboard by her mother is performed in much the same way as Lillian Gish's terror is performed in *Broken Blossoms*, via an intense physical agitation of the body combined with defensive attempts to make the body small by curling up. Carrie's lack of self-worth in the scenes that follow is again suggested by her defensive hunched-over posture, while in comparison her brief accession to normality – when she goes to the prom – involves her for the first time in the film walking with an upright stance. Then, when she has been publicly humiliated (by having a bucket of pig's blood dumped on her as she steps on to the stage to receive the 'Prom Queen' award) and unleashes a devastating telekinetic attack on all present, she suddenly becomes very still, with this punctuated by occasional sharp movements of her head which seem to initiate the different stages of the attack. As is the case with other monsters, this stillness gives us a sense of her power, especially when it is contrasted with the frantic, panicked movements elsewhere in the hall as terrified prom-nighters attempt to escape. Spacek's performance – which earned her an Oscar nomination – is a virtuoso one and subtler in its modulations between Carrie as victim and Carrie as monster than the thumbnail sketch given above might suggest. But even so, it should be clear not just how dependent the effectiveness of the film is on Spacek's artistry, but also how that performance holds together notions of the monstrous and of the victim in a way that critical-theoretical accounts of the horror have often found hard to grasp or understand.

Returning in this light to the scene with which this chapter began – the monster advancing on a potential female victim – it becomes apparent how complex such a scene can be so far as the relation of power to powerlessness is concerned. Monsters can become victims, victims can become monsters or in other ways can achieve dominance, with much of this relayed through a type of performance which foregrounds the body in motion. It is interesting that those critical accounts of horror, and especially the psychoanalytical ones, which engage with notions of the body often offer a peculiarly objectified version of the body, one that primarily fixes it as the location of sexual difference. Thinking of the body not as 'the body' but instead as someone's body, as in particular an actor's body performing physical movements associated with either subjection or dominance (or both), bestows upon that body an energised, transformative quality. It becomes a body in constant change, not a body fixed in a particular identity, be that the identity of victim or of monster. Looking at horror in this way can lead us to a more precise understanding of how horror films themselves operate in terms of scenarios involving change and transformation, scenarios within which both monsters and victims are never quite as powerful or as powerless as you might expect them to be.

CHAPTER EIGHT

Modern horror and the 1970s

The world belongs to the young. Make way for them. Let them have it.

(*Targets*, 1968)

A NEW HORROR?

It begins, or at least it seems to begin, during the 1960s with a rejection of some of the old ways. It was in this decade that certain horror films issued challenges to the established conventions of the horror genre. No longer could one assume that good and evil would be separate and distinct, and that goodness would always prevail; nor that the forces of normality would invariably be on the side of the righteous. Alfred Hitchcock's *Psycho* (1960), for example, swept aside some of the Gothic trappings of earlier horrors and offered instead a recognisably up-to-date modern world. No Transylvanian castles here and no sinister noblemen either; instead just the banality of an interrupted car journey, a motel and a shower, and the shock of the heroine being killed off long before the film's conclusion, with the killer turning out to be a boy-next-door type (albeit one with a severe mother fixation and transvestite tendencies). A cluster of horror films from 1968 provided yet more iconoclastic takes on horror's sacred conventions. In George Romero's ground-breaking *Night of the Living Dead* (1968), the 'hero' failed to save anyone and was himself shot dead by his potential rescuers, while Roman Polanski's *Rosemary's Baby* (1968) concluded with the heroine agreeing to be a mother to the recently-born Antichrist. Meanwhile Peter Bogdanovich's directorial debut *Targets* (1968), in which an ageing horror-film star (played by real-life ageing horror-film star Boris Karloff) encounters a rifle-wielding serial killer, made a pointed comparison between the redundancy of the old horror formulae and the chaotic insecurity of the modern world. Something similar happened in the opening of *Night of the Living Dead* when a young man teases his sister with a Boris Karloff impersonation just before the 'real' and all too graphic modern horror commences. The message could not be clearer. The old horror was either dying or dead; a new horror was about to be born.

According to most histories of horror, however, it is not until the 1970s that the transition from old or 'classic' horror to something more modern was finally clinched. It was the 1970s that saw the proliferation and consolidation of new attitudes and approaches which seemed more aggressive and ruthless but also more artistically ambitious and socially engaged than what had gone before in the genre. No wonder then that some horror critics and historians have come to view the 1970s as a 'golden age' of horror production, as a period in which the genre acquired – if only for a while and only intermittently – some maturity and artistic integrity as well as a sense of social responsibility.

This way of thinking about horror history is very much centred on the American horror film. Indeed, the resurgence of American horror from the late 1960s onwards might be viewed as involving a winning back of a genre-leadership that had, in part at least, been lost to European film-makers in the late 1950s. It is as if the new horror, and especially the new American horror, breathed new life into a genre that had become exhausted through the sheer repetitiveness of the by then outdated gothic period format associated most of all with Britain's Hammer studios. Horror historian Gregory Waller is not alone in arguing that 'Hammer's films reaffirm what are assumed to be the "normal" values of heterosexual romance, clearly defined sexual roles, and the middle-class family and testify to the importance and the relevance of social stability and traditional sources of authority and wisdom' (Waller, 1987, p.4). In place of Hammer's apparently conformist, pro-authority dramas played out in nineteenth-century settings, the modern American horror film offered instead contemporary settings accompanied by a rejection or a questioning of dominant social values and social authority. Moralistic conclusions in which evil was definitively defeated by the forces of good were generally replaced by more tentative or ambiguous conclusions in which good sometimes failed (*Night of the Living Dead* and *Rosemary's Baby*, for example) or evil secured a clear victory (notably *The Omen*), and, as the safety and reassurance provided by 'classic' horror – i.e. horror from the 1930s through to the 1960s – faded away, we were left instead with an altogether more menacing, challenging and overwhelming horror experience. Or at least that is how some critics and historians have come to see it.

This chapter focuses on the 1970s and, in particular, on the extent to which it actually is the first decade of something called modern horror. In part, this will involve considering how what is usually thought of as the modern horror film fits into a broader horror history. How valid is it to separate the horror genre into distinctive 'classic' and 'modern' sections? This question becomes especially significant when one takes into account the range of horror films produced outside America during the 1960s and 1970s, especially in Britain, Italy and Spain. Are these European horrors simply the backdrop against which the cutting-edge American horrors are defined, or are they also 'modern', either in a manner comparable with or in a manner different from the American version?

An appraisal of 1970s horror also needs to engage with some of the already-existing interpretations of the films in question, especially those that consider them in terms of their political and ideological significance. The idea that horror might have a political dimension, that it could provide a meaningful engagement with key social and political issues of the day, was a relatively new one back in the 1970s. This approach was associated most of all with the influential work of critic Robin Wood, who argued that 1970s American horror had the potential to be either a radical and progressive social critique, one which opened up society's power structures to a critical interrogation, or, conversely, a reactionary bolstering of an oppressive regime (Wood, 1986, pp.70–94). In any event, ultimate judgements about the value of horror films would be based on an awareness of their relationship with, and attitude towards, society's dominant ideologies. Is this a valid way of thinking about either horror in general or 1970s horror in particular? And what precisely was it about 1970s horror films that inspired such interpretations, the likes of which had not before been deployed in relation to the horror genre?

It seems from this that the very concept of 'modern horror' poses some fundamental questions about both the way we understand the historical development of the horror genre and how we seek to explain and value individual horror films. Perhaps the best way of approaching these questions is through a consideration of that messy process by which something that we now call 'modern' separates itself out from something that we now, perhaps a little patronisingly, refer to as 'classic'. How, where, when and why does the modern nightmare begin?

A QUESTION OF ORIGINS

It is relatively easy to determine when any cycle of horror production begins. You just follow the trail of sequels and rip-offs back to a commercially successful original film. Determining the start date for a more widespread, or even epochal, shift in the horror genre – such as the transition from classic to modern horror – is more difficult. The films most often identified as marking the onset of generic change have already been mentioned, namely *Psycho* in 1960 and *Night of the Living Dead* and *Rosemary's Baby* in 1968. But there seems little agreement among critics as to which of these is the most significant starting point. Robin Wood and Reynold Humphries plump for *Psycho* in their studies of the American horror film, while Gregory Waller declares definitively in his study of American horror that *Night of the Living Dead* and *Rosemary's Baby* mark the proper beginning of modern horror (Wood, 1986; Humphries, 2002; Waller, 1987). Whichever film is selected, a problem remains, however, and that is that none of them, not even the more recent productions from 1968, lead directly and immediately to sustained horror production of the type that would later be labelled 'modern'. In fact, one has to wait until the early 1970s before more films of the modern type appear – Wes Craven's *Last House on the Left* in 1972, William Friedkin's *The Exorcist* in 1973 and Tobe Hooper's *The Texas Chainsaw Massacre* in 1974 – and a regular flow of American horror does not develop until the mid-1970s.

From this perspective, early examples of modern horror such as *Psycho* and *Night of the Living Dead* start to look like isolated outposts of activity rather than like the actual beginning of anything. But is this apparent isolation simply the result of viewing them retrospectively via their relation to certain types of 1970s US horror film? It could be argued that thinking about these films instead in terms of the immediate context of their production can alert us to broader shifts occurring within the genre during the 1960s, and not just in American cinema. Seen in this way, films like *Psycho*, *Night of the Living Dead* and *Rosemary's Baby*, rather than functioning as shocking interventions into a staid horror genre, to a certain extent fit into and contribute towards what is going on around them (although at the same time one should not underestimate the innovative power of these three remarkable films). This in turn points towards a different understanding of what subsequently happens in the 1970s, both in American cinema and elsewhere, and of horror history in a more general sense.

Take *Psycho*, for example. Often seen as an important new development in Hitchcock's career as he moved from his glossy 1950s thrillers to a starker, more experimental form of film-making, it also arguably represented an attempt by the director to tap into a new horror-exploitation market that emerged towards the end of the 1950s. The break-up of the old Hollywood studio system in the late 1940s and 1950s had made it easier for independent film-makers to find outlets for their work, and this had coincided with a limited relaxation of censorship regimes in both America and western Europe. One consequence was the development of a low-budget exploitation sector consisting of films that contained what for the time was daring new subject matter often related to issues of sex and violence, with the horror genre proving a particularly useful resource in this respect. A key innovator here was Hammer, a small British company which from 1957 onwards produced a series of colour gothic horrors, including *The Curse of Frankenstein* (1957), *Dracula* (1958) and *The Mummy* (1959), that proved hugely successful in American and European markets and which encouraged other independent film companies to initiate their own horror production. So in America, one found early teen-horrors *I Was a Teenage Werewolf* (1957) and *I Was a Teenage Frankenstein* (1957) as well as a cycle of Edgar Allan Poe adaptations directed by Roger Corman at American International Pictures, including *The Fall of the House of Usher* (1960) and *Pit and the Pendulum* (1961), and a number of splatter-gore movies – among them *Blood Feast* (1963) and *Two Thousand Maniacs* (1964) – directed by cult film-maker Herschell Gordon Lewis. Numerous competitors for Hammer also emerged elsewhere, notably in Britain itself, in Italy and in Spain.

A common reading of the revival of horror's commercial fortunes in the late 1950s and early 1960s sees it as essentially a gothic moment in horror history, with period settings proving the main commercial draw. This clearly applies to Hammer's colour features as well as to Corman's Poe films and early work by Italian film-makers Mario Bava (*La maschera del demonio*, 1960), Riccardo Freda (*L'Orribile segreto del Dr Hichcock*, 1962) and Spanish director Jesus Franco (*Gritos en la noche*, 1962). However, as is so often the case in the history of the genre, other types of horror are quite easy to find, particularly those featuring contemporary settings. In Britain, for example, Anglo-Amalgamated produced a series of lurid horror-thrillers set firmly in the present, including Michael Powell's controversial *Peeping Tom* (1960), while Hammer itself produced a series of psychological thrillers with contemporary settings that were designed to cash in on both the success of *Psycho* and Hammer's own brand name. Mario Bava, Italy's premier horror film-maker of the time, also moved between period dramas and contemporary *giallo*-psychological thrillers, and in France Georges Franju's *Les Yeux sans visage* (1959) made effective use of modern settings in its story of surgical experiments gone terribly wrong. Given that since the 1930s, horror cinema has offered a mix of period and contemporary settings, with the late 1950s and early 1960s no exception to this, it seems that any simple distinction made between classic and modern horror solely on the basis of the latter taking place in the here-and-now is, to put it mildly, problematic.

The horror-related activity that was taking place in America and in Europe in the late 1950s and early 1960s was largely defined through its reliance on what might be termed a kind of shock aesthetic. Of course, earlier horror films had often deployed shocking elements as forms of dramatic emphasis, but in the late 1950s, largely as a response to new market conditions, these shocking elements became not only more graphic but also more provocative and obtrusive. In effect they functioned as spectacles or attractions in their own right and, as part of this, featured heavily in the way in which the films in question were marketed. This eminently marketable shock value resided in the inclusion of previously taboo material – for example, incest and matricide in *Psycho*, necrophilia in *L'Orribile segreto del Dr Hichcock*, cannibalism in *The Revenge of Frankenstein* (1958) – and in an increased explicitness regarding violence, gore and sexuality. Hence, for example, the graphic surgical scenes in *Les Yeux sans visage*, *Gritos en la noche* and Hammer's Frankenstein films. Hence too the overtly sexual appeal of the vampire in *Dracula* and *Brides of Dracula* (1960). To a certain extent, the now famous shock to audience's expectations provided by *Psycho*'s shower murder was also anticipated in this period by Hammer's *Dracula*, in which the ostensible hero is killed off about twenty minutes into the film, and by *City of the Dead* (1960), in which the ostensible heroine is, like Marion Crane, killed off long before the film's conclusion.

Many of these horror films also offered representations of extreme psychological states that, while often couched in Freudian terms, tended not to be figured as problems susceptible to a cure. In comparison with a film like *Cat People* (1942), for example, in which Irina's psycho-sexual issues are presented as a problem requiring a solution of some kind (albeit one not really achieved in the film), the portrayals of male neuroticism found in all of Roger Corman's Poe films and in Italian horrors such as *La maschera del demonio* and *L'Orribile segreto del Dr Hichcock* are offered more as states of being than they are as problems. Hammer horror, although most often associated with the portrayal of male authority, also contained numerous representations of anxious or diminished male characters, albeit not framed within an explicitly psychoanalytical perspective. As some critics and historians have noted, this fascination with the psychologised individual might well be related to broader social change, and in particular to shifting definitions of identity within an increasingly affluent and consumerist world. (On US horror in this period, see Jancovich, 1996; on British horror, see Hutchings, 1993a.) What is clear is that horror in the late 1950s, both in its period and in its contemporary forms, tended to foreground notions of human psychology in a more explicit and sometimes open-ended manner than before in the genre (although it is worth noting that some films, notably *I Was a Teenage Werewolf*, retained a *Cat People*-like relation between psychological problem and psychological cure). *Psycho* emerges from this not as an isolated work but instead as part of a broader continuum of horror activity, both in its shocking explicitness and in its focus on Norman Bates' apparently uncurable murderous psychopathology. This does not mean that in itself it is not distinctive and influential. It does mean that those accounts of *Psycho* which seek to separate it out completely from its fellow horror films in the interests of establishing a clear beginning for modernity within the genre are doing a disservice to what is going on elsewhere in the genre at the time of *Psycho*'s production.

Much the same can be said of the 1968 productions *Rosemary's Baby* and *Night of the Living Dead*. Critics have made a lot of the willingness of these films to jettison some established generic conventions, especially the convention which dictates that evil is ultimately defeated. However, comparable approaches are apparent across a range of other films, and not just American films or horror films. In part, this is to do with the entrance into cinema of a group of younger film-makers, in part with the industry's growing awareness that its prime audience was a youthful audience, in part with a further rolling back of censorship, and in part (although it is difficult to quantify this) with a changing social climate as young people showed themselves increasingly willing to question and protest against the values of their parents. American and British films as various as *2001: A Space Odyssey* (1968), *If . . .* (1968), *Bonnie and Clyde* (1967), *Easy Rider* (1969), *Performance* (1970) and *A Clockwork Orange* (1971) spoke of a countercultural rejection of or raging against the social establishment in much the same way as did *Targets* and *Night of the Living Dead*. (*Rosemary's Baby* is somewhat different inasmuch as it showed little interest in offering any social commentary, explicit or implicit. It probably makes more sense to view this film in the context of Polanski's work, and in particular as one of his powerful studies of urban alienation, which also included the British-produced *Repulsion* in 1965 and the French-produced *The Tenant* in 1976. It is certainly the case that, in comparison with *Night of the Living Dead*, *Rosemary's Baby* has not figured much in critical discussions of the modern American horror film.)

Dissatisfaction with some of the older forms of horror can also be found within British horror of the late 1960s and early 1970s where, as was the case in America, younger film-makers produced horror films that combined sympathy for the young with hostility to the authority embodied by older people. One thinks here of, among others, Michael Reeves's *The Sorcerers* (1967) and *Witchfinder General* (1968), Peter Sasdy's Hammer films *Taste the Blood of Dracula* (1969) and *Hands of the Ripper* (1971), Peter Sykes's Hammer film *Demons of the Mind* (1971), Piers Haggard's *Blood on Satan's Claw* (1970) and Gordon Hessler's *Scream and Scream Again* (1969), all of which depicted young men and women being assaulted, tortured and killed by monstrous older figures. In fact, it could be argued that the young British horror film-makers had rather more to react against than their American counterparts given that they were working within a horror tradition that – in the form of Hammer's horror films from the late 1950s onwards, at least – had, to a certain extent, a paternalistic quality to it, with father figures like Van Helsing in *Dracula* and *Brides of Dracula* and Father Sandor in *Dracula – Prince of Darkness* (1965) authoritatively directing the battle against the forces of evil.

In contrast, American horror films, and for that matter Italian horror films as well, had tended to lack such authority figures.

Placing films like *Psycho* and *Night of the Living Dead* within broader generic, national and international contexts reveals that changes occurring in the horror genre during the 1960s were both more pervasive and more gradual than sometimes supposed. A key moment here seems to be the late 1950s when horror production became internationalised and more attached than before to a particular kind of exploitation cinema, with this in turn leading to new forms of horror. Seeing the genre in this way necessarily complicates any sense of 1970s horror as marking a clean break with the practices associated with classic horror. Instead of thinking, say, of Hammer horror as antithetical to the sort of horror represented by *Psycho*, we can now start making connections, through a comparison of the films themselves and the contexts of their production and consumption.

One might also consider here other ways in which earlier forms of horror have been seen as distinct from horror of the 1970s. Much critical writing on modern horror has argued that 'classic' horror narratives are characterised by closure and reassurance, with the monster ultimately destroyed, normality restored and the audience left untroubled by the horror experience. For example, Andrew Tudor has distinguished between what he terms secure and paranoid horror in a manner that can readily be mapped on to a classic/ modern distinction:

> In secure horror the powers of disorder are always defeated by expertise and coercion, the genre's world authorities – whether those of science or of the state – remaining credible protectors of individual and social order. . . . In contrast, doubt is everywhere to be found in paranoid horror. Here, human actions are routinely unsuccessful, order far more precarious and boundaries between known and unknown rarely as clear as they might at first seem.

> (Tudor, 1989, pp.214–15)

But to what extent are 'classic' horror films actually defined through narrative closure? A survey of them reveals that it is often quite hard to find many straightforwardly attractive or positive authority figures. Possible candidates, including Van Helsing in Universal's *Dracula* (1931), Karl Brettschneider in *The Vampire Bat* (1933), Dr Garth in *Dracula's Daughter* (1936) and Dr Judd in *Cat People*, tend to be undermined or compromised in some way or other, and even when they either kill the monster or are involved in its defeat, this is rarely figured as a triumphant victory. Instead there is often something arbitrary about the conclusions of horror films from the 1930s and 1940s, as if the ending has been tacked on once the film's requisite running time has been reached. In part, this might have something to do with the fact that in many instances film-makers, and audiences, suspected that the monster would return in the next film in the cycle and therefore were not particularly committed to the concept of final destruction, but in part it also related to the very loosely-structured narratives that so often featured (and continue to feature) in the horror genre. In other words, while successful human intervention was usually present within a classic horror narrative, it is not clear that the fact of that intervention was in itself significant so far as an audience's response to the film was concerned. Certainly the films themselves often seemed more concerned with producing suspense, terror and pathos than they were with choreographing scenes of reassurance. It follows that perhaps classic horror cinema was not as obsessed with the protection of social authority as sometimes believed. Even Hammer horror films of the late 1950s and early 1960s, which are usually classified as 'classic horror' (although Isabel Cristina Pinedo has suggested that they represent an inter-mediary stage in horror history) contain numerous examples of the failure of authority, so that alongside the triumphant victories over evil in *Dracula* and *The Hound of the Baskervilles* (1959) exist the weak neurotic men featured in, among others, *The Mummy, The Man Who Could Cheat Death* (1959), *The Two Faces of Dr Jekyll* (1960) and *The Gorgon* (1964). (On Hammer, see Hutchings, 1993a; Pinedo, 1997.) One wonders whether it is just the age of some of these films that make them appear safe to us now in comparison with more recent horrors, and that we have forgotten both how shocking and how surprising some of these old horror movies were on their initial release.

So where does this leave the concept of 'modern horror'? Inasmuch as it is predicated on a clear-cut distinction from something called 'classic horror', it becomes decidedly problematic. Clearly both 'classic' and 'modern' function as abstractions that do not do full justice to the variety of horror production apparent at any given moment in genre history. To a large extent these abstractions were first generated by horror film-makers themselves. The generational theme that undoubtedly runs through much of post-1968 horror involved stressing and exaggerating 'the sins of the father' in order to underline the suffering of the young. From this perspective, the Boris Karloff impersonation at the beginning of *Night of the Living Dead*, for example, or the casting of an aged Karloff in *The Sorcerers* and *Targets* become emblematic, self-dramatising expressions of a new youth-centred approach to horror rather than objective statements about the nature of the old horror. It is only when later critical accounts of horror history take up these essentially youthful pro-vocations that they are transformed into something approaching orthodoxy.

The idea that modern horror erupts explosively into a staid and reactionary horror establishment – whether this be at some point in the 1960s or in the 1970s – is thus revealed as an overly dramatic version of horror's historical development, one that often obscures the various micro-histories, both cyclical and national, that comprise a broader genre history. What is needed instead is an approach that can give us a sense of gradual and uneven change, of the ebb and flow of the genre as it adapts in various ways to shifts in the industrial and social circumstances of its production. This in turn can lead to a more balanced and grounded understanding of how any sector of the horror genre is distinctive and special. In the case of horror in the 1970s, this involves considering how, why and where particular types of horror emerged during that decade, and how these types related both to each other and to earlier forms of horror.

THE QUIET BEFORE THE STORM? THE EARLY 1970S

There are a few moments in the history of horror when no one brand or type of horror film is dominant in the market place and consequently when horror production itself becomes even more varied than usual. The late 1960s and early 1970s is such a moment, and perhaps the most interesting example of this in horror history. During this period Hammer, although still active, was no longer the market leader it once had been, and while *Night of the Living Dead* and *Rosemary's Baby* had been commercially successful, neither had generated a cycle of similar productions.

What one finds in the years between 1968 and 1973 is an unruly but intriguing mix of different horror approaches and styles issuing from a range of national contexts. So in Britain, as already noted, there are a series of 'anti-father' horror films, coming in both gothic and contemporary forms, with the father in question often associated with old-school Hammer horror, along with some comedy-horror films – such as *Theatre of Blood* (1973), *The Abominable Dr Phibes* (1971) and *Dr Phibes Rises Again* (1972) – that engaged in playful terms with generic conventions. (For a discussion of the 'anti-father' films, see Hutchings, 1993a, pp.159–85; for a discussion of the *Dr Phibes* films and *Theatre of Blood*, see Benshoff, 1997, pp.208–17.) Meanwhile, in Italy, where gothic settings had gone out of fashion, directors Mario Bava and Dario Argento were developing the *giallo* horror-crime format in new and exciting directions, Bava with *Hatchet for the Honeymoon* (1969) and proto-slasher *Bay of Blood* (1971) and Argento with his 'animal' cycle – *The Bird with the Crystal Plumage* (1970), *Cat O'Nine Tails* (1971) and *Four Flies on Grey Velvet* (1971). In Spain, the werewolf movie *La marca del hombre-lobo* (1967) had inaugurated a cycle of films featuring Jacinto Molina (better known as Paul Naschy) as the lycanthropic Count Waldemar Daminsky, while the success of *La noche del terror ciego* (1971), in which the rotting corpses of the Knights Templar rise up to terrorise the modern world, also led to several sequels. In addition

Early 1970s camp horror: *The Abominable Dr Phibes* (1971) with Vincent Price as Phibes. Courtesy of MGM CLIP+STILL.

to this, Spanish horror gave us some memorable one-off projects, such as, for example, the vampire film *La novia ensangrentada* (1972), the psychological horror film *La campana del infierno* (1973), and the Spanish-British SF/gothic horror hybrid *Horror Express* (1972), a film which unlike many international co-productions managed to give the impression of being both authentically Spanish and authentically British.

In comparison with this European activity, American horror in the years leading up to 1973 was more tentative. There were considerably fewer American horror films being produced in this period than there were European ones, and most of these were isolated projects that, while often interesting in themselves, were clearly not going anywhere so far as the market or subsequent horror production was concerned. Examples included the Lovecraft adaptation *The Dunwich Horror* (1969), the occult thriller *The Mephisto Waltz* (1971) and the psychological horror film *The Other* (1972). (Critics sometimes lump in these films – and especially *The Other* – with later American horrors. However, as we will see, they are quite different from what followed, both formally and thematically.) The only discernible overarching preoccupation of American horror of the early 1970s involved the updating of the vampire story, with films like *The House of Dark Shadows* (1970, based on a popular television series), *Count Yorga – Vampire* (1970), *The Return of Count Yorga* (1971), *The Velvet Vampire* (1971), *Grave of the Vampire* (1972) and *Blacula* (1972), all featuring vampires on the loose in contemporary America, although even this quality was not specific to America but could also be found in European vampire films of the period.

This was a time characterised then both in Europe and America by a relative openness to new ideas and approaches. Much of this activity has since been obscured or overshadowed by subsequent developments in the genre, and especially by the increasing presence within horror of a particular type of American horror film dubbed as 'modern horror'. However, these horrors from the early 1970s should not be either simply subsumed into the horror to come or dismissed as rather tired examples of outdated generic formulae. Instead they represent distinctive achievements in their own right, offering as they do bold revisions of particular generic formats and conventions.

AUTEURS, FAMILIES AND THE APOCALYPSE

In the early 1970s a cluster of films appeared that, while distinct from each other in style and tone, did point the way forward to a different type of horror, one that would turn out to be more commercially successful and critically esteemed than some of the more established generic formats within the changing social and political climate of the 1970s. These films were *Last House on the Left* (1972), *Dead of Night* (1972), *The Possession of Joel Delaney* (1972) and *Sisters* (1973), and they were significant partly because of who directed them and partly because of the way in which they represented the family.

Horror auteurs

Three of these films marked the genre debuts of directors who would go on to make further significant contributions to the genre: Wes Craven, director of *Last House on the Left*, would also direct, among others, *The Hills Have Eyes* (1977) and the *Scream* films; Bob Clark, director of *Dead of Night*, would also make *Children Shouldn't Play with Dead Things* (1972), the inventive early slasher film *Black Christmas* (1974) and *Murder by Decree* (1979); and Brian De Palma, director of *Sisters*, would make, among others, *Carrie* (1976) and the controversial *Dressed to Kill* (1980). (Waris Hussein, director of *The Possession of Joel Delaney*, is the odd one out here; *Possession* was his only horror film.) In the next few years, other film directors would also commence what in many cases would turn out to be sustained and highly productive engagements with horror, notably Larry Cohen (*It's Alive* in 1974, *God Told Me To* in 1976), Tobe Hooper (*The Texas Chainsaw Massacre* in 1974, *Death Trap* in 1976, *The Fun House* in 1981) and David Cronenberg (*Shivers* in 1975, *Rabid* in 1977, *The Brood* in 1979).

Post-1972 US horror cinema can be viewed as marking the advent of the horror auteur-director. US cinema of the 1970s in general gave more opportunities to young film directors than it had before – notably, Francis Coppola, Martin Scorsese and Steven Spielberg all came to the fore in the 1970s – but horror was the only genre of the period to acquire its own customised 'movie brats' (to use the term applied by Linda Myles and Michael Pye to the new generation of film directors: Myles and Pye, 1979). Of course, there had been earlier film directors who had specialised in horror. One thinks here, to name but a few, of James Whale, Tod Browning, Erle C. Kenton and George Waggner from the 1930s and 1940s, and of Terence Fisher, Mario Bava and Roger Corman from the 1950s and 1960s. However, these figures had tended to be self-effacing industry insiders working in a variety of genres before ending up, usually by chance, as horror specialists; in occasional interviews they would often deprecate their own work and its possible cultural significance. By contrast, the new 1970s horror auteurs (of whom George Romero and the British film director Michael Reeves might be seen as late-1960s versions) had a much more emphatic presence both within the production process, with most of them writer-directors, and in the way the films were marketed and received by critics and to a certain extent by audiences as well. One of the ways in which horror got serious in the 1970s, it seems, was through its association with directors such as these who were wholeheartedly committed to the genre as a suitable vehicle for the expression of ideas and were willing to articulate this commitment in interviews and publicity material. The fact that many of the directors concerned were working independently of the Hollywood studio system further aided the impression of a kind of independence from traditional tastes and values.

Accordingly, the distinctive quality shared by *Dead of Night*, *The Possession of Joel Delaney*, *Sisters* and *Last House on the Left* is not their contemporary settings (which were hardly novel by this stage in horror history) nor in itself their critical focus on the family (it is easy to find earlier explorations of the family unit in horror), but rather their manifest desire to say something about contemporary society. *Dead of Night*, for example, is one of the few films of the early 1970s, horror or otherwise, to deal explicitly with the Vietnam conflict in its disturbing tale of a Vietnam veteran returning to his hometown as a zombie. *The Possession of Joel Delaney*, in which the spirit of a poor Puerto Rican possesses a wealthy young man, articulates what would become a key theme in 1970s horror (and also in the 1970s disaster film), namely the complacency and arrogance of the upper classes. *Sisters*, a psychological horror film about Siamese twins, offers itself as a critique of aspects of patriarchy (although the idea of Brian 'Dressed to Kill' De Palma as a 'feminist' director will undoubtedly cause some critical hackles to rise) while *Last House on the Left*'s relentless portrayal of the savagery lurking beneath the veneer of normality in its story of a middle-class family taking an awful revenge on their daughter's killers conveys a powerful sense of identity itself – individual, familial, national – being torn asunder.

Family horror, apocalyptic horror

'Family horror' is a key term in much critical writing about 1970s US horror and usually signifies films in which the monster comes from within the family (for example, the zombified son in *Dead of Night*, the monstrous baby in *It's Alive*) or comes in the form of a family (the cannibal families that feature in *The Texas Chainsaw Massacre* and *The Hills Have Eyes*) or infiltrates itself into a family (the evil children in *The Omen* and *The Godsend* or the demon that possesses the girl in *The Exorcist*). More specifically, the term is applied to those films that represent the family as a social institution, the prime function of which is to implant normative social identities (see Ryan and Kellner, 1988; Williams, 1996; Wood, 1986). Such films can be contrasted with other horror films concerned with the family that lack any obvious social dimension and which are more interested instead in exploring family relations in psychological terms – see the gothic films of Roger Corman or Mario Bava as examples of this from the 1960s, or the American film *The Other* from 1972. The family itself within 1970s US family horror is often interpreted then, by critics at least, as a microcosm of society, one which through its internal dynamics registers broader social problems. In the case of the 1970s, these problems have been related to the social divisiveness caused by, among other things, the Vietnam war, Watergate, the rise of feminism, the economic disruption of the oil crisis, and so on, with all these assaults upon traditional American values and ideals often figured in critical writing as a kind of miasma of social dissatisfaction which in some way or other infiltrates a wide range of cultural artefacts, not least horror films. If there is something wrong with the family in these films, the argument goes, that is because there is something wrong with America. This leads us to the idea of apocalyptic horror, for a characteristic of many of these films – and it is apparent in *Last House on the Left*, *Dead of Night*, *The Possession of Joel Delaney* and *Sisters* – is that they depict the collapse or destruction of the family (and, implicitly, of society as well), with much of the force of that destruction coming from within.

There are problems with thinking about horror in this way. For one thing, there is the question of how precisely these horror films relate to the social context of their production, especially given that most of the social events and trends seen as influencing the films do not feature explicitly within the films themselves. (*Dead of Night* is an exception in its explicit referencing of Vietnam.) In response to this problem, there is a tendency, as there so often is in the interpretation of horror, to offer figurative readings of horror films, readings in which elements within films acquire significance beyond the literal demands of the narrative. So, for example, the cannibal family that features in *The Texas Chainsaw Massacre* has been interpreted as representing a degraded lower class whose situation 'allegorizes the destructive psychological effects of forced unemployment' while demonic possession in *The Exorcist* has been seen as 'a metaphor for fears about independent women and female sexuality' (Ryan and Kellner, 1988, pp.182, 57). As already discussed in Chapter 5, the danger of this type of approach is that it can lead to a reductive account of films, one which fixes the meaning of elements within films in a manner that denies the complexities and ambiguities involved in the narrative process. In the case of *The Texas Chainsaw Massacre*, for example, simply stating that the monstrous family is a metaphor for a particular social class can obscure both the dramatic purposes served by the family and the ways in which the film's attitude towards it develops in the course of the narrative in a manner not necessarily determined by any metaphorical or allegorical imperatives. *The Texas Chainsaw Massacre* might be 'about' class on some level but there is so much more to it than this. As we will see in the next section of this chapter, the same applies to *The Exorcist*.

There is also the question of how this way of thinking about horror deals with notions of pleasure. If, as some critics have argued, 1970s family and apocalyptic horror films illustrate in various ways a sense of social crisis, why should audiences have paid money to experience what should by any measure have been depressing or upsetting? An assumption here appears to be that the primary yield of these films is ideological, that they are seeking either to reinforce a threatened social order or to question it. From this perspective, any pleasure afforded by horror becomes suspect, a deceptive veneer behind which ideology works, and those audiences who thought they were going to see horror films just for the purpose of entertainment are revealed as being unaware of the real reasons for their behaviour, as being in effect the dupes of ideology. This is a rather stern view of the horror genre and it has led to equally stern judgements about particular 1970s horror films based upon whether the films in question can be seen as either politically progressive or politically reactionary.

PROGRESSIVE AND REACTIONARY HORROR

Robin Wood's article 'An Introduction to the American Horror Film' – which first appeared in 1979 and, as a sign of its influence, has been reprinted several times since – sets out very clearly the possibilities within horror for both a progressive and a reactionary engagement with political and ideological issues (Wood, 1984). For Wood, horror's progressiveness lays in 'its potential for the subversion of bourgeois patriarchal norms', especially those norms associated with the family unit (Wood, 1986, p.191). This usually involves films exhibiting a degree of sympathy with and understanding of the monster, with this in turn leading to some form of critique of the social repressiveness of which the monster is a product. In other words, normality itself is called into question by the progressive horror film. In contrast, the reactionary or conservative character of horror lies in the tendency of some films to hold the monster at arm's length, so to speak, presenting it as an entity that is 'simply evil' and thereby fully endorsing social norms. This distinction between progressive and reactionary horror is not just an evaluative one. It also has implications for the way we think about horror history, with modern horror – i.e. 1970s horror – often seen by critics as more open to the progressive approach than its 'classic' predecessors.

Wood is too astute a critic to allow the progressive/reactionary distinction to become schematic, and his analyses of individual horror films are always sensitive to ambiguity and contradiction. However, his attempt to connect an understanding of horror with a concern for social justice begs some important questions both about the nature of horror films themselves and about the kinds of effect they might have on audiences. To illustrate this, let us take two examples of what might be seen as progressive 1970s horror films, *It's Alive* and the British-produced *Death Line* (1972). Both offer narratives in which the monster – the baby born to a 'normal' couple in *It's Alive*, the cannibalistic tunnel-dweller in *Death Line* – are at certain points treated with some sympathy, with this often combined with an unsympathetic treatment of the forces of normality. In *It's Alive*, this is achieved not so much through the representation of the monster itself (which remains off-screen for most of the film) but rather through its father's gradual acceptance of the monster as his own child. In *Death Line*, the sympathy largely derives from the monster's distress over the death of his mate and his desperate and rather poignant attempts to communicate with his female captive. In each case, it is possible to locate these monsters within a broader context of social repression. In *It's Alive*, this has to do with the family itself as a repressive institution, while in *Death Line* the context is more obviously economic, with the tunnel-dweller the descendent of workers trapped by a fall-in and abandoned by their employers because it would have been too expensive to rescue them. (On *It's Alive* in these terms, see Wood, 1986, pp.98–102; Williams, 1996; see Perks, 2002 for a discussion of *Death Line*.)

However, do such films necessarily lead us to an enhanced awareness of how repressive our society is? While the monsters might be viewed sympathetically in some scenes, in other scenes they remain – for want of a better term – monstrous, i.e. violent, disgusting, scary, killing innocent people and, in the case of *Death Line*, eating them as well. Wood himself acknowledged that this sense of the monster as dangerous and ugly was a constitutive feature of the horror genre, but for him horror films are progressive 'precisely to the degree that they refuse to be satisfied with this simple designation' (Wood, 1986, p.192). The implication here is that horror is a genre wholly dependent on inherently repressive categories of Otherness that relate directly to equally repressive social categories of Otherness. It follows that in a just and free world, a world in which groups are not repressed or marked as Other, there would be no horror. The progressive horror film emerges from this as a kind of anti-horror film, a film railing against the genre to which it belongs. This might explain why one occasionally detects in Wood's critical writing a certain disappointment that ultimately these films fail to reject the trappings of horror and become instead another kind of cinema, one that is revolutionary and genuinely oppositional. As Wood notes of what he sees as the 'progressive' work of Larry Cohen, 'the "thinking" of the films can lead logically only in one direction, toward a radical and revolutionary position in relation to the dominant ideological norms and the institutions that embody them, and such a position is incompatible with any definable position within mainstream cinema' (Wood, 1986, pp.101–2).

Such an approach can sometimes find it difficult to explain why people actually might enjoy horror films. Wood's description in 'An Introduction to the American Horror Film' of his disturbing encounter with a fun-seeking audience for *The Texas Chainsaw Massacre* has already been discussed in Chapter 4 of this book. In contrast to that kind of wild response, one presumes that the ideal response to a progressive horror film would involve a reasoned understanding of what the film was 'really' about. Meanwhile a reactionary horror film would encourage and/or reinforce an audience's acceptance of social repressiveness. It seems from this that horror is always deadly serious. Fun does not enter into it.

As a previous chapter in this book has indicated, trying to predict how an audience will respond to any film is always a fraught, uncertain business. Bearing this in mind, the politico-ideological readings of horror proposed by Robin Wood and other critics start to look less like observations of what the genre is actually doing – something that, in terms of audience response at least, is far from clear – and more like discursive claims for the genre issued from a broadly left-wing position. It is an approach that seeks out sites within culture that can be seen in terms of ideological resistance, and in post-1972 horror, a type of horror which undoubtedly contains some elements of social critique, it finds an object amenable to the sort of analysis in which it wishes to engage. It follows that while the readings of films that have emerged from this approach have proved both powerful and influential, they are readings predicated on a partial view of the horror genre. The key question here therefore does not involve asking whether a film was progressive or reactionary but rather identifying who is asking the question and why.

Within the progressive/reactionary paradigm, there is, of course, room for disagreement. For example, while Wood considers *The Texas Chainsaw Massacre* in progressive terms, Andrew Britton condemns the film as reactionary (Wood, 1986; Britton, 1979, p.41). But one can also step back from this approach and see horror in different ways. In the case of both *It's Alive* and *Death Line*, one could speculate that an audience, rather than taking from the films an enhanced and potentially political awareness of social repression, would leave with a more amorphous and emotional sense of sadness over the monster's clearly not fully meriting its ultimate fate. In other words, they would have engaged with the films in literal terms rather than poking beneath the surface looking for metaphorical or symbolic resonances. From this perspective, the films' negative portrayal of many aspects of the 'normal' world would, in part at least, function in the interests of producing scenes of pathos which in themselves would not necessarily have any ideological significance. Of course, whether audiences do actually respond either in this way or in the way implied by Wood's approach is a moot point. What is clear, however, is that the films themselves are characterised by a certain ambiguity that facilitates different interpretations of them. Wood himself commented on what he saw as horror's inherent ambivalence both to normality and the monster, observing that 'central to the effect and fascination of horror films is their fulfilment of our nightmare wish to smash the norms that oppress us and which our moral conditioning teaches us to revere,' although he never really considered the extent to which this quality might relate to, or perhaps undermine, any hard-and-fast distinction between progressive and reactionary horror (Wood, 1986, p.80).

This has implications for the way we think about those horror films dubbed reactionary. Two such films singled out for particular opprobrium by critics favouring the ideological approach are *The Exorcist* and *The Brood*. So far as the former is concerned, Regan's possession in *The Exorcist* has often been viewed as a condensed and coded representation of youthful rebelliousness at a time when traditional values were being brought into question by the younger generation, with Regan's gender also potentially aligning her with a concurrent feminist rejection of patriarchal definitions of femininity. Accordingly, as her possession develops, Regan finds herself under the increasing scrutiny of male authority figures, first doctors and psychiatrists and then priests. This culminates with an exorcism – which at one point involves a priest punching the little girl repeatedly in the face – in which Regan's rebelliousness, and implicitly all the social disorder she represents, is contained and effaced, with this containment shown, in true reactionary style, as a good and necessary thing.

However, such a reading fails to take account of the fact that every male authority figure in the film is either discredited or killed in the course of the narrative, and that Father Karras's climactic heroic sacrifice, when he calls the demon into himself and then commits suicide, is as much an expression of his own despair as it is an assertion of religious (or patriarchal) authority. (See Clover, 1992, for a discussion of the film in these terms.) As another aspect of this ambivalence to male authority, clearly a pleasure, or potential pleasure, offered by *The Exorcist* is seeing such authority figures humiliated and punished. (See Chapter 3 for a discussion of Regan's encounter with a psychiatrist.) Within what some consider a reactionary project, this might well be a perverse pleasure, but it is a pleasure nevertheless. From this perspective, the film's ending, far from being an unproblematically triumphant restoration of patriarchal repression, is a tentative and open conclusion that simply restores Regan to the fatherless family which, according to many critics of the film, was the main problem being addressed by the film in the first place.

David Cronenberg's *The Brood* has been described by Robin Wood as 'the precise antithesis of the genre's progressive potential' in its 'projection of horror and evil on to women and their sexuality, the ultimate dread being of women usurping the active aggressive role that patriarchal ideology assigns to the male' (Wood, 1984, pp.194–5). The female in question is Nola who is capable of giving physical shape to her rage by producing, via parthenogenetic means, monstrous children who do her murderous bidding. Nola's reign of terror is eventually concluded when her estranged husband strangles her, although a coda reveals that Nola's daughter is beginning to show signs of her mother's 'affliction'. The ideological message could not be clearer, it seems. Women existing apart from male authority are dangerous, and defensive male violence against them is therefore justifiable.

Or at least that is one interpretation of the film. However, as with *The Exorcist*, one can readily find elements within *The Brood* that ameliorate or downright contradict its apparent status as reactionary text. Most notable here is the performance of Samantha Eggar as Nola, who emerges as a far more charismatic figure than any of the unremittingly dull representatives of normality in the film. In much the same way as *The Exorcist* invites us to enjoy the destruction of normality in a manner not necessarily reversed or contained by a supposedly authoritative conclusion, *The Brood* too gives us space to enjoy the displays of Nola's power and perhaps come to some understanding of her rage at a world that appears to have exacerbated her problems. The famous scene in which she reveals her external womb to her husband can be seen as marking a disgust at female reproductivity, with the husband's appalled reaction meant to cue in an equivalent response from the film's audience. But the scene can also be viewed as marking a fascination with bodies – male and female – that underpins much of the director David Cronenberg's work, in which case the reaction of the husband, who is not presented as a particularly appealing character, is not our reaction. Again there is an ambiguity here, an interpretative room for manoeuvre, which makes it hard to fix the film once and for all within any particular evaluative category.

MAKING HORROR PUBLIC

As should by now be clear, any characterisation either of modern horror or of 1970s horror as a totality is bound to be schematic. A more modest claim that might be made for one particular section of 1970s horror, and especially – but not exclusively – US production, is that it develops a sense of horror as existing in relation to public domains and social institutions. To a certain extent, this quality can be related back to some SF/horror monster movies from the 1950s which depicted various agencies of the state mobilising to fight the monster (see, for example, *Them!* and *War of the Worlds*), but it takes on a character of its own during the 1970s. Repeatedly in 1970s horror, private, domestic and familial dramas are connected with contemporary institutions, be these state, military, legal, scientific or media-related, but without the dramas being wholly subsumed into those institutions (which is what often happened in 1950s monster movies). This is already apparent in *Night of the Living Dead*, a film that contrasts the private tribulations of the characters trapped inside the house with public events such as television broadcasts and the climactic activities of the posse. (In contrast, *Rosemary's*

Baby shows little interest in moving Rosemary from her domesticated world into any more public arenas, with this perhaps helping to explain why *Rosemary's Baby* does not serve so well as *Night of the Living Dead* as a forerunner of 1970s horror.)

Numerous historians of the horror genre have pointed to the ineffectiveness and inadequacy of social institutions in 1970s horror in comparison with earlier types of horror. But a more pointed comparison would focus on the fact that such institutions, and associated public ceremonies and events, are present at all in 1970s when they were generally absent from what had gone before in the genre, and that these provide a focus for realism within the films concerned. One thinks here of the documentary-like renditions of both hospitals and churches in *The Exorcist*, of the world of politics conjured up by *The Omen* and the world of big business in *Damien – Omen 2* (1978), of the opening hospital scene in *It's Alive*, and of the medico-scientific institutes that feature in David Cronenberg's *Rabid* and *The Brood*. In all these cases, scenes of possession, Satanism, mutation and monstrosity are located within a familial context but those families in turn are put into public spaces. This also applies for those 1970s films which lack any obvious reference to social institutions, notably Wes Craven's *The Last House on the Left* and *The Hills Have Eyes*, but which explicitly present the family itself as a social institution, one that is neatly defined against its anti-social doppelganger, the family of monsters (with both Craven's films then working to destabilise any clear sense of Otherness).

This turn towards what might be thought of as a kind of limited social realism can be seen as part of a broader engagement with social reality characterising American cinema of the period. The sense certain 1970s films, horror and otherwise, offer of connecting with a realistically presented social world arguably provides the grounds upon which both the social critiques of film-makers and the allegorical interpretations of critics are founded. It is certainly the case that some 1970s films – and one thinks in particular of the work of Larry Cohen and Wes Craven – contain social-critical elements, but it is equally certain that other films, and not just the ones dubbed reactionary by critics, seem indifferent to such things while still maintaining some kind of connection with notions of the public and the social.

Take *Audrey Rose* (1977), for example. This tale of reincarnation has not achieved much prominence in critical writing on 1970s horror cinema, probably because of its quiet self-effacement (no *Exorcist*-style vomiting or other vileness here) and the fact that it was made by Robert Wise, a director very much of the old school whose previous credits included not just *The Haunting* (1963) but also *West Side Story* (1961) and *The Sound of Music* (1965). It might be related to the 'monstrous child' cycle of films, although Ivy, the child in question, is neither evil (like Damien in *The Omen*) nor possessed by evil (as is Regan in *The Exorcist*). Instead she is, or appears to be, the reincarnation of Audrey Rose, a child who was burned to death in a car crash and whose spirit is tormented by her memories of that terrible demise. The ensuing struggle between Ivy's parents and Audrey's father over control of Ivy might be read as either expressing a reactionary hostility towards children found elsewhere in the genre, a hostility symptomatic of a broader anxiety about youthful rebellion, or in a more progressive manner revealing and criticising such hostility. The latter of these readings is probably most supportable – the innocence of both Ivy and Audrey makes it hard to blame either of them for anything – but even this way of seeing the film arguably distorts it in an attempt to make it fit into a model of 1970s horror cinema predicated on notions of social critique.

A useful comparison here is with an earlier Robert Wise film, *The Curse of the Cat People* that he, co-directing with Gunther von Fritsch, made for producer Val Lewton in 1944. There are clear narrative parallels with *Audrey Rose*. Both feature families in which a sole female child is troubled by spirits from the past – the ghost of Irina in *The Curse of the Cat People* and Audrey's spirit in *Audrey Rose* – and in which rational fathers are less sympathetic to the child's plight than their more intuitive mothers. One key difference between the two films is that in *Curse* the child survives while in *Audrey Rose* she dies, but perhaps a more important difference so far as understanding 1970s horror cinema is concerned relates to the ways in which these narrative resolutions are reached. In the case of *Curse*, the family moves towards a kind of 'cure', both for the child and itself as a unit, via its own internal psychological dynamic. In the case of *Audrey Rose*, by way of a contrast, everyone goes to court and from there to hospital. The trial of Audrey's father for kidnapping Ivy becomes a public forum for a discussion of reincarnation, and this in turn leads to an extraordinary public demonstration of hypnotic regression as Ivy becomes Audrey Rose and then dies in front of a shocked audience witnessing the event through a one-way mirror. Throughout the film Wise has repeatedly filmed Ivy through windows with her hands pushed up against the glass. On one level, this clearly relates back to Audrey's death when she was trapped behind glass in the burning car. But it has also given us a sense of looking in on this family from outside, and of Ivy in particular being on public display, in a manner that is disturbingly literalized in the final hypnosis scene. The outcome is that while the child in *The Curse of the Cat People* has been cured in private, Ivy has died very publicly in front of an audience.

It seems from this that *Audrey Rose* fits into certain trends within 1970s horror without being in any obvious way 'about' anything, least of all social repression. While some 1970s film-makers undoubtedly used horror's new public dimension to make points about society, other film-makers, like Wise, appear to have approached it more in terms of the formal and stylistic challenges it offered, with horror's new 'realism' functioning here more as an innovation designed to update and refresh the genre than as an example of political practice. Seeing 1970s horror in this way gives us perhaps a clearer sense of its variety, enables us to understand in more detail the different uses to which new subject matters and new approaches are being put in the genre, and also facilitates some international connections and comparisons. For example, the 1970s horror work of British director Peter Walker, whose films included *Frightmare* (1974) and *House of Whipcord* (1974), engages with British social institutions in a manner comparable with American horror cinema, whereas the 1970s horror films of Italian director Dario Argento studiously avoid anything even vaguely approaching a sense of social reality. (For pertinent discussions of Walker, see Chibnall, 1998; Hunt 1998, pp.142–59.)

From about 1972 to about 1979, then, American cinema produced a series of horror films which played their dramas out in public and which, because of this, attracted interpretations that made a great deal of the ability of these films, or at least some of them, to make us think critically about the world in which we lived. This chapter has suggested that such interpretations, while undoubtedly important and influential, ultimately provide a limited, one-dimensional account of horror, and that while certain films might be seen as socially critical, questions remain both about whether audiences of the time actually experienced them in that way and about whether other films, perhaps even the majority, were even remotely interested in saying anything significant about society.

One thing remains clear, however. Things were about to change in the genre, and change in a way that still has implications for the state of horror today. Social comment, directorial artistry and challenging horror experiences were all out, misogyny, directorial ineptitude and repetitive generic formula were in. Or at least that is how some saw it. In any event, the slasher film cometh.

CHAPTER NINE

Slashers and post-slashers

Please don't kill me, Mr Ghostface. I want to be in the sequel.

(*Scream*, 1996)

THE BEGINNING OF THE END

While this is the final chapter of this book, it is only final in the sense that *Friday the 13th: The Final Chapter* (1984, to date, the fourth in a series of eleven films) and *Freddy's Dead: The Final Nightmare* (1991, to date, the sixth out of eight films) are final, i.e. in a provisional and inconclusive way. The intention here is to review some of the key developments in the horror genre since the 1970s. Needless to say, doing full justice within one chapter to everything that has happened in horror during this period would be an impossible task. So instead the chapter will focus on one particularly significant horror format, namely the American slasher film. Critically derided and protested against on its first appearance in the late 1970s, the slasher has since acquired a certain status within horror production and horror criticism. One could go so far as to argue that the slasher format has provided the basis for much US horror production since the late 1970s and that, in terms of its influence at least, it is more important than some of the more critically praised 'progressive' horror films of the 1970s.

This chapter identifies the reasons for the slasher's importance (and for its notoriety as well) and traces the slasher's influence on horror production of the 1980s and 1990s. The chapter concludes with a discussion of a cycle of horror films sometimes referred to as the postmodern slashers (including *Scream, I Know What You Did Last Summer, Urban Legend* and their sequels), a cycle which, as I write this, seems to be winding down even as new developments emerge within the genre. This chapter offers itself then as a snapshot of a particular sector of the horror genre, a snapshot which captures certain patterns and trends but which is far from being the final word on a genre that, even as you read this, is changing and reinventing itself.

ORIGINAL SLASHERS

If nothing else, looking at the slasher film can illustrate how the status of particular cycles of horror production fluctuates over time. Few critics had anything good to say about the slashers – with the possible exceptions of *Halloween* (1978, usually seen as the film which inaugurated the slasher cycle) and *Dressed to Kill* (1980) – during the period of their greatest box-office popularity between the late 1970s and 1983–84. Their cheapness, crudeness and formulaic repetitiveness, along with their apparent pandering to un-sophisticated teenage audiences, led to their being seen as degrading experiences in much the same way as earlier types of horror (Hammer horror, for example) had been seen as degrading when they first appeared, degrading both in their reliance on scenarios of extreme violence and in their crass and dumb exploitative nature. In addition, however, the slasher's reliance on the stalking and terrorisation of women lead to a new charge, that of misogyny, with the films themselves branded as violent and pernicious reactions against feminism.

Clearly some of the negative reactions to these films did not emanate from the world of film criticism but rather related to feminist activity elsewhere, with this most evident in the public protests organised against *Dressed to Kill* (which, thematically and formally at least, is untypical of the slasher cycle as a whole). For film critics, and especially those on the left, the slasher too was often a reactionary and regressive development, especially in comparison with earlier social-critical US horror films. In particular, the slasher offered 'a conservative moralism regarding sexuality' which was itself just one part of a broader turn to the right that took place in American film and American society towards the end of the 1970s (Ryan and Kellner, 1988, p.191). However, from the 1990s onwards, books and articles started to appear, notable among them Carol Clover's *Men, Women and Chainsaws: Gender in the Modern Horror Film*, which questioned some of these readings, often from a explicitly feminist perspective. (See, for example, Clover, 1992; Dika, 1990; Trencansky, 2001). While not usually celebratory of the slasher, there was a willingness here to acknowledge that these films were complex and worthy of scrutiny, and that they might contain elements that had the potential to be progressive, with this especially the case so far as the representation of the female hero was concerned. (Some critics in the 1980s had also found value in certain slashers but only to the extent that they deviated from a formulaic norm; see, for example, Wood, 1986, pp.194–201. Clover is different in that she is attending to the formula itself.)

Identifying the reasons for this shift in critical attitudes is complicated by the fact that the term 'slasher', while widely used, is decidedly vague. Other terms have been deployed in relation to US horror of the late 1970s – the trade magazine *Variety* coined the term 'teenie-kill pic', Vera Dika has proposed 'stalker film', Roger Ebert uses the term 'women-in-danger films' – with particular films moved in and out of categories as seems appropriate (Dika, 1990; Ebert, 1981). Sometimes, for example, *Dressed to Kill* is included (as in Ebert) while in other accounts it is excluded (in Dika). The controversial rape-revenge drama *I Spit on Your Grave* (1978) features centrally in Ebert's article where it is linked with the likes of *Halloween* (which Ebert likes) and *Friday the 13th* (which he doesn't like), while Carol Clover deals with the film separately from the 'slashers' (and also includes films as slashers which have not been seen in that way by other critics, for example the *Nightmare on Elm Street* films: Clover, 1992). In comparison with this, Cynthia Freeland, in her book on the genre, defines the slasher in a less historical manner 'as a generic label for a movie with a psychopathic killer, usually a male, whose assumed blood lust drives him to a sort of extreme violence against women', a label which for Freeland covers films as diverse as *Peeping Tom* (1960), *Frenzy* (1972) and *Henry: Portrait of a Serial Killer* (1986) (Freeland, 2000, p.161).

Given this variety of labels and definitions, it is no wonder that Steven Schneider has suggested that the 'slasher' category is 'little more than a catch all' that lacks 'formal and historical specificity'. Nevertheless, the term 'slasher' is far more widely used – by film-makers, critics and, so far as one can tell, by audiences – than more specialised terms such as, for example, the stalker film. Even Schneider, for all his reservations about 'slasher' as a meaningful designation, offers a definition of the slasher, one which can function as a useful starting point: 'a horror film in which isolated psychotic individuals (usually males) are pitted against one or more young people (usually females) whose looks, personalities, and/or promiscuities serve to trigger recollections of some past trauma in the killer's mind' (Schneider, 2000b, p.74). The very looseness of such a definition, and indeed the vagueness of the 'slasher' term itself, is arguably its most valuable quality inasmuch as it can facilitate a more open, less proscriptive approach to this area of horror production than has sometimes been offered by critics. What is required is an approach that encompasses not only a sense of what elements slasher films – defined in the broadest sense – might have in common, but also a sense of how films like *Halloween*, *Friday the 13th*, *Dressed to Kill*, *Eyes of a Stranger* (1981), etc. are different from each other. Too often critical accounts of the slasher (or the stalker or the teenie-kill pic or women-in-danger movies), in their attempts to define clearly and precisely the films in question, end up stressing their formulaic and repetitive nature at the expense of an awareness of the distinctiveness of particular films or groups of films. Even for those accounts which seek to engage with the slasher as a complex and perhaps even progressive horror format, this can lead to a sense that these films are essentially the same, a sense remarkably similar to that exhibited by those unequivocally negative critiques of the slasher that view it simply as a mindless, artless and exploitative mass-cultural product.

The following discussion of some of the distinctive features of US horror films from the late 1970s and early 1980s seeks to strike a balance between seeing these features in terms of their pervasiveness and understanding the different ways in which they are deployed and inflected by film-makers. This will be in the interests of replacing the dull, monotonous thud of repetition frequently heard in writings about the slasher with an approach more attentive to detail, nuance and innovation.

Point of view

The slasher is generally seen as highly reliant on subjective camerawork, and in particular on a foregrounding of the killer's point of view. This emphasis is clearly present in the opening sequences of two key early slashers, *Halloween* and *Friday the 13th* (1980). In each of these, the killer's stalking of his victims is conveyed via point-of-view shots assigned to the killer. Our sense of seeing events through the killer's eyes is accentuated both by an unstable movement of the camera (a steadicam in *Halloween*, a shaky handheld camera in *Friday the 13th*) designed to convey a sense of the killer's walking, and by the way in which the victims, when first confronted by the killer, look directly at the camera. Again and again, not just in *Halloween* and *Friday the 13th* but also in numerous later slashers (and for that matter in earlier films that anticipated the slashers to come – for example, *Black Christmas* in 1974 and *The Eyes of Laura Mars* in 1978) an audience seems to be positioned, so far as their vision is concerned at least, in the place of the killer.

Having said this, the significance of this use of point of view is far from clear. One influential approach is to argue that such a technique encourages an audience to identify with the killer and thereby gain a sadistic pleasure from his (or, less commonly, her) murderous acts. As Roger Ebert notes in his 1981 critique of the slasher, 'it is a truism in film strategy that, all else being equal, when the camera takes a point of view, the audience is being invited to adopt the same point of view' (Ebert, 1981, p.55). Ebert links this with what he considers the poorly characterised or uncharacterised killer in most slashers (although he excepts *Halloween*, a film he likes, from this charge), and suggests that in such cases the killer becomes a mere vehicle for the audience's disturbing sadistic and/or misogynist desires: 'the visual strategy of these films displaced the villain from his traditional place within the film – and moved him into the audience' (Ebert, 1981, p.56).

There are problems with thinking about point of view in this way, both generally and in terms of its specific application to the slasher film. As many film critics have pointed out, simply assigning any character in a film some point-of-view shots does not necessarily lead to an audience either empathising with that character or aligning itself in some way with his/her position in the drama. Nor do film-makers need point of view to encourage our sympathies with their characters. (See Robin Wood's analysis of the opening sequences of Hitchcock's *Psycho* in this respect where he argues that point-of-view shots are only used after the director has established an audience's sympathy for the character Marion Crane: Wood, 1989, p.308). It follows that point-of-view shots from the position of an unpleasant character (e.g. the killer in a slasher film) or an inhuman character or non-character (e.g. the shark in *Jaws*) do not inevitably induct an audience into a world of sadistic pleasure. In fact, such a technique could have exactly the opposite effect, for the sight of the victim seen close-up through the killer's eyes could encourage an audience's masochistic identification with the victim's position. As Kaja Silverman has noted (although not of the slasher film), 'the fascination of the sadistic point of view is merely that it provides the best vantage point from which to watch the masochistic story unfold' (Silverman, 1980, p.5). In addition, Carol Clover has offered the suggestion that the very obtrusiveness of 'the hand-held or similarly unanchored first-person camera works as much to destabilize as to stabilize identification' (Clover, 1992, p.45).

Regardless of whether one thinks slashers promote sadism, masochism or a mixture of the two, account also needs to be taken of other possible functions served by the slasher's use of point of view. It is quite clear that this particular cinematic technique, far from having the singular meaning ascribed to it by Ebert, often involves a complex and sometimes decidedly ambiguous approach to the material. For example, the fact that the reverse shot, the shot of the person looking which usually accompanies a point-of-view shot, is often withheld in slashers until near the end of the narrative merits further consideration. One reason for this withholding of the face of the killer is, quite simply, that a number of slashers have whodunnit structures that are dependent on hiding the killer's identity – for example, *Friday the 13th*, *Prom Night* (1980), *Terror Train* (1980) and *The House on Sorority Row* (1982). From this perspective, the killer's point-of-view shot becomes not so much a focus for our identification as it does a lure, a focus for our curiosity as we ask ourselves 'Who is looking, who is the killer?' (although a sceptical Robin Wood has suggested that this use of point of view merely acts as an alibi for an audience's sadistic indulgence in the acts of the killer: Wood, 1986, p.198). In line with this, point-of-view shots seem to function in many slashers as stand-ins for a monster who is either wholly or partly absent from the film's field of vision, with these point-of-view shots diminishing or disappearing entirely once the monster is visibly present.

Another function of the killer's point of view – and one that can be related to a masochistic effect – is to do with the creation of suspense. The presence of a point-of-view shot or shots marked as belonging to an unseen or partially glimpsed killer makes us all too aware that the killer is present, with this awareness not usually available to those potential victims being stalked by the killer. This disparity between our knowledge and the victims' knowledge can induce anxiety as we, helpless spectators, anticipate the killer's attack. This anxiety can be further accentuated through the slasher's use of false point-of-view shots, shots which look like the killer's point-of-view shots but which turn out not to be (with *Halloween* an especially assiduous exponent of this strategy). In all these cases, point of view, far from signalling a sadistic empowerment of the audience, has the potential to invoke that audience's subjection and helplessness either in terms of its lack of knowledge – about who or where the killer is – or in its submission to the film's suspenseful effects. The fact that the slasher killers themselves, once revealed, usually turn out to be ugly, sexually dysfunctional and deeply unattractive creatures with whom it is hard (although not impossible) to imagine anyone identifying makes it yet clearer that, so far as point of view is concerned at least, the visual methods by which some scenes of violence are dramatised do not necessarily lead to an audience being aligned, or aligning itself, with these murderous individuals.

Thinking about point-of-view techniques in this way opens up the question of what sorts of pleasure are on offer in this type of horror film. Is it about sadism, or masochism, or a sliding back and forth between these two forms of thrilling experience? Or are other elements at play here? Vera Dika, for example, has suggested that there is a certain 'gaming' quality in audiences' responses to the slasher as they, in a very public manner, engage with – often via the noisy responses that some critics find so disturbing when experiencing this type of cinema – and enjoy the ways in which the films seek to outwit and surprise them without 'cheating' on the slasher conventions (Dika, 1990). Point of view in this respect potentially offers a thrilling and unnerving destabilisation of spatial relations that is all just part of the slasher game.

Ultimately perhaps these issues can only be resolved via reference to the various ways in which audiences have negotiated their way through this terrain. It is no doubt true, as Carol Clover has pointed out, that someone who was identifying wholeheartedly with the sadistic killer in a slasher film could well experience some discomfort when the tables are eventually turned on the killer (or, as in *Friday the 13th*, when the killer is revealed to be a woman: Clover, 1992). But it is equally true that our sadistic spectator could just focus on those elements that suit his particular fantasy and ignore or not pay much attention to the rest. Similarly, the masochistic and the gaming responses could well involve audiences' actively shaping the experience of 'slasherdom', making it do whatever they want it to do. Given that the slasher film seems to offer multiple pleasures then (as well as, for some, multiple non-pleasures), it is therefore appropriate that its use of point of view is open to such different interpretations.

Death to teenagers

Robin Wood has suggested that what has been referred to as the slasher cycle falls into two categories – the 'teenie-kill pic' and the 'violence against women' film. However, even as Wood does this, he acknowledges that these categories are only partially distinguishable from each other and that there is considerable overlap between the two (Wood, 1986, p.195). As is the case with Roger Ebert's focusing on *I Spit on Your Grave*, one gets a sense here of more variety within the area designated as 'slasher' than is sometimes supposed. Nevertheless, the emphasis placed by Wood and others on teenagers is a significant one for an important feature of the slasher is that it introduces back into horror after some years absence teenagers as principal characters.

There had been an earlier cluster of teen-horror films back in the 1950s, including such titles as *I Was a Teenage Werewolf* (1957), *I Was a Teenage Frankenstein* (1957), *How to Make a Monster* (1958) and *Blood of Dracula* (1957). These had tended to adopt within a horror context the then popular 'juvenile delinquency' narrative format in which troubled teenagers rebelled against their own families and social conventions in general. In both *I Was a Teenage Werewolf* and *Blood of Dracula*, for example, the unhappiness of the misunderstood main teenage characters is expressed via their anti-social behaviour. Both become victims of predatory adults who initially seem friendly but who really wish to use the teenagers in scientific experiments that transform them into monsters. Eventually the teenage monsters turn upon and kill those adults and are themselves then killed. In the manner of other teen-angst movies of the period (notably *Rebel Without a Cause*), one is offered a moralistic emphasis on the need for social adjustment combined, not in an entirely cohesive way, with a sense of teenagers being treated unfairly by society.

Throughout the 1960s, teenage characters in horror films, when present at all, tended to be marginal. In the pre-slasher 1970s, the genre did see several attempts to engage with (or exploit) teenagers, with perhaps Hammer's *Dracula AD 1972* (1972) the most embarrassingly ineffective and Brian DePalma's *Carrie* (1976) the most significant. But these films rarely escaped the distant and rather patronising tone that had characterised much of 1950s teen-horror. When teenagers did finally return to the centre-stage in the late 1970s, it was in a context where they were subject to terrorisation and violence and where, according to some critics, they themselves were figured as causes for concern. Ryan and Kellner put this most bluntly in their negative take on what they term the 'slash and gash' or 'slice and dice' film: 'Young teens, especially girls, are shown engaging in "immoral" activities like sex and drugs. They are killed' (Ryan and Kellner, 1988, p.191). In comparison with the calls made by 1950s teen-horror for teenagers to adapt themselves to social norms, the slasher is here considered as a much cruder and more obvious form of moralistic instruction (Don't take drugs, don't have sex . . .) backed up with lashings of punitive violence (. . . or else you die!).

The obvious question that arises from looking at slashers in this way concerns why such a format should have proved so popular with teenage audiences. In their analyses of these films, Robin Wood and Ryan and Kellner argue that they are expressions of an unresolved and probably unconscious sexual guilt, with the hedonistic lifestyle of the teenagers in the films (and by extension in the audience) simultaneously seen as attractive and deserving of punishment. As Wood puts it, 'the satisfaction that youth audiences get from these films is presumably twofold: they identify both with the promiscuity and with the grisly and excessive punishment' (Wood, 1986, p.196; also see Ryan and Kellner, 1988, p.191). The picture offered here of unsuspecting teenagers willingly showing up in cinemas to swallow the bitter pill of repression is characteristic of the ideological approach to the horror genre both in its focus on social repressiveness and in its unwillingness to engage with pleasure as anything other than a deceptive lure that hides the true ideological import of media texts. In the face of such criticism – and in the interests not of saving the slasher from ignominy but rather of trying to work out more precisely what is going on in the films themselves – it is worth thinking about the ways the teenage characters themselves are presented. For one thing, it seems clear that these films make far more varied use of their teenage characters than Wood and others are prepared to acknowledge, and that the films' judgements about and treatment of these characters do not necessarily relate in some blanket-like way to their being hedonistic teenagers in need of discipline.

Saying that the slasher film – and especially its teenie-kill variant – deals in sexual guilt is all very well in this respect, but a review of the films reveals that guilt of a different kind is often present, notably in those films where a group of teenagers are guilty either of a criminal act or of an extremely unpleasant act, with the violence subsequently directed against those teenagers a direct consequence of, and punishment for, their own nastiness. One thinks here, for example, of *Prom Night*, in which some young children's cruel teasing of a classmate leads to her death, *Terror Train*, in which an astonishingly nasty student prank causes its victim to lose his sanity, *The Burning* (1980), in which another cruel prank leaves its victim hideously scarred, and *The House on Sorority Row*, in which the female victim of yet another extremely unpleasant practical joke ends up dead. (Post-*Scream* neo-slashers *I Know What You Did Last Summer* and *Valentine* both borrow this particular narrative format.) The killer in *Prom Night* turns out to be the brother of the dead girl avenging his sister's death, the killers in *Terror Train* and *The Burning* (and *I Know What You Did* and *Valentine* as well) are the original victims come back to exact their own revenge, while the son of the dead woman in *The House on Sorority Row* systematically kills the women responsible for the death of his mother. Teenagers here are shown to be guilty not of sexual or drugs-related mis-demeanours but rather of being inconsiderate, unpleasant people; their hedonism functions merely to underline their self-absorption and lack of consideration for others. Their terrorisation and deaths might seem excessive punishment for the original 'crimes', especially given that some of them are presented with a degree of sympathy, but nevertheless they are generally seen as deserving punishment of some kind. Interestingly in this respect, the characters left alive at the end of both *Terror Train* and *The House on Sorority Row* are the ones who, while involved in the original practical jokes, have since expressed shame and sorrow for their actions. Having a conscience and being penitent, it seems, leads – some of the time, at least – to survival.

The fact that in other slasher films – notably *Halloween*, *Friday the 13th* (and its sequels), and *Hell Night* (1981) – the teenagers are not guilty in this manner and yet are still victimised and killed might suggest that here we do have a case of characters being punished for their hedonistic lifestyle. Certainly films of this type often – but by no means always – make distinc-tions between sexually active teenagers and sexually inactive teenagers. (See the following section on the final girl for more on this.) So, for example, in *Halloween*, Laurie (played by Jamie Lee Curtis) is contrasted with her two female friends mainly through her lack of a boyfriend, while in *Hell Night*, the demure Marti (played by Linda Blair) is contrasted with Denise, who within a few minutes of entering the haunted house strips off and has sex with a man she has only just met. The fact that Laurie and Marti survive while the other characters die might well suggest that virtue – defined specifically as sexual abstinence – is being rewarded here and 'immoral' behaviour punished, with, as Wood has noted, the monster thus figured as an expression of repressive forces rather than itself being the product of repression (Wood, 1986, p.195).

But is this really how these films are meant to be received? Horror historian Andrew Tudor's comment that all the young women in *Halloween* are 'appealingly characterised' and that 'there is no sense that their activities are represented as inappropriate or immoral' could reasonably be applied to a range of these slashers, and even Wood acknowledges that slashers do not make any explicit condemnation of apparently immoral behaviour (Tudor, 1989, p.202; Wood, 1986, p.196). If there is condemnation and punishment here then, it seems to be implicit and locked away on a deep, hidden level. But before diving beneath the surface of the slasher in order to recover its apparent secrets, it is worth identifying what ostensible judgements the films make about their teenage characters. Is virginity or chastity in itself really the key to survival in this type of film and, as *Scream* subsequently asserts, does sex always equal death?

There is a case to be made for the idea that if young people are being punished in these films, they are being punished not for their pleasure-seeking ways but rather for their complacency. From this perspective, the difference between Laurie and her friends in *Halloween* or Marti and Denise in *Hell Night* is less to do with sexual activity and more to do with levels of watchfulness and resourcefulness. Laurie and Marti survive because they are more alert to their environments than other teenagers and, when faced with danger, are more adaptable. (For more on this, see Hutchings, 1996). Thus the sexual activity engaged in by teenagers renders them vulnerable not because of its 'sinfulness' but rather because it involves a diminution in their awareness of the dangerous world around them. This helps to explain why Jeff in *Hell Night*, who is presented as equally virtuous as Marti, dies while she lives: he might be virtuous but he is just not paying enough attention.

In both types of slasher, the one in which the teenagers are culpable of some crime or other unpleasantness and the one in which the teenagers are, so to speak, 'innocent', the danger they face tends to emanate from the past, either as the direct consequence of the past actions of the teenagers themselves or as something that relates to a past associated with the teenagers' community or location but of which they are not fully aware and for which they are not responsible. So in *Halloween* the killer Michael Myers returns to his home town of Haddonfield, in *Friday the 13th* teenagers at Camp Crystal Lake suffer because of something that happened at the camp back in the 1950s, and in *Hell Night* teenagers blunder into a house which too contains terrible secrets from a half-remembered past. It follows that if these films do have a message (and perhaps for some audiences they are just thrilling experiences which have no significance beyond the thrills), then it is not the decidedly negative 'Don't have sex, don't take drugs, etc.' – activities which are more incidental to the dramas than some critics suppose – but instead the urgent and arguably more positive and life-affirming injunctions to 'Take care!' and 'Watch out!' Take care because your actions, especially the nasty ones, can and will have unpleasant consequences (including your own death). Watch out because the world in which you live has secrets that can and will harm you. This quality of the films might well help to explain why audiences of the time (and audiences since) often express a certain impatience with, and take pleasure at the violent comeuppance of, those teenagers who blunder through slasher scenarios completely unaware of the danger they are in.

Having said this, it cannot be denied that much of the more graphic violence in these films is directed against female teenagers, and that many slashers – although by no means all of them – place a remarkable emphasis on the terrorising of women. The issue of whether the slasher is an intrinsically or at least predominantly misogynist horror format is therefore still one that requires some consideration.

Final girls

The fact that critical attitudes to the slasher movie have shifted somewhat and become less condemnatory since the early 1990s can in part at least be assigned to the influence of Carol Clover's book about the modern horror film *Men, Women and Chainsaws* and especially its conceptualisation of 'the final girl'. Clover's starting point was the earlier perceptions of the slashers as irredeemably misogynist films that presented the slaughter of young women for the entertainment of a predominantly male adolescent audience. For Clover, one of the most interesting features of the slasher seemed to fly in the face of this way of seeing it, namely the convention that it needed to be a woman who ended up fighting and defeating the monster-killer – for example, Laurie in *Halloween*, Alice in *Friday the 13th*, Ginny in *Friday the 13th: Part 2* (1981), Marti in *Hell Night*, or Katherine in *The House on Sorority Row* – and that the actions of this female would receive the audible approval of the slasher's audience. Clover dubbed this heroic female the final girl.

According to Clover, what separated the final girl from other women so far as her gender identity was concerned was her boyishness: 'her smartness, gravity, competence in mechanical and other practical matters, and sexual reluctance set her apart from the other girls and ally her, ironically, with the very boys she fears or rejects, not to speak of the killer himself' (Clover, 1992, p.140). Not unlike the killer, who for Clover was a similarly liminal figure, the final girl hovered uncertainly between masculinity and femininity, with this sense of a gender confusion carried over into the ways in which an audience, and especially a male audience, might have responded to the female hero. While Clover does not reject entirely the idea that the slasher offers some sadistic pleasures, she does argue that the male audience for this type of film is, in effect, sent on a pleasurable journey through what is felt as a masochistic and feminising (inasmuch as it is unmanning) experience, both through that audience's increasing empathy with the boyish final girl – 'a congenial double for the adolescent male' – and through its willing subjection to the shocks administered by the films themselves (Clover, 1992, p.51). What this suggests is that nothing is what it seems in the slasher, that a scenario in which a male killer (and, of course, not all slasher-killers are male) stalks and kills a female can involve males – both in the film and in the audience – being in some way feminised, and some women – especially the final girls – becoming masculinised to some degree.

The psychoanalytical nature of Clover's approach to the slasher brings some problems of its own. (For a detailed discussion of psychoanalytical approaches to horror in general, see Chapter 3.) For one thing, there is the question of whether it involves not just the privileging of the hidden and obscure over the manifestly obvious, but also reading too much psychoanalytical significance into particular details, for example the final girl's alleged boyishness. For another, there is the foregrounding apparent within it of gender at the expense of other types of difference (to do with class, race, etc.). Given that mainstream cinema frequently invites us to identify or empathise with characters who are different from us in some way – with this often involving a crossing of class, racial, generational and national boundaries as well as gender-specific ones – one has to wonder whether the slasher's apparent invitation to male spectators to step away temporarily from their gender identities is that special or distinctive. In addition to this, what are we to make of the evidence (which admittedly is largely anecdotal) that women formed a significant part of the audience for the original slashers?

These issues focus most of all upon the figure of the final girl herself, and in particular on the question of whether her characterisation is consistent across the range of slashers. In other words, to what extent is Clover's conceptualisation of the final girl an abstraction that serves certain functions within her account – notably to be the epitome of gender confusion – but which obscures a sense of how specific 'final girls' are different from each other? Consider in this respect the following candidates for 'final girldom': Laurie in *Halloween*, Alice in *Friday the 13th*, Marti in *Hell Night* and Katherine in *The House on Sorority Row*. (The first three of these films are cited by Clover; the fourth is one of the less well-known slashers.) Are they all boyish? Marti seems the most obvious example of this, with her masculine-sounding name and her ability to repair cars, a skill which ultimately saves her life. Laurie too has a gender-neutral name, and Jamie Lee Curtis, the actor who plays her, possesses a certain androgynous quality which has been exploited by some film-makers (notably Kathryn Bigelow in the thriller *Blue Steel*, 1990) but not, one feels, by John Carpenter, director of *Halloween*, for here Laurie remains, in visual terms at least, resolutely female throughout. It is interesting in this light that while Marti uses her skills as a mechanic to save herself, Laurie fights back with domestic implements – a knitting needle, a coathanger – more associated with femininity. Having said this, one thing that Marti and Laurie do have in common is that from the very beginning of the films in which they

The first final girl: Laurie Strode (Jamie Lee Curtis) in *Halloween* (1978).

appear they are separated out in a schematic way from other women in the film. This is apparent in their clothes, which are more modest than those worn by the other females, and in their abstinence from sexual activity. They are different, then, but this can be thought of as a difference between women rather than a difference that betrays or compromises the femininity of particular women.

Alice in *Friday the 13th* and Katherine in *The House on Sorority Row* are different again. Alice is not initially separated out from her fellow campers, either visually or in terms of her behaviour, and she only gradually emerges as the sole survivor/final girl. As with Laurie, it is hard to think of her in 'masculine' terms; even her climactic act of decapitating the killer with an axe resembles, in her facial expression and in her panicked movement, her performance of terror elsewhere in the film (and, as if to underline this, the use of slow motion here recalls the use of slow motion to depict the first female victim's terror in the film's opening sequence). In *The House on Sorority Row*, Katherine's difference from the group only really becomes apparent when she displays anxiety about her fellow sorority sisters' attempt to cover up the housemother's death. Her difference from the rest, and her ultimate survival, derives then from her moral status.

All these final girls share some qualities – especially watchfulness and resourcefulness – which in our culture and under certain circumstances can be viewed as masculine, and in their fight for survival they will often deploy knives and other stabbing implements that might be thought of as having phallic connotations (although of course this is debatable). But the danger in Clover's approach is that in order to establish a slasher scenario involving a gender disruption that then reaches out into the audience, she accentuates these 'masculine' elements when in many other respects these representations of women are more conventional than she is prepared to acknowledge. The idea of the 'damsel in distress' is a long-standing one in our culture, and not just in film; and the final girl, in her various forms, can readily be placed within such a category. Watchfulness and resourcefulness, especially when played out in the domestic settings of most slashers, can take on a feminine character. (For an earlier example of this, see 'persecuted women' films from the 1940s such as *Rebecca*, *Gaslight* and *Secret Beyond the Door*.) As for the violence of the final girls, and their willingness and ability to fight back, it is worth noting that this nearly always occurs in the context of the final girl's running away rather than arising from a conscious decision on her part to face the monster. (Compare her in this respect with the much more aggressive final girls who show up in the later *Nightmare on Elm Street* films.) Moreover, the final girl does not always succeed in defeating the killer and saving herself. In *Halloween* (and also in *Halloween 2*), Laurie has to be saved by Dr Loomis, while in *The House on Sorority Row* – in a climax that virtually repeats the conclusion of the early 1970s proto-slasher *Black Christmas* – the final girl collapses into sedated unconsciousness with the killer still active in the house in which she is trapped. Only Alice in *Friday the 13th* and Marti in *Hell Night* get to kill the killer, and in Alice's case her triumph is undermined by the sudden appearance – possibly in a dream – of Jason, son of the killer, while in Marti's case, having impaled the killer on some railings, she walks away exhausted in what turns out to be an understated conclusion. The conclusion in which Clover shows most interest, that of *Texas Chainsaw Massacre 2* (1986) in which the final girl swings a chainsaw around in victorious celebration, is untypical then of the way that slashers usually end.

This could help to explain why, for all the critical attention paid in the 1990s to the final girl, not many people seemed to notice her as a significant generic innovation at the time of the slasher's original popularity in the late 1970s and early 1980s. Although one can only take anecdotal evidence so far, my own recollection of seeing these films back then was that I was most taken, especially in the case of *Halloween*, by the shock tactics on offer which, in their attempts to make an audience jump, might have been decidedly mechanical but which also were frequently very effective. I'm sure I noticed that women were turning out to be the ultimate survivors in this new type of horror film, but this clearly did not register as that striking. Perhaps this was because I was able to relate these female characters back to female characterisation in earlier horrors – some of the 1960s gothic work of Mario Bava or Roger Corman, for example, or the 'persecuted women' films already mentioned. To a certain extent, the final girls' violence set them apart, but that violence was usually the panicked product of a much more conventional female terror rather than something that interrupted that terror in some surprising way.

It could be argued that Clover's influential reading of the slashers is not just retrospective but also revisionary, fixing as it does upon certain elements within the films and interpreting them in the light of subsequent developments in American film, particularly the introduction of the female hero into action films and thrillers – for example, *Aliens* (1986), the *Terminator* films (1984 and 1991), *Thelma and Louise* (1991) and *The Silence of the Lambs* (1991) – where previously they had been a marginal presence. Women in these films tended to be more emphatically aggressive, violent and – perhaps – masculine than their final girl predecessors. In retrospect, the slashers can be seen as anticipating or even inaugurating this change, but in themselves they are much more tentative ventures into emergent new gender roles in US cinema.

Another way of thinking about these films, one that is perhaps more connected with the original context of their production and consumption, is in terms of terror. The prime aim of these films is to scare the audience, to put the audience in suspense, to make the audience jump. As Clover herself has noted, this aim is a distinctive one in genre history. Beforehand, shocks had tended to be placed firmly within, and subordinated to, particular narrative structures. In the slasher, however, the delivery of shocks seems to become the main point of the film, with the narratives organised around the shock sequences rather than the other way round. Within such a context, the women in the films – and especially the final girl – become the prime vehicles for the expression of terror. No doubt this is because our culture provides numerous conventions for conveying female terror and relatively few for male terror: as Clover notes, 'Abject terror . . . is gendered feminine' (Clover, 1992, p.51).

Whether or not this makes these films misogynist either in intent or in effect is difficult to tell. While the negative responses to the slashers have tended to leave a historical trace – in the form of appalled reviews and in records of the protests against them – the responses of the audiences who made these films commercially successful are by now largely lost to history. It is all very well to say that an audience got sadistic thrills from the slasher or instead experienced the slasher in 'feminising' terms but, aside from some limited anecdotal evidence and in the absence of any substantial research on the slasher audience, it is hard to prove either way. In any event, and as already indicated in an earlier chapter, those audiences, so far as one can tell, are heterogeneous and generally unpredictable. Ultimately then, the slasher, far from being a bad object or perhaps even a good object, starts to look more enigmatic than might have been supposed. In all sorts of ways – in its deployment of point of view, in its representation of teenagers and women – it might seem perfectly straightforward, but a closer inspection reveals that this is far from being the case.

To a certain extent, this is true of horror cinema in general. Over the years, the genre has provoked a more polarised critical response than most other mainstream film genres, with critics either loathing or (more rarely) approving of horror. These responses have often focused on the possible effects of horror films on their audiences, on the nature of the horror audience, or the relation of these films to broader cultural concerns and issues. As has been the case with the slasher film, the films themselves have sometimes been obscured by these various attempts to fix once and for all the meaning and status of horror itself.

POST-SLASHERS

The slasher format changed significantly during the first half of the 1980s. While an emphasis on teenage protagonists being stalked and killed by a serial killer was retained, these 'post-slasher' films were more willing than their predecessors to embrace both supernatural themes and a self-reflexive humour. (I am indebted for the term 'post-slasher' to Conrich, 2003.) This was apparent in the various sequels to archetypal slashers *Halloween* and *Friday the 13th*, in which any vestigial sense of Michael Myers and Jason Voorhees being realistically motivated characters was firmly pushed to one side in favour of seeing them as supernatural or quasi-supernatural entities. But this change was most apparent in what, in commercial terms at least, would turn out to be the major US horror cycle of the 1980s, the *Nightmare on Elm Street* series of films inaugurated by director Wes Craven in 1984 in which child-murderer Freddy Krueger returns from the dead to stalk through the nightmares of his teenage victims.

This turn to the supernatural, especially when coupled with the jokiness of much post-1984 US horror, seemed to mark the definitive end of the 'serious' and 'mature' horror associated by some critics with the 1970s. As if to underline what appeared to those increasingly exasperated critics as an onset of generic mindlessness, many 1980s US horrors belonged to monster-franchises (notably Jason/*Friday the 13th*, Michael/*Halloween* and Freddy/*Nightmare on Elm Street*) that, according to some at least, were dependent on the production of repetitious, lowest-common-denominator panderings to an unsophisticated and undemanding teenage audience. Horror historian Paul Wells has argued that this type of production inaugurated the 'McDonaldisation' of horror, while Andrew Tudor has suggested that although earlier forms of horror had been dependent upon sequels, in 1980s horror 'it is as if the concept of a "sequel" – or, if you like, the process of "sequelling" – has itself become a major convention of the genre, a phenomenon fully understood and, more important, expected and embraced by a generically competent horror audience' (Wells, 2000, pp.93–7; Tudor, 2002, pp.106–7).

Of course, one can challenge the assumption made by much critical writing on this period that the films which make up the various horror franchises are all more or less the same, i.e. unimaginative reproductions of a commercially winning formula. If one takes the *Nightmare on Elm Street* cycle of films, for example, it is quite easy to find changes and innovations occurring from one film to the next. Perhaps unsurprisingly, the character of Freddy Krueger becomes more central as the cycle proceeds and is given an increasingly complicated backstory, and a story arc develops through the cycle that at any point requires, or expects, a knowledge of previous events in earlier *Elm Street* films. In addition, there are stylistic differences between the films – with, for example, *Nightmare on Elm Street 5: The Dream Child* (1989) more visually 'gothic' than its predecessors – and, perhaps, qualitative ones as well, with some of the films better made than others.

Of course, the question remains of whether differences like these (and comparable ones can be found in the other horror franchises of the 1980s) are of any significance. Clearly, for some critics they are merely superficial and dispensable tinkerings that fail to disguise the fact that essentially this is the same old formula being repeated yet again for gullible audiences. For others, notably the fan following for each of the franchises, such differences can be significant and can provide a basis for discussion of the achievements of the franchise in question. As we have already seen in this book, this sort of disagreement between critics and horror audiences is not uncommon in the history of the genre. Similarly, the strategy adopted by a number of critics of putting a distance between themselves and what is perceived as a exploitative, sequelized mass-cultural product (as well as the audience for such product) is a familiar one in horror criticism. It does not follow that because of this the horror fans will always be right and the anti-franchise critics always wrong; debates about the value of this type of horror film will no doubt produce a number of viable pro- and anti- positions (and, in any event, not all horror fans are supporters of the 1980s horror franchises). However, it is fair to say that the preponderance of sequels – highlighted in the 1980s by the practice of numbering them rather than coming up with a different title, as was the case with earlier horror sequels – among the 1980s post-slashers seems less of a problem for fans who, closer to the genre and its processes, are more prepared to embrace the idea of the sequel as a challenge to the franchise film-makers to develop the franchise in interesting ways, than it is for some critics who seem distressed by the very idea of the sequel itself.

So far as the values of the post-slasher are concerned, Paul Wells has suggested that the monsters in the *Friday the 13th* and *Nightmare on Elm Street* films

> *become the frisson in valueless worlds informed by boredom, inadequacy and the sense that nothing is surprising anymore . . . the real cynicism lies in the fact that there is no particular answer or response to the problem of the monster. Jason is anonymous and randomly brutal, Freddy is perverse, vengeful and petty, and yet there are no values, standards, ideals or traditions with which to challenge them.*
>
> (Wells, 2000, pp.96–7)

Here what is seen as the repetitious hollowness of the films produces a cynical black humour that is voiced most eloquently by Freddy Krueger as he cracks bad jokes while killing his teenage victims, and it also leads to a self-referentiality which Wells associates with the postmodern (more on which below). In other words, for Wells, these films do not engage in any meaningful way with social reality but instead provide little more than a series of empty frissons organised around notions of the chase.

Against this view of 1980s franchise horror, one might argue that some of the virtues promoted by the original slashers – namely the need to be alert and to be able to transform that alertness into physical defensive violence – are carried over into, and transformed by, the post-slashers. It is notable in this respect (especially in the *Elm Street* films) that the post-slasher final girls tend to be far more proactively violent than their slasher predecessors.

(See Trencansky, 2001 for a discussion of this.) One thinks here, for example, of Nancy luring Freddy Krueger into a series of home-made booby traps in the first *Nightmare on Elm Street* film and of Alice taking him on martial-arts style in *A Nightmare on Elm Street 4: The Dream Master* (1988); another iconic image in this respect is that of the heroine of *The Texas Chainsaw Massacre 2*, swinging a chainsaw around her head in celebration of her victory. No slasher heroine from the early 1980s sought out and delivered (or celebrated) violent retribution as emphatically as this. It is as if the movement away from the downbeat, low-budget realism of the original slashers to the more obviously fantasy-based settings of the 1980s post-slashers facilitated more extreme and stylised representations of the teenage responses to the threat posed by the monster.

Significantly, this is often coupled with a distrust of adult authority figures – especially parental ones – and a sense that, when it comes to a fight with Freddy or Jason, the teenagers are to all intents and purposes on their own. While the 1980s post-slashers usually lack 1970s-style references, coded or otherwise, to broader social issues and generally seem detached from any obvious (or obscure) political agenda, they do arguably offer their own teenage-centred version of a resistance to social norms. The key 1980s monster in this respect is Freddy Krueger, who in the course of the *Elm Street* cycle becomes the voice of monstrous parenthood, mocking the aspirations of the teenage protagonists in a manner comparable with that of the teenagers' own unsympathetic parents and emerging as a force against which the teenagers must constantly struggle in order to acquire a sense of self-worth.

At the same time, Freddy (along with some of the other 1980s monsters) has become a popular icon for the teenage horror audience, a kind of hero in his own right. To a certain extent, this popularity might be seen as reflecting a teenage nihilism and, perhaps, a conservative identification with the forces of social repression. However, there are arguably other less censorious elements at play here. It is certainly the case that not all the teenage characters in the *Elm Street* films are offered as identificatory figures; some are decidedly complacent and slow-on-the-uptake, and Freddy's attacks upon them could be seen, in part at least, as an expression of the knowledgeable teenage horror audience's impatience with such attitudes. In other ways, too, Freddy is presented as a knowledgeable figure, knowledgeable not only about teen culture and teen humour but also about the world conjured up by the films themselves. Many of his killings, which usually take the form of elaborate practical jokes, involve an inventive, self-reflexive play with a cinematic medium that, in Freddy's razor-tipped hands, is transformed into something decidedly pliable. Cinematic space itself becomes elastic, with sinister locations appearing from nowhere and other more familiar settings mysteriously vanishing; conventional notions of scale are altered by characters being made unfeasibly small or large; and modes of representation themselves can change (for example, in *Freddy's Dead: The Final Nightmare*, an unfortunate teenager finds himself trapped in a computer game). (For more on the *Elm Street* films in these terms, see Hutchings, 1996.)

Freddy's status as, in effect, a Master of Ceremonies presiding over a flaunting of the fictional nature of the drama has sometimes led to the *Elm Street* films being seen in terms of postmodernism where postmodernism itself is simply, and somewhat questionably, associated with self-reflexivity and pastiche. The problem with this (aside from the very narrow definition of postmodernism that it involves) is that throughout its history the horror genre has frequently laid bare its own fictional devices, either for the purposes of making fun of itself or for exploring and meditating on the appeal of fearful fiction. It follows that if the *Nightmare on Elm Street* films – and other knowing horror films from the 1980s – are different from what has gone before in the genre, this is probably a relative difference rather than an absolute one. However, given that the term 'postmodern horror' has recently gained some currency in discussions of US horror of the 1980s and 1990s, with particular reference to the 'neo-slasher' *Scream* films, it is worth thinking further about how apt and useful such a designation actually is.

POSTMODERN SLASHERS?

In a recent essay, Andrew Tudor questions the usefulness of 'postmodern horror' as a critical term. While for Tudor, 'postmodern horror' might just about be acceptable as a somewhat arbitrary descriptive label for a number of recent horror films, the term brings with it theoretical and historical complications that can lead to our understanding of the films themselves becoming obscured. There is probably very little that could be added to Tudor's lucid account of the ways in which contemporary horror films should, and should not, be seen as postmodern (Tudor, 2002). What I want to do here, by way of a contrast, is introduce a somewhat simpler – although not entirely straightforward – use of the term 'postmodern', one proffered by my local multiplex cinema back in 1998 on a flyer advertising films to be shown in the coming week. On that flyer *Urban Legend* (1998) is described as a 'postmodern horror film'. Within the context of the intended readership for the flyer, the meaning of the label 'postmodern horror' here is perfectly clear and, needless to say, has absolutely nothing to do with postmodern theory; it means that *Urban Legend* is a film like *Scream* (1996). But what does the label 'like *Scream*' actually mean?

When *Scream* first appeared in 1996, it was generally seen as a smart and innovative piece of work that, paradoxically, owed much of its originality to its knowing references to earlier horror films, and especially the slashers of the late 1970s and early 1980s. Its famous opening sequence, in which an unseen, mobile phone-wielding killer tests his intended victim's knowledge of scary movies before slaughtering her in the style of the slasher, set the tone for a film in which the teenage protagonists quickly realise that they are trapped in a slasher-like scenario and, with varying degrees of success, attempt to use that knowledge to evade the killer.

This knowingness about genre conventions has often been credited to Wes Craven, the director of all three *Scream* films, whose association with horror goes back to the 1970s genre 'classics' *The Last House on the Left* (1972) and *The Hills Have Eyes* (1977) and whose *A Nightmare on Elm Street* helped to establish the self-conscious post-slasher format of the 1980s. In particular, his *A New Nightmare* (1994), the sixth film in the *Elm Street* cycle and the first since the original *A Nightmare on Elm Street* to be directed by Craven himself, has often been seen as anticipating the self-reflexivity to come in Craven's career. This is hardly surprising given that *A New Nightmare* features members of cast and crew from the first *Elm Street* film (including Wes Craven) playing themselves as they confront the 'real' Freddy Krueger. However, this form of self-reflexivity and self-awareness, which is extreme even by the standards of the *Elm Street* cycle, is quite different from that offered by the *Scream* films (although some interesting comparisons could be made between *A New Nightmare* and *Scream 3*, both of which are set in the Hollywood film industry). As Andrew Tudor has noted, the relatively realistic *Scream* and its sequels do not blur the line between film and film-makers in the manner of *A New Nightmare* (aside from a few in-joke cameo appearances – Craven himself in *Scream*, Jay, Silent Bob and Carrie Fisher in *Scream 3*), nor do they offer the distorted, dream-like worlds of the *Elm Street* films generally. Instead, the knowingness of *Scream* is primarily the knowingness possessed by its characters about the situations in which they find themselves (Tudor, 2002).

The phenomenal commercial success of *Scream* meant, inevitably, that sequels and other films hoping to benefit from that initial success – precisely by 'being like *Scream*' – quickly appeared, among them *Scream 2* (1997), *Scream 3* (2000), *I Know What You Did Last Summer* (1997), *I Still Know What You Did Last Summer* (1998), *Halloween: H20* (1998), *Urban Legend* (1998), *Urban Legends: Final Cut* (2000), *Cherry Falls* (2000), *Valentine* (2001), *Final Destination* (2000) and *Final Destination 2* (2003). Perhaps the most striking thing about these films (with, for obvious reasons, the exception of the *Scream* sequels) is that they clearly do not see 'being like *Scream*' as involving the inclusion of knowing references to old horror films. There is the occasional gesture in the direction of *Scream*'s genre-knowingness – for example, *Urban Legends: Final Cut* is set in a university film school, most of the characters in *Final Destination* are named after directors or actors associated with horror

The neo-slasher: Neve Campbell with Rose McGowan in *Scream* (1996). Courtesy of Miramax Film Corp.

cinema – but generally these films seek to relate themselves to the *Scream* franchise in other ways. Given that, for critics at least, it is precisely that knowingness about horror which defines *Scream*'s brand of postmodern horror, the apparent lack of knowingness in other films means that they tend to be seen as 'relatively straightforward stalk and slash', to use Andrew Tudor's phrase. But is this actually the case? Is there a way of linking these films together that does not end up relegating some of them to the ignominy of 'stalk/slashdom' and which can also cast a new light on the role played by genre knowingness in this type of horror?

While most of these films make use of slasher narrative formats, it is clear that in other respects they are very different from the original slashers. They have higher production values and the young actors who appear in them, many of whom are cast from American television, are considerably more glamorous. Characterisations, while still fairly schematic, tend to be more detailed and rounded than was the case with the slashers. (So far as the *Scream* films are concerned, the input of talented writer Kevin Williamson, who also wrote *I Know What You Did Last Summer* as well as creating the television series *Dawson's Creek*, is undoubtedly important in this regard; a case could be made for the *Scream* films reflecting his sensibility more than they do Wes Craven's.) There is less of a concern with the moral value of virginity (although, as noted above, the original slashers might not be as judgemental about this as has sometimes been supposed), with the young protagonists' sexual activities presented as a normal part of their lives, and with *Scream* and *Cherry Falls* mocking the idea of virginity's moral superiority. There is a greater focus on the interpersonal dynamics of groups of young people, with this in turn leading to a diminution in the status of the final girl figure. While these films still generally hold on to the idea of having a central female protagonist, she is rarely as isolated here as she is in the likes of *Halloween* and *Friday the 13th*. Instead, and this is particularly true of the *Scream* and the *I Know What You Did Last Summer* films, it is the young protagonists acting in concert with each other who manage to defeat the killer. (See Trencansky, 2001 for an interesting discussion of what she sees as the reactionary sexual politics of the neo-slashers in comparison with the original slasher movies.)

To a certain extent, the 'postmodern slasher' can be thought of as a reaction against the post-slasher franchises of the 1980s, most of which by the mid-1990s were showing distinct signs that they had outstayed their welcome at the box office. Refusing both the supernatural scenarios associated with 1980s horror (with the exception of the *Final Destination* films) and the focus on the monster – be this Freddy Krueger, Jason Voorhees or Michael Myers – as that which bound the film or films together, the postmodern slashers offered a different sort of franchise or cycle, one in which the common element linking the films was instead a whodunnit structure populated by predominantly young characters and often (although by no means always) organised around a particular concept of which the characters in the films had some awareness. In the case of the *Scream* trilogy, the films are linked by the idea that the activities of the killer will in some way or other reference horror movie conventions, in the two *Urban Legend* films, the connection is murders being done in the style of urban legends, in *Cherry Falls* the concept involves a serial killer only targeting virgins, while in the two *Final Destination* films it involves characters miraculously surviving accidents only to discover that Death is very unhappy about this situation and is seeking to rectify it by arranging further fatal 'accidents' for them. For those films that generated a sequel, in only one (*I Still Know What You Did Last Summer*) does the monster/killer in the first film survive into the sequel, as was usually the case with the 1980s franchises. Instead, what typically survive are a few of the young people and, more importantly, the concept. (Given that Death in the *Final Destination* films never actually appears, it could be argued that this figure functions more as a concept/narrative premise than it does as a conventional movie monster.)

It is the films which lack this kind of concept – most notably *I Know What You Did Last Summer* and *Valentine* – that are often seen, unjustly in my view, as relatively straightforward slasher throwbacks, even though such films usually possess enough of the qualities outlined above to render them, for marketing purposes at least, 'like *Scream*'. *I Know What You Did Last Summer* in particular is a striking example of 1990s horror in its subtle depiction of teenage disappointment and failure, and in this respect it is quite unlike anything one would find in the original slasher cycle. Even in those horror films which do rely on a concept of some kind, it is striking how intermittently that concept features. In both the *Scream* trilogy and the two *Urban Legend* films, for example, there are lengthy sequences in which no mention is made either of horror conventions or of urban legends and where an audience is clearly being invited to respond as they would to any suspense/horror sequence, i.e. with apprehension and, where appropriate, shock and surprise. What is perhaps the best-known sequence to emerge from this type of horror – the opening sequence of *Scream* – is therefore untypical of the cycle as a whole in its seamless merging of movie-referencing and 'stalk and slash'.

The idea that self-reflexivity is the primary distinguishing feature of this type of horror, while no doubt influential (and providing the basis for the designation of these films as postmodern), has led to a marginalisation of other elements in the films which are as important, if not more so, than their 'postmodern' qualities. For instance, it is not unreasonable to see these films as developing the emphasis made in the slashers and post-slashers on the need for the young protagonists – and by implication the young audience – to be alert. The whodunnit structures adopted by these films involve their characters having to probe into the past – either their own past or the past of their community – in order to make sense of the present and then be able to act decisively on the basis of the knowledge thus acquired. That these characters – and sometimes the killers too – are often more media-savvy than their slasher predecessors might be seen as bestowing a postmodern tinge on proceedings, but in an important sense this kind of awareness is the product of something more fundamental to the films, namely their commitment to producing more detailed, rounded and sympathetic characterisations of their young protagonists and their culture than was apparent before in teenage horror. To put it another way, *Scream*'s references to horror movies are arguably motivated not by some postmodern agenda but rather by the fact that the horror being referenced is a significant part of the cultural experience of its characters, an experience which *Scream* itself wants to take seriously. It is interesting in this respect that all these films bear the mark of teenage television drama – in the casting of some of their principals, in the input of TV writer Kevin Williamson into some of them, in their willingness to explore adolescent traumas – to the extent that it might make more sense to think of them not as 'postmodern horror' but rather as 'teenage soap horror'.

The outcome of this change in emphasis is twofold. First, it takes the 'gaming' experience offered by the original slashers on to another level. Back in the late 1970s and early 1980s, the game involved the film-makers trying to make an audience jump while the audience was constantly attempting to second-guess the film-makers. While the 1990s film-makers are still facing that challenge, they also present fictional worlds in which the characters themselves are often aware of the rules of the game and are using that knowledge in their attempts to survive. It might be 'the rules of the horror movie' in the *Scream* films or the rules involved in Death's plan in the *Final Destination* films (namely, you die in the order you were meant to die in the original accident but if you escape the next accident you go to the bottom of Death's list and if you can somehow arrange to experience clinical death and then be brought back to life you get removed from the list entirely and are safe). Even in those films where there are no obvious 'rules' (*I Know What You Did Last Summer*, for example) the struggle for survival involves not just avoiding the killer (as tended to be the case in the original slashers) but also trying to work out the scheme of things that produced the situation of danger in the first place.

The second outcome of the 1990s approach to horror is, perhaps surprisingly, a sense of pathos attendant upon the more developed characterisations we find in this type of horror. While playing the game might provide a rush of adrenaline (for the protagonists in the films and for the audiences for the films), losing the game means that you die. Perhaps here we finally get to the heart of these 'postmodern slashers' as they seek to transform death into an exciting game that can be played and (sometimes) won. Ultimately, it is a reassuring fantasy. There must be rules, these films seem to tell us, if only we can work out what they are. But at the same time there is always the prospect of failure and death. That these films are willing to acknowledge this, while still holding on to the fantastic possibility that the game can be won, suggests that some maturity has finally entered the critically derided world of the teenage horror film.

THE VIEW FROM HERE AND NOW

As ever, the horror film moves on. As the 'films like *Scream*' cycle fades away, other groupings and trends emerge. Recent years have seen the horror genre's encounter with new digital technologies – in *The Blair Witch Project* (1999), *My Little Eye* (2002), *28 Days Later* (2002) – and the internet – *My Little Eye* (again), *Feardotcom* (2002). With the *Ring* films (*Ring* and *Ring 2* in 1998 and *Ring 0* in 2000) from Japan and *The Eye* (2002) from Hong Kong, Asian film-makers have shown that they are capable of assimilating some of the conventions of western horror cinema into a distinctly non-western genre product (and western film-makers have returned the compliment by remaking *Ring* as a Hollywood film). There has been a welcome resurgence of the British horror film, with the likes of *Long Time Dead* (2002), *28 Days Later* (again), *My Little Eye* (yet again), *Dog Soldiers* (2002) and *Deathwatch* (2002), and some continental European genre films of note, including from Germany *Anatomie* (2000) and from France *The Brotherhood of the Wolf* (2001). There has also been a renewed interest in the ghost story, with *The Sixth Sense* (1999), *What Lies Beneath* (2000), *The Others* (2001) and *The Devil's Backbone* (2001), although this particular trend appears to have been a short-lived one.

Years from now we might look back at this time and see patterns emerging that are not immediately apparent to us today. From today's perspective, the perspective of the here and now, we seem to be at one of those intriguing moments in genre history where there is no single dominant generic type or format. Instead we are confronted with different types of horror film jostling for our attention. But to a certain extent perhaps, this has always been the case. Our retrospective views of horror history have often tidied up the genre in their attempts to categorise and make sense of it, stressing the importance of some generic types and marginalising or ignoring others. From the perspective of the here and now, whether your here and now is Britain in 2003 or, say, America in the mid-1930s, things are never that simple and generic patterns never that obvious. Accordingly, and in the face of much critical writing on horror that sees it as being an essentially formulaic and predictable mass-cultural product, this book has tried to give a sense of the sheer sprawl and messiness of the genre and the way in which it does not fit neatly into critical categories. Even in this chapter's discussion of the slasher film, often viewed as the most formulaic of all horror formats, I have emphasised the differences between films (and if I had had more space would have emphasised those differences even more). This is because what I find so fascinating about horror is precisely its changeability and its unpredictability, and this book stands as a record of that fascination. I have no idea what the future of the horror genre might be but I look forward to it with keen interest.

This book is now finished. Let the horror continue . . .

FURTHER READING

A good starting point for further reading on horror cinema is the work of Robin Wood. His seminal article, 'An Introduction to the American Horror Film', which first appeared in 1979, is collected with other writings on horror in Wood's *Hollywood from Vietnam to Reagan* (1986). While my own book has taken issue with various aspects of Wood's approach, this has (I hope) been done in a respectful manner. I very much admire Wood's criticism, both for its insights and for its accessible, jargon-free prose style. In particular, his development of the idea that horror has an ideological dimension, and that the genre reveals and sometimes critiques social inequalities, has proved very influential.

Probably the most important book written on horror in recent years is Carol Clover's *Men, Women and Chainsaws: Gender in the Modern Horror Film* (1992). Its psychoanalytical approach might not be to everyone's taste but its discussion of the complexities of horror spectatorship is compelling and important. Barbara Creed's *The Monstrous-Feminine: Film, Feminism, Psychoanalysis* (1993) also offers an interesting exploration of horror cinema from a psychoanalytical perspective, with particular reference to the representation of the maternal and the abject. For those keen to avoid psychoanalytical theory (not an easy thing to do in horror criticism), Noel Carroll's *The Philosophy of Horror* (1990) and Andrew Tudor's *Monsters and Mad Scientists* (1989) are well worth consulting for their insights into horror's codes, conventions and structures.

There are numerous studies of specific periods or types of horror production. Notable among these are Rhona Berenstein's *Attack of the Leading Ladies: Gender, Sexuality and Spectatorship in Classic Horror Cinema* (1996), Reynold Humphries *American Horror: An Introduction* (2002), Mark Jancovich's *Rational Fears: American Horror in the 1950s* (1996), Kim Newman's *Nightmare Movies* (1988), a study of post-1968 American and European horror, and *American Horrors* (1987), a collection of essays edited by Gregory Waller. Also highly recommended are two books by one of horror's leading historians, David Skal, *Hollywood Gothic* (1990), a definitive account of the production of the 1931 *Dracula*, and *The Monster Show: A Cultural History of Horror* (1993).

Critical studies of horror directors include Steve Chibnall's *Making Mischief: The Cult Films of Pete Walker* (1998), Michael Grant (ed.), *The Modern Fantastic: The Films of David Cronenberg* (2000), my own *Terence Fisher* (2002) and Maitland McDonagh's *Broken Mirrors, Broken Minds: The Dark Dreams of Dario Argento* (1991). *Cronenberg on Cronenberg* (1992, edited by Chris Rodley) gives an opportunity for one of the genre's most lucid film-makers to express himself, while Doug Bradley's *Sacred Monsters: Behind the Mask of the Horror Actor* (1996) provides some unique insights from the perspective of a horror performer (Bradley played Pinhead in the *Hellraiser* films).

Some of the most interesting material written on horror has been in the forms of essays and reviews. Selections of this material can be accessed in a number of collections and readers, including Steve Chibnall and Julian Petley (eds), *British Horror Cinema* (2002), two volumes edited by Barry K. Grant, *Planks of Reasons: Essays on the Horror Film* (1984) and *The Dread of Difference: Gender and the Horror Film* (1996), Mark Jancovich (ed.), *Horror: The Film Reader* (2002), Kim Newman (ed.), *Science Fiction/Horror Reader: A Sight and Sound Reader* (2002), and Alain Silver and James Ursini (eds), *Horror Film: Reader* (2000).

The following reference books are all highly recommended for both the range and depth of their coverage of the genre: Phil Hardy (ed.), *The Aurum Film Encyclopedia: Horror* (1985), Kim Newman (ed.), *The BFI Companion to Horror* (1996), and Jack Sullivan (ed.), *The Penguin Encyclopedia of Horror and the Supernatural* (1986).

Finally, and somewhat self-indulgently, I would like to recommend two rather aged volumes, Denis Gifford's *A Pictorial History of Horror Movies* (1973) and David Pirie's *A Heritage of Horror: The English Gothic Cinema 1946–1972* (1973), which together comprised my own starting point. These were the first books I ever read on horror. Each in its own way (and they are very different from each other) confirmed for me that horror was a valuable part of culture, that it was worth thinking about and talking about. I am indebted to them both.

BIBLIOGRAPHY

Altman, R. (1999) *Film/Genre* (BFI, London).

Baird, R. (2000) 'The Startle Effect: Implications for Spectator Cognition and Media Theory', *Film Quarterly* 53 (3) 12–24.

Barker, M. (1984) *The Video Nasties* (Pluto Press, London).

Baudry, J.-L. (1986a) 'Ideological Effects of the Basic Cinematographic Apparatus' in Rosen, P. (ed.) *Narrative, Apparatus, Ideology* (Columbia University Press, New York) 286–98.

Baudry, J.-L. (1986b) 'The Apparatus: Metapsychological Approaches to the Impression of Reality in the Cinema' in Rosen, P. (ed.) *Narrative, Apparatus, Ideology* (Columbia University Press, New York) 299–318.

Belton, J. (1985) 'Technology and Aesthetics of Film Sound' in Elisabeth Weis and John Belton (eds) *Film Sound: Theory and Practice* (Columbia University Press, New York) 63–72.

Benshoff, H. (1997) *Monsters in the Closet: Homosexuality and the Horror Film* (Manchester University Press, Manchester).

Benshoff, H. (2000) 'Blaxploitation Horror Films: Generic Reappropriation or Reinscription', *Cinema Journal* 39 (2) 31–50.

Berenstein, R. (1996) *Attack of the Leading Ladies: Gender, Sexuality and Spectatorship in Classic Horror Cinema* (Columbia University Press, New York).

Biskind, P. (1983) *Seeing is Believing* (Pluto Press, London).

Bonitzer, P. (1981) 'Partial Vision: Film and the Labyrinth', *Wide Angle* (4) 56–63.

Bradley, D. (1996) *Sacred Monsters: Behind the Mask of the Horror Actor* (Titan Books, London).

Britton, A. (1979) 'The Devil, Probably: The Symbolism of Evil' in Wood, R. *et al.* (eds) *The American Nightmare* (Toronto Film Festival, Toronto) 34–42.

Carroll, N. (1984) 'Ape and Essence' in Grant, B. (ed.) *Planks of Reason: Essays on the Horror Film* (Scarecrow, Metuchen, NJ) 215–44.

Carroll, N. (1990) *The Philosophy of Horror, or Paradoxes of the Heart* (Routledge, New York and London).

Carroll, N. (1996) 'Prospects for Film Theory: A Personal Assessment' in Bordwell, D. and Carroll, N. (eds) *Post-Theory: Reconstructing Film Studies* (University of Wisconsin Press, Madison) 37–68.

Chibnall, S. (1998) *Making Mischief: The Cult Films of Pete Walker* (Fab Press, Guildford).

Chibnall, S. and Petley, J. (eds) (2002) *British Horror Cinema* (Routledge, London).

Clarens, C. (1967) *An Illustrated History of the Horror Film* (Putnam, New York). (Later published as *Horror Movies: An Illustrated Survey* (Martin Secker & Warburg, London, 1968.)

Clover, C. (1992) *Men, Women and Chainsaws: Gender in the Modern Horror Film* (BFI, London).

Conrich, I. (2003) 'The *Friday the 13th* Films and the Cultural Function of a Modern Grand Guignol' in Lafond, F. (ed.) *Cauchemars Americains: Fantastique et Horreur dans le Cinema Moderne* (Les Editions du CEFAL, Lihge) 103–18.

Creed, B. (1993) *The Monstrous-Feminine: Film, Feminism, Psychoanalysis* (Routledge, London).

Dadoun, R. (1989) 'Fetishism and the Horror Film' in Donald, J. (ed.) *Fantasy and the Cinema* (BFI, London) 39–62.

Dika, V. (1990) *Games of Terror: Halloween, Friday the 13th, and the Films of the Stalker Cycle* (Associated University Presses, London and Toronto).

Doty, A. (1993) *Making Things Perfectly Queer* (University of Minnesota Press, Minneapolis).

Doty, A. (2000) *Flaming Classics: Queering the Film Canon* (Routledge, London).

Douglas, M. (1984) *Purity and Danger: An Analysis of the Concepts of Pollution and Taboo* (Ark, London).

Dyer, R. (1997) *White* (Routledge, London).

Ebert, R. (1981) 'Why Movie Audiences Aren't Safe Anymore', *American Film* March 54–6.

Elsaesser, T. (1989) 'Social Mobility and the Fantastic' in Donald, J. (ed.) *Fantasy and the Cinema* (BFI, London) 23–38.

Erb, C. (1998) *Tracking King Kong: A Hollywood Icon in World Culture* (Wayne State University Press, Detroit).

Evans, W. (1984) 'Monster Movies: A Sexual Theory' in Grant, B. (ed.) *Planks of Reason: Essays on the Horror Film* (Scarecrow, Metuchen, NJ and London) 53–64.

Fiske, J. (1992) 'The Cultural Economy of Fandom' in Lewis, L. (ed.) *The Adoring Audience: Fan Culture and Popular Media* (Routledge, London) 30–49.

Freeland, C. (2000) *The Naked and the Undead: Evil and the Appeal of Horror* (Westview Press, Boulder, CO).

Freud, S. (1990) 'The Uncanny' in *The Penguin Freud Library, vol. 14: Art and Literature* (Penguin, Harmondsworth) 335–76.

Gaines, J. (1992) *Contested Culture: The Image, The Voice, and the Law* (BFI, London).

Gifford, D. (1973) *A Pictorial History of Horror Movies* (Hamlyn, London).

Gorbman, C. (1987) *Unheard Melodies: Narrative Film Music* (Indiana University Press, Bloomington and Indianapolis).

Grant, B. (ed.) (1984) *Planks of Reason: Essays on the Horror Film* (Scarecrow Press, Metuchen, NJ and London).

Grant, B. (ed.) (1996) *The Dread of Difference: Gender and the Horror Film* (University of Texas Press, Austin).

Grant, M. (ed.) (2000) *The Modern Fantastic: The Films of David Cronenberg* (Flicks Books, Trowbridge, Wiltshire).

Grotjahn, M. (1958) 'Horror – Yes It Can Do You Good', *Films and Filming* November 9.

Guerrero, E. (1990) 'Aids as Monster in Science Fiction and Horror Cinema', *Journal of Popular Film and Television* 18 (3) 86–9.

Hammond, P. (1978) *The Shadow and Its Shadow: Surrealist Writings on Cinema* (BFI, London).

Hardy, P. (ed.) (1985) *The Aurum Film Encyclopedia: Horror* (Aurum, London).

Hawkins, J. (2000) *Cutting Edge: Art-horror and the Horrific Avant-garde* (University of Minnesota Press, Minneapolis).

Hill, D. (1958/59) 'The Face of Horror', *Sight and Sound* 28 (1) 6–11.

Hollinger, K. (1996) 'The Monster as Woman: Two Generations of Cat People' in Grant, B. (ed.) *The Dread of Difference: Gender and the Horror Film* (University of Texas Press, Austin) 296–308.

Humphries, Reynold (2002) *American Horror: An Introduction* (Edinburgh University Press, Edinburgh).

Hunt, L. (1992) 'A (Sadistic) Night at the Opera: Notes on the Italian Horror Film', *The Velvet Light Trap* (30) 65–75.

Hunt, L. (1998) *British Low Culture: From Safari Suits to Sexploitation* (Routledge, London).

Hutchings, P. (1993a) *Hammer and Beyond: The British Horror Film* (Manchester University Press, Manchester).

Hutchings, P. (1993b) 'Masculinity and the Horror Film' in Kirkham, P. and Thumim, J. (eds) *You Tarzan: Masculinity, Movies and Men* (Lawrence and Wishart, London) 84–94.

Hutchings, P. (1996) 'Tearing Your Soul Apart: Horror's New Monsters' in Sage, V. and Lloyd-Smith, A. (eds) *Modern Gothic: A Reader* (Manchester University Press, Manchester) 89–103.

Hutchings, P. (2002) *Terence Fisher* (Manchester University Press, Manchester).

Jancovich, M. (1992) *Horror* (Batsford, London).

Jancovich, M. (1996) *Rational Fears: American Horror in the 1950s* (Manchester University Press, Manchester).

Jancovich, M. (2000) '"A Real Shocker": Authenticity, Genre and the Struggle for Distinction', *Continuum: Journal of Media and Cultural Studies* 14 (1) 23–35.

Jancovich, M. (ed.) (2002) *Horror: The Film Reader* (Routledge, London).

Jenkins, H. (1992) *Textual Poachers: Television Fans and Participatory Culture* (Routledge, London).

Jenkins, H. (1995) 'Historical Poetics' in Hollows, J. and Jancovich, M. (eds) *Approaches to Popular Film* (Manchester University Press, Manchester) 99–122.

Jenks, C. (1992) 'The Other Face of Death: Barbara Steele and *La Maschera del Demonio*' in Dyer, R. and Vincendeau, G. (eds) *Popular European Cinema* (Routledge, London) 149–62.

Jenson, J. (1992) 'Fandom as Pathology: The Consequences of Characterization' in Lewis, L. (ed.) *The Adoring Audience: Fan Culture and Popular Media* (Routledge, London) 9–29.

Kaminsky, S. (1974) *American Film Genres: Approaches to a Critical Theory of Popular Film* (Pflaum, Dayton, OH).

Kermode, M. (1997) 'I was a Teenage Horror Fan: or "How I Learned to Stop Worrying and Love Linda Blair"' in Barker M. and Petley J. (eds) *Ill Effects: The Media/Violence Debate* (London, Routledge) 57–66.

Knee, A. (1996) 'Gender, Genre, Argento' in Grant, B. (ed.) *The Dread of Difference: Gender and the Horror Film* (University of Texas Press, Austin) 213–30.

Kristeva, J. (1982) *The Powers of Horror* (Columbia University Press, New York).

Lovell, A. (1975) *Don Siegel: American Cinema* (BFI, London).

Mayne, Judith (1993) *Cinema and Spectatorship* (Routledge, London).

McDonagh, M. (1991) *Broken Mirrors, Broken Minds: The Dark Dreams of Dario Argento* (Sun Tavern Fields, London).

Mendik, X. (2000) *Tenebre/Tenebrae* (Flicks Books, Trowbridge, Wiltshire).

Metz, C. (1985) 'Aural Objects' in Elisabeth Weis and John Belton (eds) *Film Sound: Theory and Practice* (Columbia University Press, New York) 154–61.

Mulvey, L. (1975) 'Visual Pleasure and Narrative Cinema', *Screen* 16 (3) 6–18.

Myles, L. and Pye, M. (1979) *The Movie Brats* (Faber, London).

Naha, E. (1982) *The Films of Roger Corman* (Arco Publishing, New York).

Neale, S. (1980) *Genre* (BFI, London).

Newman, J. (1990) 'Shirley Jackson and the Reproduction of Mothering: *The Haunting of Hill House*' in Docherty, B. (ed.) *American Horror Fiction* (Macmillan, London) 120–34.

Newman, K. (1988) *Nightmare Movies* (Bloomsbury, London).

Newman, K. (ed.) (1996) *The BFI Companion to Horror* (BFI, London).

Newman, K. (ed.) (2002) *Science Fiction/Horror Reader: A Sight and Sound Reader* (BFI, London).

O'Flinn, P. (1986) 'Production and Reproduction: The Case of *Frankenstein*' in Humm, P. *et al.* (eds) *Popular Fictions: Essays in Literature and History* (Methuen, London) 196–221.

Paul, W. (1994) *Laughing Screaming: Modern Hollywood Horror and Comedy* (Columbia University Press, New York).

Perks, M. (2002) 'A Descent into the Underworld: *Death Line*' in Chibnall, S. and Petley, J. (eds) *British Horror Cinema* (Routledge, London) 145–55.

Pinedo, I. (1997) *Recreational Terror: Women and the Pleasures of Horror Film Viewing* (State University of New York Press, Albany).

Pirie, D. (1973) *A Heritage of Horror: The English Gothic Cinema 1946–1972* (Gordon Fraser, London).

Punter, D. (1996) *The Literature of Terror, vol. 1: The Gothic Tradition* (Longman, London).

Rathgeb, D. (1991) 'Bogeyman from the Id: Nightmare and Reality in *Halloween* and *A Nightmare on Elm Street*', *Journal of Popular Film and Television* 19 (1) 36–43.

Richardson, M. (1991) 'The Psychoanalysis of Count Dracula', an excerpt from the article 'Psychoanalysis of Ghost Stories', first published in 1959, reprinted in Frayling, C. (ed.) *Vampyres: Lord Byron to Count Dracula* (Faber, London) 418–22.

Rockett, W.H. (1982) 'The Door Ajar: Structure and Convention in Horror Films that Would Terrify', *Journal of Popular Film and Television* 10 (3) 130–6.

Rodley, C. (ed.) (1992) *Cronenberg on Cronenberg* (Faber, London).

Ryan, M. and Kellner, D. (1988) *Camera Politica: The Politics and Ideology of Contemporary Hollywood Film* (Indiana University Press, Bloomington and Indianapolis).

Sanjek, D. (1990) 'Fans Notes: The Horror Film Fanzine', *Literature/Film Quarterly* 18 (3) 150–9.

Schneider, S. (2000a) 'Monsters as (Uncanny) Metaphors: Freud, Lakoff, and the Representation of Monstrosity in Cinematic Horror' in Silver, A. and Ursini, J. (ed.) *Horror Film Reader* (Limelight Editions, New York) 167–92.

Schneider, S. (2000b) 'Kevin Williamson and the Rise of the Neo-Stalker', *Post-Script* 19 (2) 73–87.

Sconce, J. (1995) '"Trashing the Academy": Taste, Excess and an Emerging Politics of Cinematic Style', *Screen* 36 (4) 371–93.

Silver, A. and Ursini, J. (eds) (2000) *Horror Film: Reader* (Limelight, New York).

Silverman, K. (1980) 'Masochism and Subjectivity', *Framework* (12) 2–9.

Skal, D. (1990) *Hollywood Gothic: The Tangled Web of Dracula from Novel to Stage to Screen* (Andre Deutsch, London).

Skal, D. (1993) *The Monster Show: A Cultural History of Horror* (Plexus, London).

Skal, D. (1996) *V is for Vampire: The A–Z Guide to Everything Undead* (Penguin, Harmondsworth).

Stoker, B. (1993) *Dracula* (Penguin, Harmondsworth) (orig. published 1897).

Stoker, B. (1996) *Jewel of the Seven Stars* (Oxford University Press, Oxford) (orig. published 1903).

Sullivan, J. (ed.) (1986) *The Penguin Encyclopedia of Horror and the Supernatural* (Penguin, Harmondsworth).

Taubin, A. (1992) 'Invading Bodies: *Alien 3* and the Trilogy', *Sight and Sound* 2 (3) 8–10.

Trencansky, S. (2001) 'Final Girls and Terrible Youth: Transgression in 1980s Slasher Horror', *Journal of Popular Film and Television* 29 (2) 63–73.

Tudor, A. (1973) *Theories of Film* (Secker & Warburg, London).

Tudor, A. (1989) *Monsters and Mad Scientists: A Cultural History of the Horror Film* (Blackwell, Oxford).

Tudor, A. (2002) 'From Paranoia to Postmodernism? The Horror Movie in Late Modern Society' in Neale, S. (ed.) *Genre and Contemporary Hollywood* (BFI, London) 105–16.

Twitchell, J. (1985) *Dreadful Pleasures: An Anatomy of Modern Horror* (Oxford University Press, New York and Oxford).

Tyler, P. (1971) *Magic and Myth of the Movies* (Secker and Warburg, London).

Walkowitz, J. (1992) *City of Dreadful Delights: Narratives of Sexual Danger in Late-Victorian London* (Virago, London).

Waller, G. (ed.) (1987) *American Horrors: Essays on the Modern American Horror Film* (University of Illinois Press, Urbana and Chicago).

Wells, P. (2000) *The Horror Genre: From Beelzebub to Blair Witch* (Wallflower, London).

Wiegman, R. (1993) 'Feminism, "the Boyz" and Other Matters Regarding the Male' in Cohan, S. and Rae Hark, I. (eds) *Screening the Male* (Routledge, London) 173–93.

Williams, L. (1984) 'When the Woman Looks' in Doane, M. *et al.* (eds) *Revision: Essays in Feminist Film Criticism* (University Publications of America, Frederick, MD) 83–99.

Williams, L. (1995) 'Film Bodies: Gender, Genre, and Excess' in Grant, B. (ed.) *Film Genre Reader 2* (University of Texas Press, Austin) 140–58.

Williams, L. (2000) 'Discipline and Fun: *Psycho* and Postmodern Cinema' in Gledhill, C. and Williams, L. (eds) *Reinventing Film Studies* (Edward Arnold, London) 351–78.

Williams, T. (1996) *Hearths of Darkness: The Family in the American Horror Film* (Fairleigh Dickinson University Press, Madison, NJ).

Wood, R. (1976) *Personal Views: Explorations in Film* (Gordon Fraser, London).

Wood, R. (1984) 'An Introduction to the American Horror Film' in Grant, B. (ed.) *Planks of Reason: Essays on the Horror Film* (Scarecrow Press, Metuchen, NJ and London) 164–200.

Wood, R. (1986) *Hollywood from Vietnam to Reagan* (Columbia University Press, New York).

Wood, R. (1989) *Hitchcock's Films Revisited* (Faber, London).

Young, E. (1996) 'Here Comes the Bride: Wedding Gender and Race in *Bride of Frankenstein*' in Grant, B. (ed.) *The Dread of Difference: Gender and the Horror Film* (University of Texas Press, Austin) 309–37.

FILMOGRAPHY

Abbott and Costello Meet Frankenstein US, 1948, dir. Charles T. Barton
Abby US, 1974, dir. William Girdler
Abominable Dr Phibes, The Britain, 1971, dir. Robert Fuest
Adventures of Robin Hood, The US, 1938, dir. Michael Curtiz
Alien Britain, 1979, dir. Ridley Scott
Aliens US, 1986, dir. James Cameron
American Werewolf in London, An Britain, 1981, dir. John Landis
Amityville Horror, The US, 1979, dir. Stuart Rosenberg
Anatomie Germany, 2000, dir. Stefan Ruzowitzky
Audrey Rose US, 1977, dir. Robert Wise

Bat, The US, 1926, dir. Roland West
Bat, The US, 1959, dir. Crane Wilbur
Bat Whispers, The US, 1930, dir. Roland West
Bay of Blood (*Ecologia del Delitto, Twitch of the Death Nerve*) Italy, 1971, dir. Mario
    Bava
Beast With Five Fingers, The US, 1946, dir. Robert Florey
Ben Hur US, 1959, dir. William Wyler
Beyond, The (*L'Aldila*) Italy, 1981, dir. Lucio Fulci
Bird with the Crystal Plumage, The (*L'uccello dalle piume di cristallo*) Italy, 1970,
    dir. Dario Argento
Birds, The US, 1963, dir. Alfred Hitchcock
Black Cat, The US, 1934, dir. Edgar G. Ulmer
Black Christmas Canada, 1974, dir. Bob Clark
Black Room, The US, 1935, dir. Roy William Neill
Blackenstein US, 1973, dir. William A. Levey
Blacula US, 1972, dir. William Crain
Blade US, 1998, dir. Stephen Norrington
Blair Witch Project, The US, 1999, dir. Daniel Myrick and Eduardo Sanchez
Bless the Child US, 2000, dir. Chuck Russell
Blob, The US, 1958, dir. Irvin S. Yeaworth, Jnr
Blob, The US, 1988, dir. Chuck Russell
Blood Beast Terror, The Britain, 1967, dir. Vernon Sewell
Blood Feast US, 1963, dir. Herschell Gordon Lewis
Blood for Dracula (*Dracula cerca sangue di vergine e . . . mori di sete*) Italy, 1973,
    dir. Antonio Margheriti and Paul Morrissey
Blood from the Mummy's Tomb Britain, 1971, dir. Seth Holt
Blood of Dracula US, 1957, dir. Herbert L. Strock
Blood on Satan's Claw Britain, 1970, dir. Piers Haggard

Blow Out US, 1981, dir. Brian De Palma
Blue Steel US, 1990, dir. Kathryn Bigelow
Bonnie and Clyde US, 1967, dir. Arthur Penn
Bram Stoker's Dracula US, 1992, dir. Francis Ford Coppola
Breakdown US, 1997, dir. Jonathan Mostow
Bride of Frankenstein US, 1935, dir. James Whale
Brides of Dracula, The Britain, 1960, dir. Terence Fisher
Broken Blossoms US, 1919, dir. D.W. Griffith
Brood, The Canada, 1979, dir. David Cronenberg
Brotherhood of the Wolf, The (*Le Pacte des loups*) France, 2001, dir. Christophe Gans
Burning, The US, 1980, dir. Tony Maylam

Cabinet of Dr Caligari, The Germany, 1919, dir. Robert Wiene
Campana del infierno, La (*The Bell of Hell*) Spain, 1973, dir. Claudio Guerin Hill
Candyman US, 1992, dir. Bernard Rose
Candyman 2: Farewell to the Flesh US, 1995, dir. Bill Condon
Candyman 3: Day of the Dead US, 1999, dir. Turi Meyer
Cannibal Holocaust Italy, 1979, dir. Ruggero Deodato
Carrie US, 1976, dir. Brian De Palma
Carrie 2: The Rage US, 1999, dir. Katt Shea
Casablanca US, 1942, dir. Michael Curtiz
Cat and the Canary, The US, 1927, dir. Paul Leni
Cat and the Canary, The US, 1939, dir. Elliot Nugent
Cat and the Canary, The Britain, 1978, dir. Radley Metzger
Cat Creeps, The US, 1930, dir. Rupert Julian
Cat O'Nine Tails (*Il gatto a nove code*) Italy, 1971, dir. Dario Argento
Cat People US, 1942, dir. Jacques Tourneur
Cherry Falls US, 2000, dir. Geoffrey Wright
Children Shouldn't Play with Dead Things US, 1972, dir. Bob Clark
City of the Dead (*Horror Hotel*) Britain, 1960, dir. John Llewellyn Moxey
Clockwork Orange, A Britain, 1971, dir. Stanley Kubrick
Conde Dracula, El Spain/Italy/Germany, 1970, dir. Jess Franco
Copycat US, 1995, dir. Jon Amiel
Count Yorga – Vampire US, 1970, dir. Bob Kelljan
Creature from the Black Lagoon, The US, 1954, dir. Jack Arnold
Cronos Mexico, 1993, dir. Guillermo Del Toro
Curse of Frankenstein, The Britain, 1957, dir. Terence Fisher
Curse of the Cat People, The US, 1944, dir. Robert Wise and Gunther von Fritsch
Curse of the Mummy's Tomb, The Britain, 1964, dir. Michael Carreras
Curse of the Werewolf, The Britain, 1961, dir. Terence Fisher

Damien – Omen 2 US, 1978, dir. Don Taylor
Dark Waters Britain/Italy/Russia, 1994, dir. Mariano Baino
Dead of Night Britain, 1945, dir. Alberto Cavalcanti, Charles Crichton, Basil Dearden
    and Robert Hamer
Dead of Night (*The Night Walk, Deathdream*) Canada, 1972, dir. Bob Clark
Death Line (*Raw Meat*) Britain, 1972, dir. Gary Sherman
Death Trap (*Eaten Alive*) US, 1976, dir. Tobe Hooper
Deathwatch Britain, 2002, dir. Michael J. Bassett
Demons of the Mind Britain, 1971, dir. Peter Sykes

Deranged Canada/US, 1974, dir. Jeff Gillen and Alan Ormsby
Devil's Backbone, The (*El Espinazo del Diablo*) Spain, 2001, dir. Guillermo del Toro
Diaboliques, Les France, 1955, dir. Henri-Georges Clouzot
Dr Black, Mr Hyde US, 1976, dir. William Crain
Dr Jekyll and Mr Hyde US, 1920, dir. J. Charles Haydon
Dr Jekyll and Mr Hyde (John Barrymore version) US, 1920, dir. John S. Robertson
Dr Jekyll and Mr Hyde US, 1931, dir. Rouben Mamoulian
Dr Jekyll and Mr Hyde US, 1941, dir. Victor Fleming
Dr Phibes Rises Again Britain, 1972, dir. Robert Fuest
Dr Terror's House of Horrors Britain, 1964, dir. Freddie Francis
Doctor X US, 1932, dir. Michael Curtiz
Dog Soldiers Britain, 2002, dir. Neil Marshall
Don't Look Now Britain, 1973, dir. Nicolas Roeg
Dracula US, 1931, dir. Tod Browning
Dracula Britain, 1958, dir. Terence Fisher
Dracula US, 1979, dir. John Badham
Dracula – AD 1972 Britain, 1972, dir. Alan Gibson
Dracula – Dead and Loving It US, 1995, dir. Mel Brooks
Dracula Has Risen From the Grave Britain, 1968, dir. Freddie Francis
Dracula – Prince of Darkness Britain, 1965, dir. Terence Fisher
Dracula 2000 US, 2000, dir. Patrick Lussier
Dracula's Daughter US, 1936, dir. Lambert Hillyer
Dressed To Kill US, 1980, dir. Brian De Palma
Dunwich Horror, The US, 1969, dir. Daniel Haller

Easy Rider US, 1969, dir. Dennis Hopper
Ed Gein US, 2000, dir. Chuck Parello
End of Days US, 1999, dir. Peter Hyams
Event Horizon US, 1997, dir. Paul Anderson
Evil Dead, The US, 1982, dir. Sam Raimi
Evil Dead 2, The US, 1987, dir. Sam Raimi
Exorcist, The US, 1973, dir. William Friedkin
Exorcist 2: The Heretic US, 1977, dir. John Boorman
Exorcist III, The US, 1990, dir. William Peter Blatty
Eye, The (*Gin Gwai*) Hong Kong/Singapore, 2002, dir. Oxide Pang and Danny Pang
Eyes of a Stranger US, 1981, dir. Ken Wiederhorn
Eyes of Laura Mars, The US, 1978, dir. Irvin Kershner

Fall of the House of Usher, The (*House of Usher*) US, 1960, dir. Roger Corman
Fallen US, 1998, dir. Gregory Hoblit
Fatal Attraction US, 1987, dir. Adrian Lyne
Feardotcom US, 2002, dir. William Malone
Fiend Without a Face Britain, 1958, dir. Arthur Crabtree
Final Conflict, The Britain, 1981, dir. Graham Baker
Final Destination US 2000, dir. James Wong
Final Destination 2 US, 2003, dir. David R. Ellis
Fly, The US, 1986, dir. David Cronenberg
Fog, The US, 1980, dir. John Carpenter
Four Flies on Grey Velvet (*Quattro mosche di velluto grigio*) Italy, 1971,
    dir. Dario Argento

Frankenstein US, 1910, dir. J. Searle Dawley
Frankenstein US, 1931, dir. James Whale
Frankenstein Created Woman Britain, 1967, dir. Terence Fisher
Frankenstein Meets the Wolf Man US, 1943, dir. Roy William Neill
Frankenstein Must Be Destroyed Britain, 1969, dir. Terence Fisher
Freaks US, 1932, dir. Tod Browning
Freddy's Dead: The Final Nightmare US, 1991, dir. Rachel Talahay
Frenzy Britain, 1972, dir. Alfred Hitchcock
Friday the 13th US, 1980, dir. Sean S. Cunningham
Friday the 13th Part 2 US, 1981, dir. Steve Miner
Friday the 13th Part 3 US, 1982, dir. Steve Miner
Friday the 13th: The Final Chapter US, 1984, dir. Joseph Zito
Frighteners, The US, 1996, dir. Peter Jackson
Frightmare Britain, 1974, dir. Peter Walker
Fun House, The US, 1981, dir. Tobe Hooper

Gaslight US, 1944, dir. George Cukor
God Told Me To (*Demon*) US, 1976, dir. Larry Cohen
Godsend, The US, 1980, dir. Gabriel Beaumont
Gold Diggers of Broadway US, 1929, dir. Roy Del Ruth
Gold Diggers of 1935 US, 1935, dir. Busby Berkeley
Gold Diggers of 1937 US, 1937, dir. Lloyd Bacon and Busby Berkeley
Golem, The Germany, 1913, dir. Henrik Galeen and Paul Wegener
Gorgon, The Britain, 1964, dir. Terence Fisher
Gorilla, The US, 1927, dir. Alfred Santell
Grave of the Vampire US, 1972, dir. John Hayes
Great Expectations Britain, 1946, dir. David Lean
Gritos en la noche (*The Awful Dr Orloff*) Spain, 1962, dir. Jesus Franco

Halloween US, 1978, dir. John Carpenter
Halloween 2 US, 1981, dir. Rick Rosenthal
Halloween: H20 US, 1998, dir. Steve Miner
Hands of the Ripper Britain, 1971, dir. Peter Sasdy
Hannibal US, 2001, dir. Ridley Scott
Hatchet for the Honeymoon, A (*Una hacha para la luna de miel*) Italy, 1969,
    dir. Mario Bava
Haunting, The Britain, 1963, dir. Robert Wise
Haunting, The US, 1999, dir. Jan de Bont
Hell Night US, 1981, dir. Tom DeSimone
Hellraiser, Britain, 1987, dir. Clive Barker
Hellraiser 2: Hellbound, Britain, 1988, dir. Tony Randel
Hellraiser 3: Hell on Earth, US, 1992. dir. Anthony Hickox
Hellraiser: Bloodline, US, 1996, dir. Alan Smithee (a much-used pseudonym which in
    this case stands for Kevin Yagher)
Hellraiser: Hellseeker, US, 2002, dir. Rick Bota
Hellraiser: Inferno, US, 2000, dir. Scott Derickson
Henry – Portrait of a Serial Killer US, 1986, dir. John McNaughton
High Noon US, 1952, dir. Fred Zinnemann
Hills Have Eyes, The US, 1977, dir. Wes Craven
Holocaust 2000 Italy/Britain, 1977, dir. Alberto de Martino

Horror Express (*Panico en el Transiberiano*) Spain/Britain, 1972, dir. Eugenio Martin
Hound of the Baskervilles, The, Britain, 1959, dir. Terence Fisher
House of Dark Shadows US, 1970, dir. Dan Curtis
House of Dracula US, 1945, dir. Erle C. Kenton
House of Frankenstein US, 1944, dir. Erle C. Kenton
House of Whipcord Britain, 1974, dir. Peter Walker
House on Haunted Hill, The US, 1959, dir. William Castle
House on Sorority Row, The US, 1982, dir. Mark Rosman
How to Make a Monster US, 1958, dir. Herbert L. Strock
Hunchback of Notre Dame, The US, 1923, dir. Wallace Worsley

I Know What You Did Last Summer US, 1997, dir. Jim Gillespie
I Spit On Your Grave US, 1978, dir. Meir Zarchi
I Still Know What You Did Last Summer US 1998, dir. Danny Cannon
I Walked with a Zombie US, 1943, dir. Jacques Tourneur
I was a Teenage Frankenstein US, 1957, dir. Herbert L. Strock
I was a Teenage Werewolf US, 1957, dir. Gene Fowler Jnr
If . . . Britain, 1968, dir. Lindsay Anderson
In the Mouth of Madness US, 1995, dir. John Carpenter
Incredibly Strange Creatures Who Stopped Living and Became Mixed-Up Zombies, The US, 1963, dir. Ray Dennis Steckler
Inferno Italy, 1980, dir. Dario Argento
Innocents, The Britain, 1961, dir. Jack Clayton
Invasion of the Bodysnatchers US, 1956, dir. Don Siegel
Invisible Man, The US, 1933, dir. James Whale
Island of Lost Souls US, 1932, dir. Erle C. Kenton
It Came from Outer Space US, 1953, dir. Jack Arnold
It! The Terror from Beyond Space US, 1958, Edward L. Cahn
It's Alive US, 1974, dir. Larry Cohen

Jaws US, 1975, dir. Steven Spielberg
Jeepers Creepers US, 2001, dir. Victor Salva

Keep, The US, 1983, dir. Michael Mann
King Kong US, 1933, dir. Merian C. Cooper and Ernest B. Schoedsack
King of Kings US, 1961, dir. Nicholas Ray
Kiss, The US, 1988, dir. Pen Densham
Kiss the Girls US, 1997, dir. Gary Fleder

Last House on the Left, The US, 1972, dir. Wes Craven
Last Moment, The US, 1923, dir. J. Parker Read Jnr
Last Warning, The US, 1929, dir. Paul Leni
Legend of Hell House, The Britain, 1973, dir. John Hough
Leopard Man, The US, 1943, dir. Jacques Tourneur
Life Without a Soul US, 1916, dir. Joseph W. Smiley
Little Caesar US, 1930, dir. Mervyn LeRoy
Lodger, The Britain, 1926, dir. Alfred Hitchcock
London After Midnight US, 1927, dir. Tod Browning
Long Time Dead Britain, 2002, dir. Marcus Adams
Lost Weekend, The US, 1945, dir. Billy Wilder
Love at First Bite US, 1979, dir. Stan Dragoti

Macabre US, 1958, dir. William Castle
Mad Love US, 1935, dir. Karl Freund
Man Who Could Cheat Death, The Britain, 1959, dir. Terence Fisher
Man Who Laughs, The US, 1928, dir. Paul Leni
Manhunter US, 1986, dir. Michael Mann
Marca del hombre-lobo, La (*Hell's Creatures*) Spain, 1967, dir. Enrique Lopez Eguiluz
Mark of the Vampire US, 1935, dir. Tod Browning
Mary Reilly US, 1996, dir. Stephen Frears
Maschera del demonio, La (*Black Sunday, The Mask of Satan, Revenge of the Vampire*) Italy, 1960, dir. Mario Bava
Mask of Fu Manchu, The US, 1932, dir. Charles Brabin and Charles Victor
Masque of the Red Death, The Britain, 1964, dir. Roger Corman
Mephisto Waltz, The US, 1971, dir. Paul Wendkos
Mimic US, 1997, dir. Guillermo del Toro
Monk, The France/Germany/Italy, 1972, dir. Ado Kyrou
Monster, The US, 1925, dir. Roland West
Most Dangerous Game, The (*The Hounds of Zaroff*) US, 1932, dir. Irving Pichel and Ernest B. Schoedsack
Mummy, The US, 1932, dir. Karl Freund
Mummy, The Britain, 1959, dir. Terence Fisher
Mummy, The US, 1999, dir. Stephen Sommers
Mummy Returns, The US, 2001, dir. Stephen Sommers
Mummy's Curse, The US, 1944, dir. Leslie Goodwins
Mummy's Ghost, The US, 1944, dir. Reginald LeBorg
Mummy's Hand, The US, 1940, dir. Christy Cabanne
Mummy's Shroud, The Britain, 1967, dir. John Gilling
Mummy's Tomb, The US, 1942, dir. Harold Young
Murder by Decree Britain, 1979, dir. Bob Clark
Murders in the Rue Morgue US, 1932, dir. Robert Florey
My Little Eye Britain, 2002, dir. Marc Evans
Mystery of the Wax Museum US, 1933, dir. Michael Curtiz

New Nightmare, A US 1994, dir. Wes Craven
Night of the Lepus US, 1972, dir. William F. Claxton
Night of the Living Dead US, 1968, dir. George Romero
Night Stalker, The US, 1971, dir. John Llewllyn Moxey
Nightbreed US, 1990, dir. Clive Barker
Nightmare on Elm Street, A US, 1984, dir. Wes Craven
Nightmare on Elm Street 4: The Dream Master, A US, 1988, dir. Renny Harlin
Nightmare on Elm Street 5: The Dream Child, A US, 1989, dir. Stephen Hopkins
Noche del terror ciego, La (*Tombs of the Blind Dead*) Spain, 1971, dir. Amando de Osorio
Nosferatu Germany, 1922, dir. F.W. Murnau
Nosferatu the Vampire Germany, 1979, dir. Werner Herzog
Novia ensangrentada, La (*The Blood Spattered Bride*) Spain, 1972, dir. Vicente Aranda
Now Voyager US, 1942, dir. Irving Rapper

Of Mice and Men, US, 1939, dir. Lewis Milestone
Old Dark House, The US, 1932, dir. James Whale
Omen, The US, 1976, dir. Richard Donner

One Exciting Night US, 1922, dir. D.W. Griffith
Orribile segreto del Dr Hichcock L' (*The Terrible Secret of Dr Hichcock*) Italy, 1962, dir. Riccardo Freda
Other, The US, 1972, dir. Robert Mulligan
Others, The France/Spain/US, 2001, dir. Alejandro Amenabar

Peeping Tom Britain, 1960, dir. Michael Powell
People Under the Stairs, The US, 1991, dir. Wes Craven
Performance Britain, 1970, dir. Donald Cammell and Nicolas Roeg
Phantasm US, 1979, dir. Don Coscarelli
Phantom of the Opera, The US, 1925, dir. Rupert Julian
Pit and the Pendulum US, 1961, dir. Roger Corman
Plague of the Zombies, The Britain, 1966, dir. John Gilling
Poltergeist US, 1982, dir. Tobe Hooper
Possession of Joel Delaney, The US, 1972, dir. Waris Hussein
Predator US, 1987, dir. John McTiernan
Prince of Darkness US, 1987, dir. John Carpenter
Profondo Rosso (*Deep Red*) Italy, 1975, dir. Dario Argento
Prom Night Canada, 1980, dir. Paul Lynch
Psycho US, 1960, dir. Alfred Hitchcock
Psycho 2 US, 1983, dir. Richard Franklin
Public Enemy, The US, 1931, dir. William A. Wellman

Rabid Canada, 1977, dir. David Cronenberg
Raven, The US, 1935, dir. Louis Friedlander *aka* Lew Landers
Rear Window US, 1954, dir. Alfred Hitchcock
Rebecca US, 1940, dir. Alfred Hitchcock
Rebel Without a Cause US, 1955, dir. Nicholas Ray
Red Dragon US, 2002, dir. Brett Ratner
Relic, The US, 1997, dir. Peter Hyams
Reptile, The Britain, 1966, dir. John Gilling
Repulsion Britain, 1965, dir. Roman Polanski
Return of Count Yorga, The US, 1971, dir. Bob Kelljan
Revenge of Frankenstein, The Britain, 1958, dir. Terence Fisher
Ring (*Ringu*) Japan, 1998, dir. Hideo Nakata
Ring 0 Japan, 2000, dir. Norio Tsuruta
Ring 2 Japan, 1998, dir. Hideo Nakata
Rosemary's Baby US, 1968, dir. Roman Polanski
Rouge aux lèvres, Le (*Daughters of Darkness*) Belgium, 1971, dir. Harry Kumel

Satanic Rites of Dracula, The Britain, 1973, dir. Alan Gibson
Scars of Dracula Britain, 1970, dir. Roy Ward Baker
Scream US, 1996, dir. Wes Craven
Scream 2 US, 1997, dir. Wes Craven
Scream 3 US, 2000, dir. Wes Craven
Scream and Scream Again Britain, 1969, dir. Gordon Hessler
Scream Blacula Scream US, 1973, dir. Bob Kelljan
Secret Beyond the Door, The US, 1948, dir. Fritz Lang
Secret of the Blue Room US, 1933, dir. Kurt Neumann
Sei donne per l'assassino (*Blood and Black Lace*) Italy, 1964, dir. Mario Bava
Seven US, 1995, dir. David Fincher

Seventh Victim, The US, 1943, dir. Mark Robson
Shadow of a Doubt US, 1943, dir. Alfred Hitchcock
Shining, The Britain, 1980, dir. Stanley Kubrick
Shivers Canada, 1975, dir. David Cronenberg
Shock US, 1946, dir. Alfred L. Werker
Silence of the Lambs, The US, 1991, dir. Jonathan Demme
Sisters US, 1973, dir. Brian De Palma
Sixth Sense, The US, 1999, dir. M. Night Shyamalan
Sleepy Hollow US, 1999, dir. Tim Burton
Son of Dracula US, 1943, dir. Robert Siodmak
Son of Frankenstein US, 1939, dir. Rowland V. Lee
Sorcerers, The Britain, 1967, dir. Michael Reeves
Sound of Music, The US, 1965, dir. Robert Wise
Spellbound US, 1945, dir. Alfred Hitchcock
Student of Prague, The Germany, 1913, dir. Stellan Rye and Paul Wegener
Suspiria Italy, 1977, dir. Dario Argento

Targets US, 1968, dir. Peter Bogdanovich
Taste the Blood of Dracula Britain, 1969, dir. Peter Sasdy
Tenant, The (Le Locataire) France, 1976, dir. Roman Polanski
Tenebrae (Tenebre) Italy, 1982, dir. Dario Argento
Terminator, The US, 1984, dir. James Cameron
Terminator 2: Judgement Day US 1991, dir. James Cameron
Terror, The US, 1928, dir. Roy del Ruth
Terror Train Canada/US, 1980, dir. Roger Spottiswoode
Texas Chainsaw Massacre, The US, 1974, dir. Tobe Hooper
Texas Chainsaw Massacre 2, The US, 1986, dir. Tobe Hooper
Theatre of Blood Britain, 1973, dir. Douglas Hickox
Thelma and Louise US, 1991, dir. Ridley Scott
Them! US, 1954, dir. Gordon Douglas
Thing, The US, 1982, dir. John Carpenter
Thing from Another World, The US, 1951, dir. Christian Nyby
Three Faces of Eve, The US, 1957, dir. Nunnally Johnson
Tingler, The US, 1959, dir. William Castle
Torso (I corpi presentano tracce di violenza carnale) Italy, 1973, dir. Sergio Martino
Tower of London US, 1939, dir. Rowland V. Lee
28 Days Later, Britain, 2002, dir. Danny Boyle
Two Faces of Dr Jekyll, The Britain, 1960, dir. Terence Fisher
Two Thousand Maniacs US, 1964, dir. Herschell Gordon Lewis
2001: A Space Odyssey US, 1968, dir. Stanley Kubrick

Unknown Treasures US, 1926, dir. Archie Mayo
Urban Legend US, 1998, dir. Jamie Blanks
Urban Legends: Final Cut US, 2000, dir. John Ottman

Valentine US, 2001, dir. Jamie Blanks
Vampire Bat, The US, 1933, dir. Frank Strayer
Vampire in Brooklyn US, 1995, d, Wes Craven
Vampire Lovers, The Britain, 1970, dir. Roy Ward Baker
Vampyr Denmark, 1932, dir. Carl Dreyer
Velvet Vampire, The US, 1971, dir. Stephanie Rothman

Village of the Damned Britain, 1960, dir. Wolf Rilla
Voluntad del muerto, La US, 1930, dir. George Melford

Wait Until Dark US, 1967, dir. Terence Young
War of the Worlds US, 1953, dir. Byron Haskin
Werewolf, The US, 1913, dir. Henry MacRae
Werewolf of London, The US, 1935, dir. Stuart Walker
West Side Story US, 1961, dir. Robert Wise
What Lies Beneath US 2000, dir. Robert Zemeckis
When a Stranger Calls US, 1979, dir. Fred Walton
White Zombie US, 1932, dir. Victor Halperin
Witchfinder General (*The Conqueror Worm*) Britain, 1968, dir. Michael Reeves
Wolf Man, The US, 1941, dir. George Waggner

Yeux sans visage, Les (*Eyes without a Face*) France, 1959, dir. Georges Franju

INDEX

All titles refer to films unless otherwise indicated.

CPSIA information can be obtained
at www.ICGtesting.com
Printed in the USA
BVHW071944120719
553339BV00006B/63/P